The Great University Gamble

THE GREAT UNIVERSITY GAMBLE

Money, Markets and the Future of Higher Education

Andrew McGettigan

PlutoPress
www.plutobooks.com

First published 2013 by Pluto Press
345 Archway Road, London N6 5AA

www.plutobooks.com

Distributed in the United States of America exclusively by
Palgrave Macmillan, a division of St. Martin's Press LLC,
175 Fifth Avenue, New York, NY 10010

British Library Cataloguing in Publication Data
A catalogue record for this book is available from the British Library

ISBN 978 0 7453 3294 9   Hardback
ISBN 978 0 7453 3293 2   Paperback
ISBN 978 1 8496 4764 9   PDF eBook
ISBN 978 1 8496 4766 3   Kindle eBook
ISBN 978 1 8496 4765 6   EPUB eBook

Library of Congress Cataloging in Publication Data applied for

This book is printed on paper suitable for recycling and made from fully managed
and sustained forest sources. Logging, pulping and manufacturing processes are
expected to conform to the environmental standards of the country of origin.

10   9   8   7   6   5   4   3   2   1

Typeset from disk by Stanford DTP Services, Northampton, England
Simultaneously printed digitally by CPI Antony Rowe, Chippenham, UK and
Edwards Bros in the United States of America

Contents

List of Figures and Tables

Preface

In 2010 a series of events brought me to the realisation that I knew hardly anything about what was happening in English universities, despite having been around them as a student, lecturer and employee for the best part of 20 years.

The main catalyst was the decision by Middlesex University to close its highest rated research department, the Centre for Research in Modern European Philosophy, where I had pursued my own doctorate a few years before. Eventually, during that summer's vacation, the centre was transferred across London to Kingston University, leaving behind the undergraduate courses and the academics who taught them.* Philosophy finally disappeared from Middlesex in the summer of 2012.

Decisions such as this are motivated by markets and the manner in which money moves around the higher education system. Middlesex was expanding overseas and philosophy had a limited role in its future vision. At the same time, Middlesex has been able to keep the annual research income awarded for the performance of Philosophy, roughly £175,000 in 2009/10, although no such research is now undertaken there. The relevant funding body 'does not monitor staffing changes'. The money will continue to come in until 2015 and can be directed to other ends. Middlesex, in effect, was able to strip its own assets.

The 2010 general election took place as events were unfolding at Middlesex ushering in a Coalition which, on receipt of the Browne review into university financing, took the decision to raise the maximum tuition fee at publicly funded universities from £3,375 to £9,000 per year. The complexity of the scheme, which underpins these fees with unfamiliar 'income contingent repayment loans', is

---

* Anonymous accounts of this movement from staff and students with its extensive online and press coverage (including the twelve-day student occupation of Middlesex's Mansion House building) can be found in *Radical Philosophy*, 162, Dossier: Universities, July/August 2010, pp. 40–7, and, in more detail, on the website for the Save Middlesex Philosophy group (www.savemdxphil.com), the student-led focus for the protests. My own account can be found at www. afterall.org/online/the-matter-at-middlesex: Andrew McGettigan, 'The Matter at Middlesex' *Afterall online*, 8 September 2010.

notorious: many politicians and commentators do not understand the system, nor do academics, students and parents.

But beyond the headline prices, a more profound transformation of money and markets is being pushed through without democratic oversight or parliamentary scrutiny. The contention of this book is that the government is taking a gamble with English higher education but without presenting its plans or reasoning to the public. It intends to shift resources to the most selective universities, while exposing the majority of higher education institutions to new commercial pressures. Direct funding is slashed and formerly 'private' providers will be nurtured into the sector so as to undercut established provision.

The gamble would be won if this new form of competition were to drive up standards overall. To quote a much-loved phrase of Andrew Lansley and David Willetts, 'it is the rising tide that lifts all the boats'. In this way, the quiet, piecemeal reforms to higher education funding are consistent with the second wave of public sector reform seen in health and in primary and secondary education. Unlike in these areas, however, where a decade of transformation culminated in set-piece primary legislation (the 2011 Education Act and the 2012 Health and Social Care Act), the changes in higher education have yet to stabilise and the promised Bill has been delayed. This means there are still opportunities to resist the worst of the plans.

This book is therefore a primer in two senses. Politically, it attempts to set out the measures afoot and as such illustrate what is at stake in otherwise obscure developments. Chiefly, it anticipates that any HE Bill which does materialise will be technical and presented as an attempt to rationalise arcane legislation. It will, however, be about new forms of privatisation, in particular, facilitating the entry of private equity into a sector that appears ripe for value extraction.

From below, the book is written for those who, as I did in 2010, find themselves confused by what is happening in the institutions with which they are associated, whether as students, academics, staff or potential applicants. It attempts to provide a one-stop resource for interpreting management and governor decisions. If you do not understand the context in which corporate strategic decisions are made, then you cannot subject those decisions to questioning. This is dangerous – the occupant of the vice-chancellor's office does not know best.

To that end, it is the book I wish I had to hand back then. It pulls together two years of immersion in the technical side (the mechanics and vocabulary) of the issues of funding, recruitment

markets, bond issues, joint ventures and other possibiliti
the potential buyout of established universities by privat
had to become a freelance 'policy wonk' in order to wor
was going on – this book aims to spare you that chore.

As universities and colleges are forced to operate in commercial terrain, it is basic business imperatives that come to the fore. Our habits of thought about higher education are no longer appropriate for this new terrain. This book sets out to be a guide.

To conclude these opening remarks with a few caveats:

First, this book is pitched for a general readership. As a primer and an overview I have had to restrict full discussion of some aspects. For some there will be insufficient detail in parts.

Second, I regret that there is almost no discussion of education or the lived transformative experience of study and teaching in this book. In the world of education policy and financing, there is little of this dimension. Hopefully, the material in this book is haunted by this absence and will spur readers to think about how we ended up on our current path.

Third, this terrain is live, with new almost weekly developments requiring continual revision of the manuscript. To the best of my knowledge, this book describes the state of play at the end of November 2012.

Finally, as a football fan, I consider higher education to be on a cusp of a transformation akin to that which befell the sport 20 years ago, when the breakaway Premier League and Sky TV money combined with the regulatory arbitrage of corporate restructuring to reroute the financial circuits of the game. We are about to witness something similar in higher education: a new elite will cement its position by monopolising resources in new ways, while the majority of institutions will be left to scrap in a new market swamped with cheap degree providers. We have a chance to avert the worst excesses and even avoid this fate, but it depends on what we do before the 2015 election.

Acknowledgements

This book is the product of two years' work. There are a lot of people to thank for their help and support.

In the early days of my researches Christian Kerslake, Andy Goffey, Alfie Meadows, Matthew Charles and Marina Vishmidt encouraged me to persist with my investigations.

Afterall and *Radical Philosophy* provided me with the first opportunities to write about universities. In that regard, I will thank in particular Pablo Lafuente, Melissa Gronlund, Peter Osborne, Stella Sandford, Peter Hallward and David Cunningham.

The summer of 2011 saw the formation of the 'Alternative White Paper' working group in response to the government's plans for higher education. Over the course of a few months, I had the opportunity to develop the ideas that frame *The Great University Gamble* through concerted online exchanges with the group's members: especially, Simon Szreter, Gill Evans, Howard Hotson, Kate Tunstall and James Ladyman.

At that time, I also had the great fortune to meet Gurminder Bhambra and John Holmwood. Both have been consistently supportive of this book and the broader activism it intends to inform.

For periods of my research, especially into the darker side of student loans and university financing, I was lucky to have been supported by *Research Fortnight* and the Intergenerational Foundation. I would like to thank William Cullerne Bown, Ehsan Masood, Liz Emerson, Antony Mason and Angus Hanton. They allowed me to pursue a line of research which otherwise would have stalled.

Des Freedman asked me to speak at the launch for *The Assault on Universities* (also from Pluto Press) in October 2011. That invitation led directly to this book. My especial thanks to him and all involved in the production of the book. David Castle has been a supportive editor, particularly in so far as the government's shifting legislative plans upset our original publication deadlines.

For collegiality and technical advice, John Thompson, Sukhdev Johal, Nick Barr, David Palfreyman, Dennis Farrington, Roger Brown, Bahram Bekhradnia, Gavan Conlon, Samuel Mesfen and Philip Stokoe have been exemplary.

Others who have provided me with insight, support and debate include: Liam Burns, Chaminda Jayanetti, Mark Bergfeld, Graeme Wise, Mark Leach, Nina Power, Richard Hall, Martin McQuillan, David Kernohan, Richard Cochrane, Nathan Charlton and Catherine Walsh.

I'd like to single out for thanks: Marian Hobson, who examined my doctorate in contemporary French philosophy, and has proved a persistent champion of my work in this new area; and Chris Newfield, whose excellent *Unmaking the Public University* about the threats against state-funded higher education in the USA provided both stimulation and a potential model for writing about UK higher education, despite the crucial differences.

More personally, friends and family have had to put up with me while churning out material: the McGettigans are owed 'a social soirée'!

Special thanks to Katherine Ibbett, Richard Mc Kenny and James McKay for moral support and clear-eyed observations. A pep talk from Andrew Morris during a trip round Liverpool's pubs provided a boost at a key time. Over the last 20 years, Jonathan White and I have debated pretty much everything there is to debate; since he is also an expert on higher education and privatisation, his presence in this book extends way beyond the direct citations of his work.

Clunie Reid probably saw the worst of me. My thanks and love to her: 'without whom not'.

The book though is dedicated to Pete Mellows. Together Pete and I attended the demonstrations against the tripling of the tuition fee cap and the abolition of EMA back in the Autumn and Winter of 2010. Unfortunately he did not live to see those measures undone.

'A tender man who loved justice'. In memoriam.

Abbreviations

AoC – Association of Colleges

BIS – Department of Business, Innovation and Skills
BTEC – *Formerly* Business and Education Technology Council

CAT – College of Advanced Technology
CNAA – Council for National Academic Awards
CPI – Consumer Price Index
CSR – Comprehensive Spending Review

DAP – Degree Awarding Powers
DWP – Department of Work and Pensions

EMA – Education Maintenance Allowance
ERA – Education Reform Act 1988

FE – Further Education
FEC – Further Education Corporation
FHEA – Further and Higher Education Act 1992

GDP – Gross Domestic Product

Hefce – Higher Education Funding Council for England
HEI – Higher Education Institution
HE in FE – Higher Education in Further Education
Hepi – Higher Education Policy Institute
HESA – Higher Education Statistics Agency
HNC – Higher National Certificate
HND – Higher National Diploma
HTS – Highly Trusted Sponsor

ICR Loans – Income Contingent Repayment Loans
ILEA – Inner London Education Authority

KIS – Key Information Sets

LEA – Local Education Authority

NPV – Net Present Value
NSP – National Scholarship Programme
NSS – National Student Satisfaction Survey

OBR – Office for Budgetary Responsibility
Offa – Office for Fair Access
OFT – Office for Fair Trading
OIA – Office of the Independent Adjudicator

PSND – Public Sector Net Debt

QAA – Quality Assurance Agency
QR funding – Quality-related Research funding

RAB – Resource Accounting and Budgeting
RAE – Research Assessment Exercise
REF – Research Excellence Framework
RPI – Retail Price Index

SLC – Student Loan Company
SNC – Student Numbers Controls
SSI – Small and Specialist Institutions
STEM – Science, Technology, Engineering, Mathematics

UCAS – Universities and Colleges Admissions Service
UGC – University Grants Committee
UKBA – UK Border Agency
UUK – Universities UK
VAT – Value Added Tax

Introduction: Privatisation – The Plan and the Gamble

In May 2010, the UK Coalition government formed under an overarching narrative: austerity measures had to be introduced to restore economic health, given the large and increasing public sector deficit (the difference between annual income and expenditure). Its political ending was envisaged as follows: the structural deficit would be eliminated by 2015, the rate of increase of the national debt would have been slowed to zero in relation to GDP, and that year's general election would be fought on the platform of economic competence. Public funding therefore had to be cut across the board and the budgets used to fund higher education could not be immune.

The government department responsible for English higher education – the Department for Business, Innovation and Skills (BIS) – chose to concentrate its reductions on the block grant received by universities and colleges for undergraduate provision. In the Comprehensive Spending Review of October 2010, the Chancellor, George Osborne, announced that by 2014/15 the block grant would be cut from nearly £5 billion to roughly £2 billion, an annual saving of £3 billion, with many subjects seeing all central funding removed. This measure protected the independent science and research budgets while effecting a change necessary to create a new regulated market in higher education.

However, something else is afoot: the government is not simply implementing a change driven by temporary difficulties; it does *not* intend to restore the block grant when national finances improve. Instead, austerity is the occasion which makes the prominent changes more acceptable politically: 'there is no alternative'.

In order to maintain an equivalent level of financing for universities, higher tuition fees must make up for the shortfall. A vote in December 2010, which precipitated public protests outside Westminster, raised the maximum fee permissible at a state-funded university to £9,000, a sizeable increase on the 2011/12 fee of £3,375.

Understandably, headlines focused on this dramatic rise in price and its apparent expense for graduates, while obscuring the greater burden placed on the publicly backed student loan scheme, which requires an *increase in upfront* government borrowing. In the medium term, Public Sector Net Debt is projected to grow by an additional £20 billion as a result. Aided by accounting conventions, BIS is able to show a reduction in departmental expenditure, but, perversely, the standard narrative about deficit reduction and borrowing does not apply here.

Instead, the move to a generalised fee and loan regime is part of a more profound transformation of higher education and the public sector in general. The agenda is to create a lightly regulated market of a diverse range of private companies with direct public funding to institutions diluted to homeopathic levels. An experiment is being conducted on English universities; one that is not controlled and that in the absence of any compelling evidence for change threatens an internationally admired and efficient system.

As I write two years on, with the economic strategy unravelling, pressures to cut funding further are mounting, while a promised Higher Education Bill has been delayed. Now is the time to set out what agenda the government has been pursuing, how it has been pursued without democratic mandate or oversight, and how it is now being extended without parliamentary scrutiny. For the time being, the legislative change necessary to fully realise its ambitions has been stymied by focused pressure, but the government may be gathering its strength for a push before 2014. David Willetts, the Minister for Universities and Science, hopes to be 'ingenious' and to legislate retrospectively once the effects of his policies become clearer: as it stands he intends to use the powers put in place by the previous Labour administration to pursue a privatisation agenda, opening space for private equity and commercial companies to operate within the public higher education system and distribute profits out to backers, shareholders and owners.

Much of what any Bill would propose will appear obscure and technical; it will be presented as the rationalisation of historical anomalies, the removal of 'unfair' restrictions, and as liberating for individual institutions. The aim, however, will be to break what appears to its ideologues as a state monopoly in higher education.

As this book will set out, there is large mixture of cock-up and compromise in these developments, with BIS, the department responsible for universities, under extended pressure from the Treasury to control costs, while also recently losing out to the Home Office and the UK Border Agency over student visas at London Metropolitan University. The broader aim and strategy can be pieced together as one which is consistent with the reforms of the

NHS under Andrew Lansley and primary and secondary education under Michael Gove. What is introduced is the idea that health and education can be offered and run in a manner akin to utilities such as gas and electricity. 'Public Service Reform is an omnibus term. We should understand it to embrace economic services as well as social services – telecoms, water, rail and postal services as well as health, education and policing.'[1]

What is challenged, eroded or destroyed in all these areas is democratic accountability, the disappearance of a public service in a positive sense.

PRIVATISATION: AIMING FOR A REGULATED SECTOR OF PRIVATE COMPANIES

Markets of this kind have to be created. David Willetts is committed to creating a 'level playing field' for any qualified provider able to recruit. The basic building blocks have been put in place without the need for primary legislation.

First, cut the block grant to public universities *entirely* in those areas where private providers are able to compete; thereby removing a 'subsidy' which allows the established universities and colleges to charge lower tuition fees. In a speech to the vice-chancellors of England's universities in February 2011, David Willetts said:

> Currently, one of the main barriers to alternative providers is the teaching grant we pay to publicly-funded HEIs [higher education institutions]. This enables HEIs to charge fees at a level that private providers could not match, and so gives publicly-funded HEIs a significant advantage. Our funding reforms will remove this barrier, because all HEIs will – in future – receive most of their income from students via fees. This reform, of itself, opens up the system.[2]

To confirm, austerity is the cover for an end desired for other reasons.

Second, BIS is rapidly expanding a scheme they inherited from Labour to 'designate' courses at private providers for student support. That is, students on such courses are able to access loans to pay up to £6,000 for fees while also being able to access maintenance grants and loans, used to cover costs of living while studying, on the same terms as those at the established universities. Under such arrangements, the private providers find a further impediment removed: students do not need to pay fees upfront and can more easily study full-time owing to maintenance support.

Third, it has announced changes to regulations governing the protected title of 'university', which would allow institutions with only 1,000 students to apply. Although this will benefit some smaller higher education institutions currently within the state system, its main aim is anticipatory: offering new entrants to the market access to a title which can boost market perceptions. ('University' will effectively be a kitemark within the new market.)[3]

These reforms remove barriers to 'market entry' and enable more 'providers' to compete within the state system: the first two changes obviously alter the separation of private and public providers. But market entry barriers are also about quality control – determining the standards of the public system.

It is part of the general conservative ideology that bottom-up consumerism, having funding follow the student, will drive up quality. Both Lansley and Willetts hold to the credo that 'competition is a tide which lifts every boat'. As Willetts elaborates:

> The case for our higher education reforms is quite simply that they will lead universities to focus far more intensively than ever before on the quality of the teaching experience because they will be competing for students who bring their funding with them.[4]

First, it is not clear that quality here will mean academic quality, rather than general student experience: the evidence points to investment in non-teaching facilities, such as sports centres, social facilities and landscaped campuses, to attract applicants. Second, there are obvious inefficiencies in this competition as increasing resources have to be devoted to recruitment and marketing. Which leads to the third point.

The cost of financing higher education through the botched loan scheme means that the Treasury has insisted on an overall cap on student numbers. This creates a zero sum game where the sector is unable to expand overall and individual institutions are fighting for market *share*. This has the potential to turn inefficiencies into something potentially destructive. Especially if the new providers prove capable of disrupting the market.

Importantly, competition will be competition on *price* at least in terms of headline fees and initial graduate debt. New providers will offer a cheaper tier of provision that might steal away applicants from the more expensive middle seam of higher education institutions, who will be labouring under recruitment restrictions which prevent them from out-competing market entrants. This is desirable from the Treasury perspective as it has the potential to drive down the costs of the system. But it is hard to reconcile this situation with the promise of improved quality in general: as we will see, the government wants to promote 'value for money' rather than standard quality.

In the longer term, these measures are designed to create a wholly different *system* with markets determining what is offered. The overall impact on public life is unclear, but certain subjects are threatened, individual graduates will be more indebted, while the broader civic or public missions of universities that have defined their histories may be undermined by a challenge from private training providers who have no such interest and will therefore strip back unprofitable overheads: for example, they are not required to participate in widening participation or access initiatives. Nor do they pursue research.

In effect, the majority of universities will need to become more akin to commercial operations, charging for services. Faced with competition from profit-distributing entities with rich backers, it is not clear whether maintaining charitable status will be viable in the long-run for most.

THE DEMOCRATIC DEFICIT

This book concentrates on explaining this vision, how it is meant to work, and in particular the culture it engenders within universities. It is an attempt to explain what is going on in an area where there is little public debate. Without the planned legislation, and the national attention generated, there is a democratic deficit here.

Creeping reform is inconsistent with democratic oversight. What debates there have been, have been about fee levels; what has been put out to consultation often lacks concrete proposals. In the 2011 Higher Education White Paper and its accompanying technical consultations, key issues were couched in obscure paragraphs, which when consulted upon revealed no further detail, only open-ended questions. Secrecy surrounded some of the reviews, such as that being conducted by the financial investors, Rothschild, into 'monetising the loan book'. A piece of jargon which masks something more than a simple sale of student loans to third parties. One concrete example can be proffered to illustrate this charge. The vote on tuition fees in December 2010 was a 'snap vote' called with little notice and with little time scheduled in the House of Commons: a tactical means to curtail debate both inside and outside Parliament.

Besides protests, what we have seen is largely lobbying conducted by either privateers or the vice-chancellors, through Universities UK (akin to the CBI) or the various 'mission groups'. The interests of these do not match those of academics, students or the public in general. Universities, increasingly acting like corporations, were paid off: overall universities had expected to see an increase in annual income, albeit unevenly distributed, with the cost passed on to the individual graduate and the underwriter of the loans: the Treasury or taxpayer.

However, the September 2012 figures from UCAS – the higher education organisation overseeing undergraduate applications – showed that accepted places at English universities were down by over 50,000 students compared to 2011. These results cast doubt on the competency of vice-chancellors and their ability to understand the government's plans.

WHY A GAMBLE?

The government is taking a huge gamble with England's universities, introducing uncertainty into a stable and productive system, though one not without its faults. On almost every international survey, once size of population and the economy are factored in, English higher education demonstrates excellent value for money in relation to the public spending that supports it.

Concerns ought to be to the fore given the pace of change. The rush to implement these changes before the next general election in 2015 itself creates dangers and entirely avoidable short-term challenges for universities who in some cases need to replace £40 million per year in public funding. It is not clear what the impact on academic quality will be: this is not a controlled experiment.

A small elite of institutions will benefit. As they are allowed to expand, and their prestige supports higher fees, they will be better positioned to monopolise resources. It is the fate of the remaining majority of UK universities to be the stakes in this game. Most university leaders may think that they may be lucky enough to thrive in the new setting, but we should expect a diminution in the number of universities in England, whether through merger or collapse, and prospective students are likely to soon face less choice as to where and what to study.

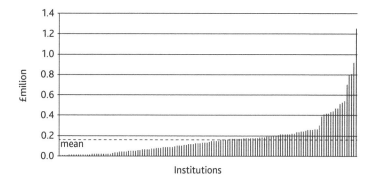

Figure 0.1   Annual income by English higher education institutions, 2010–11

Source: HESA 2011

Figure 0.1 shows the distribution of annual incomes by higher education institution in England for 2010/11. The mean annual income is £170 million. Note it only shows *income*, not wealth or assets or endowments, those measures which favour Oxford and Cambridge even further. These disparities are a historical legacy but they will be exacerbated by the new regime as those institutions which are the richest will be able to generate higher levels of income from undergraduate study than previously.

On the former regime, each institution received the same funding for the same activity – that is, a sociology student at Huddersfield or Nottingham produced the same income. That will not now be the case over the medium term: fees produce funding differentials. There are therefore a number of institutions – the mass of mass higher education – whose operating conditions will be transformed and potentially rendered unviable. So any question as to who benefits would need to clearly demarcate the self-positioning, constantly lobbying elite and new private providers primed to enter the 'level playing field' from the middle tier.

What motivates this gamble (which as yet lacks any clear controls on its outcome) is not hard to find. On the one hand, the clear intent of the government is to make universities more customer-, business- and industry-focused. Tightening the purse strings encourages institutions into such collaborations; universities are able to attract other sources of income if they are forced to do so as part of a 'knowledge economy' and export-oriented strategy. As Peter Mandelson, then in charge of BIS, wrote in 2009:

Universities will need to seek out other sources of funding, from overseas sources as well as domestic ones. The experience of the last decade suggests there is considerable capacity to do this. New money has come from creating greater economic benefits from the knowledge they generate or the teaching expertise they provide and from philanthropic sources of income and increased international earnings.[5]

Again, that universities are *able* to do so, does not mean that it is the broader interest of society that they should, if it involves re-orientation away from public benefit objectives and reduces universities to private training providers with no interest in promoting public goods.

But why destabilise and possibly sacrifice the rest of the system? There are free market ideologues in both Coalition partners who simply see increasing competition and student consumerism as the battering rams with which to overcome university inertia. Further, the efficiency of the English higher education system indicates that it is ripe for privatisation. Opening new outlets for capital is a boon to the financial services sector backing the Conservative Party. The Bureau of Investigative Journalism detailed the figures: half of the £12.2 million donated to Conservative Central Office in 2010/11 originated there, with hedge fund managers and financiers providing £2.69 million.[6]

Willetts held twelve meetings with representatives from private equity firms and education multinationals prior to the publication of the Higher Education White Paper in June 2011. These meetings were organised by Hawkpoint: corporate finance advisors specialising in mergers and acquisitions. Attendees included: Pearson plc, Kaplan, Duke Street, Sovereign Capital, Warburg Pincus, A4E. They are keen to gain access to publicly backed student loans and thereby enter a market which has been described by some analysts as 'Treasure Island'. Representatives from Hefce, the Higher Education Funding Council for England, which is designated to become the sector's regulator, were also in attendance.[7]

Ultimately, these aspects come together in a single ideological aim. The broader vision in the UK is to roll back the state to a minimum function – to broker deals between finance and private sector provision. This continues a strand of 1980s public policy but one revivified by improvements in data management and, yes, financial derivatives. The government will remove itself from as many public services as possible, whether through reduced funding or, where it has administrative responsibility, sale.

Willetts and his counterpart, the Education Secretary, Michael Gove, favour a new wave of public sector privatisation. In response, we must develop new methods of analysis and concepts which grasp the transformation we are living through. Above all, we need to be attuned to inflections of 'privatisation', which in common parlance is normally limited to the transfer of assets and responsibilities from the state to the private sector. In higher education, we see different processes, policy considerations and initiatives:

1. Marketisation or external privatisation, whereby new operations with different corporate forms are allowed to enter the state system to increase competition. This might be seen as dissolving the distinction between separate public and private sectors.
2. Commodification – the presentation of higher education as solely a private benefit to the individual consumer; even as a financial asset where the return on investment is seen in higher earnings upon graduation.
3. Independence from regulation – private providers accessing the student loan book are not bound by numbers controls and do not have to comply with reporting or monitoring requirements nor widen participation initiatives.
4. Internal privatisation – the changes to revenue streams within institutions so that for example, direct public funding is replaced by *private* tuition fee income.

We could add to this list:

5. The outsourcing of jobs and activities to the private sector and management consultants, which has become widespread in England.
6. Changes to the corporate form and governance structures of universities.
7. The entry of private capital and investment into the sector through buyout and joint ventures with established institutions.

THE ALTERNATIVE

Yet there remains a third revolution, perhaps the most difficult of all to interpret. We speak of a cultural revolution, and we must certainly see the aspiration to extend the active process of learning, with the skills of literacy and other advanced communication, to all people rather than to limited groups, as comparable in importance to the growth of democracy and the rise of scientific industry. This aspiration has been and is being resisted, sometimes openly, sometimes subtly, but as an aim it has been formally acknowledged, almost universally.

Raymond Williams, *The Long Revolution*

What many would call for is a proper debate about the purpose of universities and higher education in the twenty-first century and how they should be funded. Instead we have the hope that the market solution, that has not been presented to the public, will sort those questions out and that we will not be left with a polarised sector featuring a handful of selective universities (privatised to all intents and purposes) and a selection of cheap degree shops offering cut-price value for money.

Is education a consumer good that benefits from market reforms? It is not consumed in the same way as gas, electricity and water, where privatisation has hardly been an overwhelming success. What alternative vision of public education is available? A proper debate would throw up genuine problems, question assumptions, and discuss the solutions to be implemented. We sit at the end of a century of expansion – both in the number of institutions and the number of people participating in tertiary education. This is not without complexities or problems. We have a system which has formed over time. It was, in Raymond Williams's term, a 'long revolution' involving the transformation of individuals and institutions.

We ought to be putting the question of purpose first and asking what we want from higher education in the twenty-first century. In 1944, the Association of University Teachers set out the core goals of the university as: the pursuit and dissemination of knowledge; the formation of young people as individuals; and the study of social problems and problems of citizenship. The Robbins Report of 1963 outlined four aims: (i) instruction in skills; (ii) promoting the 'general powers of the mind'; (iii) the advancement of learning; and (iv) the transmission of a common culture and common standards of citizenship. We can add to these lists professional and vocational training.

The market envisaged by Willetts depends on universities, already private, exempt charities, acting increasingly like companies chasing commercial ends. The well-known principal-agent problem is exacerbated in universities as vice-chancellors, or their equivalents, act as if they are principal (owners) and chief executive (agent) in one person. That is, it is not simply that a top-down managerial culture has gained the upper hand, 'command and control', but that it has become autocratic.

Attention has been focused on the exorbitant salaries paid to vice-chancellors, but it would be better to consider what that reflects: broken corporatism. A different form of corporatism would be forged about collegiality: a community of scholars and students involved in running the institution needs to be developed. This would be open, participative and accountable to the broader community: an 'independent public body' in the terms of the recent von Prondzynski review into Scottish university governance.[8]

Such a set-up would be better able to promote the public goods associated with universities and would address the democratic issue of participation. In the words of Anthony Crosland: higher education institutions should be aspire to be 'relevant, vibrant, deserving of public support',[9] not simply prestigious, selective and reassuringly expensive.

OVERVIEW OF THE BOOK

Beyond the headlines about fees it is therefore important to articulate and set out the extent of the government's plans and consider their likely consequences. Chiefly, moving to a loan system in large part creates the necessary conditions for a new market in undergraduate recruitment, which in turn will lead to a new phase in 'privatisation'.

The focus of this book will be on the political economy of institutions in this new environment. It is designed to be a primer on how money is moving in new ways through the system. It will provide an overview of the issues and implications. For this reason, there will be less attention to students than some might have expected. This book will not help you decide whether you should pursue higher education or not; it will help you think about what higher education should look like and how it is being transformed today.

Unfortunately, given the constraints under which this book was produced, there are a number of themes that deserve fuller treatment but which cannot be dealt with in these pages. These include research, part-time study, postgraduate study, business and industry collaboration, further education and issues such as widening participation, social mobility and the class dynamics of education.

The book is also entirely focused on England, since the changes described are taking place in that part of the United Kingdom: fleeting reference will be made to Scotland, Wales and Northern Ireland for whom education is a devolved issue.

The book is divided into four parts and builds incrementally from a short history of recent policy and funding decisions to set out how the new market in higher education is supposed to work. In particular, it emphasises the polarising effect of the rigged market and the need to seek new income streams.

The first Part will cover recent policy history and the expansion since the late 1980s before continuing with the basics of tuition fees and student loans. The government is offering a revised, publicly backed loan scheme. The complexity of this unfamiliar scheme and the high figures involved have dominated debate. As it involves varying level of repayments for 30 years (or earlier in some cases of very high earners) it is difficult for individuals to assess how much they will repay in total. Those working within higher education may be inclined to skip those chapters, but there are nuances in there which are often misunderstood – particularly around the specifics of the income contingent repayment loans. Loans will be examined in more detail in the final section of the book.

Part 2 is concerned with the new market in undergraduate recruitment. Its four chapters cover everything from the government's complex numbers controls to the planned entry of new private providers into the sector through the creation of a 'level playing field'.

Part 3 will concentrate on 'privatisation'. The implications of such competition will lead to upheaval: transforming institutions from within but also from without through mergers, buyouts and the potential transformation of established charities into other forms. This section will also look at the issue of corporate form, bond issues and other factors altering the internal functioning of established universities.

In a departure from most writing on the subject, the fourth Part will look at the problems with the loan scheme from a fiscal and macroeconomic perspective. How will this and future governments *manage* the liabilities used to create the loan scheme? What does it mean for politics and policy that the outstanding balances on individual loan accounts are predicted on official figures to reach

£191 billion by 2046? What risks are engendered? This section introduces the term 'financialisation' to describe how loans produce information and therefore have the potential to produce a new generation of performance metrics.

The sections are designed to be relatively self-contained and to be used as a basic reference point as well as to be read straight through. At the end of the book, you will find a glossary and an index.

Part 1
The Basics of HE Funding

The fundamentals of higher education funding are set out here. Chapter 1 covers the recent policy history culminating in the events of 2010: the formation of the Coalition government, the delivery of the Browne review into undergraduate funding, and the subsequent decision to cut direct funding to universities. Chapter 2 looks at tuition fees and why the average fee in 2012 was above the government's desired figure of £7,500 per year. Chapter 3 examines student loans and their repayment terms.

1
The Mass Higher Education System and its Funding

To understand the new level of tuition fees in England and the cuts to direct grant funding of institutions, one needs to understand the recent history of the sector, which has been transformed in the last 20 years or so by an initially rapid expansion. This has placed the funding of students and the financing of universities at the centre of policy debate and brought the Treasury into the dominant position when it comes to decision-making.

THE ADVENT OF A MASS SYSTEM

Expansion of higher education began under Kenneth Baker, Secretary of State for Education in the Thatcher government. Initiated by the 1988 Education Reform Act and the 1992 Further and Higher Education Act, participation rates by age cohort leapt from around 15 per cent in 1988 to close to 35 per cent within a decade. Contrary to popular misunderstandings, this participation rate was not the simple result of polytechnics being reclassified as universities: those attending polytechnics were already included in the *higher education* participation statistics. But, the polytechnics and their successor institutions did expand, some dramatically: Hatfield Polytechnic, as it became the University of Hertfordshire, saw an expansion in its student numbers from around 5,000 to over 30,000 during the 1990s.

Figure 1.1 illustrates the dramatic spike in participation between 1988 and the mid 1990s. The two lines on the graph reflect different methods of measuring the initial participation rate in higher education. The lower line shows the Age Participation Index (API) of those under 21 as a percentage of the cohort, which has more recently been replaced by the Higher Education Initial Participation Rate (higher line) which covers those aged between 17 and 30.[1] Doubts about API methodology mean that is only used here to illustrate the *relative change in participation.*

There are now over one million Home undergraduates studying full-time and many more part-time, not to mention postgraduates

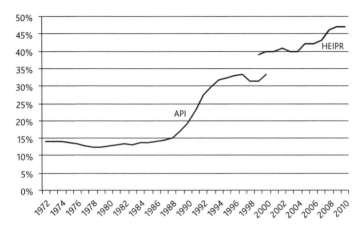

Figure 1.1   Participation of young people in HE as percentage of age cohort (England)

Source: John Thompson and Bahram Bekhradnia, *Male and Female Participation and Progression in Higher Education*, Hepi, 2010; *Higher Education in Facts and Figures*, Universities UK, 2012

and students from outside the EU. Despite populist and popular grumblings, this approach, expanding to meet demand, has largely found cross-party support, underpinning both Baker's initiative and Tony Blair's 1997 election campaign mantra of 'Education, Education, Education', which set a new target of 50 per cent of school leavers moving on to higher education. In some ways, the advent of a mass system is the consummation of the 1963 Robbins Report which argued that 'courses of higher education should be available for all those who are qualified by ability and attainment to pursue them and who wish to do so'.[2]

FUNDING THE MASS SYSTEM

The flipside to expansion is the question of funding. Figure 1.2 shows the funding per student in 2006/7 prices between 1948 and 2009.

Funding per student declined precipitously in real terms from 1981 and declined even faster with the expansion of the late 1980s and early 1990s. The last two major reviews of higher education, Dearing (1997) and Browne (2010), focused on this question of funding. Dearing recommended a means-tested upfront fee of £1,000 per year, the introduction of which stabilised the per-student resourcing (black squares in Figure 1.2). This move established the principle of 'co-payment', whereby the benefit accruing to the

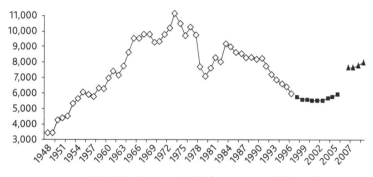

⬦ Historic funding per student (no private contributions)
▪ Historic funding per student (incorporating up front fees)
▲ Historic funding per student (incorporating differential fees)

Figure 1.2   University funding per full-time student in England, 1948–2009 (at 2006/7 prices)

Source: London Economics (BIS Research Paper Number 10), *Review of Student Support Arrangements in Other Countries*, September 2010, www.bis.gov.uk/assets/biscore/corporate/docs/r/10–670-review-student-support-in-other-countries.pdf

private individual from higher education should be reflected in more than taxation on higher earnings.

In 2004, Labour pushed through the contentious policy of 'variable fees', winning its passage by only four votes despite its large parliamentary majority. A new maximum fee was set at £3,000 per year. (Thereby introducing the legislation used by the Coalition for its snap vote in December 2010.) These fees, however, were no longer paid upfront and were instead covered by an expansion of the student loan scheme, which had previously been restricted to loans to cover some of the costs of maintenance while studying.

All institutions soon moved to this new fee level and no pricing variation occurred at undergraduate level. It is important to note that, in contrast to the latest reforms, these fees did not replace any central funding but provided *additional* resourcing to universities and college and so restored per-student funding to a level comparable to the 1980s (black triangles in Figure 1.2). Advocates of fees have in mind the manner in which their introduction broke with government rationing of resources.

THE BROWNE REVIEW

In 2009, Peter Mandelson, then Labour Secretary of State for Business, Innovation and Skills, published a report, *Higher*

Ambitions, which set out a vision for a more entrepreneurial higher education sector less reliant on central funding.[3] (In the course of 2010, the Labour government announced a reduction in the higher education budget for 2010/11 of £135 million.)

Subsequently, a review panel was established, led by John Browne, formerly chief executive of BP. Its remit was to set in place a sustainable system of financing higher education that would lighten the burden on public finances, but also enable the sector to expand to meet the current unmet demand for undergraduate education. Its final recommendations were published in October 2010 as *Securing a Sustainable Future for Higher Education*, after the change in government.[4] A short report of 60 pages, it had eight main recommendations:

1. Massive reduction in direct grants including the removal of direct public funding for arts, humanities and social science degrees.
2. The abolition of the current tuition fee cap allowing universities to set whatever fees they wished.
3. A levy scheme, or 'soft cap', requiring universities to *return an increasing proportion of those higher fees to central coffers* for each thousand pound increment above £6,000 (see Table 1.1). It was designed to dissuade universities from setting fees indiscriminately, since universities do not bear the cost of non-repayment on loans, the Exchequer does.

Table 1.1   Browne's proposed fee levy

Nominal Fee	£6,000	£7,000	£8,000	£9,000	£10,000	£11,000	£12,000
Levy per additional £1,000	none	40%	45%	50%	55%	65%	75%
Percentage of total fee received by institution	100%	94%	89%	85%	81%	77%	73%

Source: *Securing a Sustainable Future*, 2010, p. 37

4. A change to the parameters of the loan scheme so that repayments would only begin once the graduate was in receipt of more than £21,000 per annum from 2016.
5. The introduction of *real* interest rates on the loans, i.e., above inflation, which were previously subsidised against the government's cost of borrowing.
6. The removal of all institutional recruitment caps (bar medicine and dentistry).

7. An increase in maintenance loans, grants and other financial support to full-time students.
8. Extending access to loans for tuition fees to part-time students.

On the one hand, the proposed system would be more 'sustainable' by having more funding return as loan repayments. On the other hand, removing all 'supply-side' restrictions on universities by abolishing fee and recruitment caps would mean on average that institutions would receive more income providing demand remained constant.

While there was consensus on the objectives of the reform of higher education funding (increasing participation, improving quality of provision, and making the funding solution sustainable), the solution of opening up competition by removing all direct public support and hiking fees was not unanimously received. Indeed the sole piece of research commissioned by the review revealed that: 'Most full-time students and parents ... believed that the government should pay at least half the cost of higher education. This is because the personal benefits of higher education were seen by many to match the benefits to society.' This striking finding did not appear in the final report and had to be revealed through a Freedom of Information request produced by *Times Higher Education*.[5]

The report argued that it had balanced the trade-off between public and private benefits accruing to the individual, but its private sector-style solutions reflected the background of its Chairman and several of its members, with CVs that included stints at the management consultancy firm McKinsey.

THE GOVERNMENT'S RESPONSE

Although the previous Labour administration had commissioned the Browne review, when it reported in October 2010 many of its suggestions were acceptable to the Conservatives now in government. The first recommendation, cutting direct central funding to institutions, was accepted. The Comprehensive Spending Review later in October announced the reduction in central grants to universities and colleges: around £3 billion per year by 2014/15 when the new regime is to be fully implemented. BIS will no longer offer any direct funding for degrees in the arts, humanities, business, law and social sciences, thus removing one impediment to competition from private providers. (The new higher fees will replace lost funding and therefore do not significantly alter the per-student funding seen in Figure 1.2.)

In a formal response to Browne the following month, the proposed interest rate taper and the higher loan repayment threshold (£21,000 in 2016 as opposed to £15,000 today) were both accepted. However, the 'levy', Item 3 above, proved unpopular with universities who wanted to keep more of, and more control over, the higher fees they expected to receive. In addition, the removal of a maximum tuition fee cap (Item 2) was unacceptable to the junior Coalition partners, the Liberal Democrats. Their 2010 Election manifesto had committed to abolishing tuition fees; they had actively campaigned around the issue and had signed an NUS pledge promising to vote against any increase.

Instead, a compromise was reached with a new maximum tuition fee (and no levy). Through a snap vote held in the House of Commons on 9 December 2010, the maximum fee allowed was raised from £3,375 per year to £9,000 for undergraduates commencing their studies in September 2012. Almost two years later, Nick Clegg, the Deputy Prime Minister and Leader of the Liberal Democracts, felt compelled to issue a filmed apology to the nation: not for the policy, but for signing the NUS pledge.

It was a political coup to bring that vote forward using existing secondary legislation *before* publishing a White Paper and detailed proposals on the actual functioning of the loan scheme and the new market in undergraduate recruitment. No detail could be examined; the House of Lords, which voted the following week, was deprived of its now conventional role as a *revising* chamber.

Had the new maximum fee moved through Parliament slowly, accompanying primary legislation, it may have been lost and split the Coalition. As it was the vote narrowly passed. This abuse had the desired effect of spiking the guns of those opposing the remainder of the plans and confusing potential activists about just what had been won or lost on that occasion.

MISTAKE AND COMPROMISE

Browne had warned the government not to cherry-pick from his proposals and to treat them as a coherent whole, but political compromises and mistakes frustrated this further. With no levy as per Browne to encourage universities to set lower fees, the government proposals contained only the bare maximum of £9,000 per year. In early 2011, most universities moved to set their fees for

2012 entry at this level, thus challenging the Coalition's pledge that the average, mean figure would be £7,500 per year. Treasury models had been constructed on that latter assumption in Autumn 2010.

However, a huge mistake had been committed in the rush to push through the snap vote. It had been assumed that a quango, the Office for Fair Access (for more on Offa see Chapter 2), had powers to negotiate with universities wishing to charge more than £6,000 per year and to limit what was set. This would have enabled direct control of higher education expenditure and underpinned Vince Cable's public assertion that only in 'exceptional circumstances' would any university set the maximum fee. But Offa has no such legislative powers. It can only determine whether or not a publicly funded higher education institution should be able to charge more than £6,000 in tuition fees. Depriving any institution of the higher level of fees is the so-called 'nuclear option' available to Offa.

A second problem resulted from compromise. On the eve of the December 2010 vote, only a last-minute concession persuaded 27 Liberal Democrats to vote in favour (21 voted against and 8 abstained). That concession committed to ensuring that the repayment threshold of £21,000 in 2016 would be increased annually in line with average wage inflation.

BIS's intention had been to review the threshold every five years. A review could decide to freeze the threshold, move it up or move it down. It is a straightforward mechanism for ensuring the sustainability of the loan scheme since the threshold both triggers when former students start repaying *and determines the amount repaid monthly* (see Chapter 3 for more detail). The concession to index-link the threshold altered the workings of the scheme in its fundamentals and introduced problems not intended in its original design. In effect, were this pledge to come into force from 2017 it would *lower* repayments and therefore increase the burden on the Treasury and the taxpayer.

The government therefore had to manage two problems, one the *larger than expected loan outlay* owing to higher fees, and the other, a compromise that meant that *repayments are likely to be lower* than was anticipated back in Autumn 2010. This combination threatened the viability of the scheme and ensured that Browne's aim to expand the system had to be rejected: supply-side restrictions on numbers would have to be maintained. Indeed, planned numbers were reduced by 10,000 owing to the expense of the government borrowing needed to finance the new higher loans.

THE 2011 HIGHER EDUCATION WHITE PAPER

The White Paper setting out in full the government's detailed plans had been due in early 2011 but was repeatedly delayed and was only published in late June. The delay was largely attributable to this need to fix the finances on which the government's plans had been based.

Students at the Heart of the System concentrated entirely on the reform of undergraduate education. Such a document is supposed to set out a clear vision for future changes to policy and legislation, but this one was a frustrating read. Mostly covering measures already undertaken, much of the detail one might have expected was displaced into a series of reviews and consultations (I counted at least fifteen) that launched, reported and concluded at various points over the following months.

The political function of the various consultations was to map out what might actually require primary legislation and to gauge in advance where opposition might lie. Following the eruption of opposition prior to the December 2010 vote, the government has been keen to avoid the focus for protest that primary legislation – with its long progress through Parliament – would represent. Instead, the plans were to be implemented little by little in piecemeal fashion using various means. These methods include budgetary cuts, instructions to quangos, secondary legislation, and what are termed 'statutory instruments' (which can even be issued quietly over the summer while parliamentary representatives are on holiday: they come into law *if no objections are tabled*). As far as possible the government is using powers that already exist or giving existing bodies new tasks.

The major new announcement in the document concerned the new restrictions on undergraduate recruitment. These market reforms, designed to drive down price but also allow the more prestigious universities greater freedom to expand, are set out in detail in Part 2.

However, the complicated recruitment mechanisms it introduced combined with the off-putting nature of the leap to £9,000 annual fees seems to have contributed to a large reduction in places. At the beginning of September 2012, UCAS was reporting that there were 50,000 fewer accepted places for 2012 entry as compared to 2011. Although a drop in places was also seen after the higher fees were introduced in 2006, this was only around 15,000 lower – a third of the impact. The Treasury may welcome this development, but the university sector does not.

2
Tuition Fees

This chapter and the following set out the fundamental reforms initiated by the Coalition government. This will look at the new higher fees and funding regime. These changes are profound and have been achieved without primary legislation and with limited parliamentary scrutiny.[1] Although higher fees are not the whole story, the move to what is primarily a fees system is the essential condition for implementing a new kind of market in undergraduate provision, which will be the subject of Part 2.

First, when fees were introduced in 1998, and when they were increased to £3,000, this was *additional funding*. Now, it is replacement funding covering the removal of the central block grant to universities. Such a shift to fees combined with a cut to grants effects the true intent of the reforms: 'opening up the system' to private money and operations. In so far as fees replace public funding, we see an *internal privatisation* of the university, even if the loan used to pay the fees is publicly backed. Second, money will now increasingly follow the student, which is the central tenet of the proposed market in undergraduate recruitment. This is the chief market reform. Third, the higher fee encourages the applicant to consider undergraduate study as a form of 'human capital' investment, or the purchase of a financial asset, the returns on which are to be seen after graduation in the form of higher earnings. As 'In Defence of Public Higher Education' summarises:

> These changes will encourage students to think of themselves as consumers, investing only in their own personal human capital with a view to reaping high financial rewards, and discourage graduates to think of their university education as anything other than something purchased at a high price for private benefit.[2]

FEES REPLACE FUNDING

With the increase of the maximum tuition fee to £9,000 and the average fee after waivers for 2012 being around £8,100, we should

---

Devolution and Tuition Fees

Since 1999 higher education policy has been devolved to the legislative bodies governing Wales, Scotland and Northern Ireland with the exception of the research councils and the Quality Assurance Agency which have UK-wide remits. There is a separate Higher Education Funding Council for each administration.

While the UK Coalition government has extended its policy for English universities into student-led market reforms, the devolved administrations have resisted this tendency and kept a stronger measure of state control. This is most clearly evidenced in tuition fee policy, where there are four different policies (note that EU students not from the UK must be treated equivalently to 'Home' applicants).

All applicants applying to English universities are able to be charged up to £9,000 full-time, but the Welsh authorities commit to paying the amount above £3,465 for Welsh students.

Welsh institutions can charge up to £9,000, but the Welsh authorities will again pay the difference above £3,465 for Welsh students *and EU students*.

Scottish institutions are free for Scottish and EU applicants, but applicants from the rest of the UK can be charged up to £9,000.

Northern Irish institutions can charge up to £9,000, but for Northern Irish and EU applicants *the maximum fee is capped at £3,465.*

---

not assume that all universities will be better resourced than they were previously.[3] How does this translate into per student resource for different courses?

The fees supplant the central grant that was paid by government to universities directly. Nearly £3 billion has been cut from this revenue stream. In 2011/12, the Higher Education Funding Council for England (a quango managing the distribution of public money to universities) divvied up the undergraduate teaching budget given to it by BIS. A grant was paid to each HEI reflecting the number of 'Home or EU' undergraduates, their mode of study (full-time or part-time), and the kind of degree they were pursuing.

Behind the scenes, degrees are categorised into four bands: A, B, C and D. This categorisation reflects the different resources each subject is thought to need. For example, it differentiates between a laboratory-based degree (Band B) and a course like philosophy, requiring only a library and classroom (Band D). Band B received

£5,484 in grant per student *in addition to the fees charged* (excluding London weighting), Band D, £2,709.

In 2011/12, students would have seen none of this: they would have paid the same fee whichever institution they chose and whatever subject they opted to study. Choice was not steered by a consideration of more or less expensive courses. The fee for full-time study, £3,375, the maximum charged by all universities, was then supplemented by the grant. (Students from outside of the EU pay 'full cost' fees. These are unregulated and are therefore higher than fees charged to other students and are largely determined by what the market will bear.) Table 2.1 compares the funding in 2011/12 with that which commenced in 2012/13 in simplified form.[4]

Table 2.1 Comparative funding for full-time undergraduate study per student

Indicative Subjects	Band	Typical Grant 2011/12	Plus £3,375 fee	Grant 2012/13	Including Maximum Fees (£9,000)	Including Target fee (£7,500)
Clinical Medicine & Clinical dentistry, Veterinary Science	A	£14,601	£17,976	£10,000	£19,000	n/a
Laboratory-based subjects (Science, Pre-Clinical Medicine) Engineering & Technology	B	£5,484	£8,859	£1,500	£10,500	£9,000
Intensive teaching, studio or fieldwork, inc. Art, Design & Mathematics	C	£3,898	£7,273	None	£9,000	£7,500
Arts & Humanities Law & Business	D	£2,709	£6,084	None	£9,000	£7,500

Source: Hefce, 2012 (www.hefce.ac.uk/learning/funding/201213/faq.htm#q4)

The first thing to note is that the 2012 cuts to the teaching budget translate into the removal of all such central funding for Band C and Band D subjects, with Band A and B subjects receiving a proportionate reduction in funding. The government insists, however, that a £9,000 fee should not be the norm:

§1.7 We [BIS] have consistently said that we believe graduate contributions of £9,000 should apply only in exceptional circumstances. Institutions would need to charge considerably less than this to offset reductions in HEFCE funding, and higher charges impose higher costs for the public purse because of the generous subsidies in the loan system.[5]

Second, were universities to set the government's desired fee of £7,500, as shown in the rightmost column, then the subjects located in Bands A, B and C would generate only a modicum of additional revenue. As we will see below there are also additional costs to factor in, especially in relation to the funding of access initiatives. In response to concerns around the funding of particular subjects, Hefce has introduced a new division within Band C – creating Band C1 and Band C2. C1 subjects will include archaeology, creative and performing arts, design, information science, software engineering and some media studies. From 2013/14, Hefce is proposing to restore £250 per year in grant for full-time undergraduates.[6]

Band D subjects find themselves in a different situation to the other subjects. Like those in Band C they now receive no central grant, but the reduction from £2,709 to none is a lower overall reduction in resourcing than the roughly £4,000 loss facing Bands A, B and C. On this basis, Willetts has rebutted accusations that the arts and humanities are being singled out in these reforms.[7] Any institution setting £9,000 fees for these courses ought to be making a large surplus.

We will look at pricing considerations later, but things are more complicated. The issues for arts and humanities at universities relate more to the competition to which they will now be subject from new private providers. While the Russell Group may be able to maintain £9,000 fees for these subjects, other institutions may have to go lower. Additionally, some Band D subjects may suffer from the reorientation of the system towards professional and vocational outcomes, possibly threatening the liberal arts model.

Finally, there may be even the temptation for universities to use the surplus from Band D subjects to cross-subsidise more expensive subjects and even research. The Association of Business Schools is particularly concerned about their ability to retain significant proportions of their revenues.

OTHER FUNDING

There are three other funding streams that are relevant to the setting of fees:

London Weighting

After its initial absence from official policy and then an interim allocation for 2012/13, Hefce is proposing to restore a specific 'London Weighting' grant in 2013/14. Universities are labour intensive operations with staffing counting for around 55 to 60 per cent of total expenditure on average. Salaries paid to academics in London are weighted according to whether the institution is located within 'Inner' or 'Outer' London – grant funding from Hefce will now reflect this. Its proposed rates per full-time student are shown in Table 2.2.

Table 2.2   London weighting

Price group	Inner London rate	Outer London rate
A	£1,174	£734
B	£499	£312
C	£382	£239
D	£294	£184

Source: Hefce, 2012

Widening Participation

Hefce maintains a 'widening participation' budget of around £140 million. This is used to provide grants to institutions to cover the extra costs of teaching and retaining students from disadvantaged backgrounds. This is in addition to the National Scholarship Programme (NSP) and access arrangements (see below), but there are suggestions that this budget may be lost once the new access arrangements are bedded in.

Small and Specialist Institutions (SSI)

Hefce offers several 'targeted allocations' for institutions with particular needs, for example its 'small and specialist' institution grants. These have been awarded to institutions with particularly intensive models of tuition and expensive specialist resources for 'professional-standard performance spaces such as theatres or dance studios, or dedicated practice spaces' (institutions apply for these directly and although a list of such institutions is available the amounts awarded are not normally made public).

Although the 'college fee' was abolished in 1997, money from the SSI budget was paid to Oxford and Cambridge in recognition of the extra costs associated with its interview and tutorial system.[8]

This was meant to be phased out, but Hefce continues to pay it. For 2012/13, this looks to be £7 million, with Oxford receiving £4.2 million and Cambridge £2.7 million.[9] Providing the wealthiest institutions in the country with such *grants* is an anomaly that needs to be ended.

ADDITIONAL COSTS

So far, this chapter has explained the manner in which the overall structure of the funding regime works. In order to get a firmer grasp, we need to consider two additional costs facing institutions in the new funding regime: recruitment and marketing; bursaries and scholarships.

Recruitment and Marketing

The block grant was a predictable source of income for institutions since student demand was such that most institutions had no trouble meeting their recruitment caps even if applications for particular courses fluctuated with fashions. The new market is supposed to make institutions more responsive to applicants and students, but the rapid implementation of the reforms means that many HEIs will see £40–50 million removed from their annual budgets within three to four years. This creates institutional uncertainty.

Replacing that income with fees means that recruitment now becomes much more of an issue, while the artificial restrictions on recruitment that we will look at in Chapter 5 make it harder for some universities to meet their targets. With no one quite sure yet how overall and specific demand will fluctuate given the higher fees, additional resources will have to be diverted to marketing. (Note that this is one aspect in which a market mechanism is *less efficient* than central funding.) Londoners in particular will have seen many more adverts on the underground and on buses than in previous years.

Already in January 2012, the Higher Education Statistics Agency reported that between 2008 and 2011, numbers of marketing and PR staff had increased by 5 per cent, whilst reductions were seen in other administrative staff.[10]

Access Agreements

When introducing the new maximum tuition fee of £9,000 per year, the Coalition stipulated that those seeking to charge over £6,000 per year must approach the Office for Fair Access (Offa) to negotiate an 'access agreement'. Institutions that are able to charge fees under £6,000 *do not have to do so*. This is a new development since on the old legislation *all publicly funded institutions charging fees had to have such measures in place*. Private providers who offer only training and can therefore offer cheaper fees thereby avoid any public mission in widening participation in higher education.

Access agreements require institutions to set aside an agreed percentage of the additional fees on certain initiatives. These measures can include:

- improving the mix of applications received from 'lower-income backgrounds and other groups that are under-represented in higher education' (outreach initiatives) such as: 'students from lower socio-economic groups and neighbourhoods in which relatively few people enter higher education; students from some ethnic groups or sub-groups; students who have been in care; and disabled students';[11]
- providing additional support to those students who are accepted, in the form of fee waivers or maintenance bursaries to help towards living costs;
- or specialist initiatives to improve retention and successful completion amongst such students.

Different institutions have agreed different targets and spending commitments in relation to their historical performance. But nationally, between 20 to 30 per cent of the additional fee above the £6,000 threshold is being used to fund those projects. Offa calculates that by 2016/17, £671.8 million per year will be spent on access measures (26.7 per cent of the amount charged over £6,000); this compares with the commitment to spend £403.1 million on access measures in 2011/12, around an extra £270 million.[12] This represents an additional cost and further erodes the ability of institutions to charge under £7,500.

Once access agreements are combined with the centrally funded National Scholarship Programme,[13] which will by 2014/15 provide £150 million of additional support to students from households where income is under £25,000, estimated spend will increase to around £800 million in 2016/17.[14] This breaks down into:

- £298.3 million on maintenance support, e.g., bursaries and scholarships (£295.3 million in 2015/16);
- £241 million on fee waivers (£260.6 million in 2015/16);

- £58 million on student *choice* of either maintenance support or fee waivers (£24.7 million in 2015/16);
- £110.6 million on outreach (£108 million in 2015/16);
- £101.6 million on retention (£83.7 million in 2015/16).

Offa

The Office for Fair Access is an 'arms-length' quango funded by BIS. It was set up in 2004 'to promote and safeguard fair access to higher education' prior to the introduction of higher tuition fees in 2006/7. Its primary means of achieving this is the access agreements it negotiates with each HEI seeking to charge tuition fees above the basic level of £6,000. Offa then monitors the performance of the HEI against the targets agreed to 'promote access by under-represented groups'.[15]

There is some current controversy around the powers that Offa has under the terms of the 2004 Higher Education Act. The new Coalition government had believed that Offa could impose limits on the fees charged by universities above the basic level. It cannot do so and, while it has the power to refuse permission to charge more than £6,000, it is not clear under what conditions any such sanction would be invoked. This is the so-called 'nuclear option'.

Further, it is crucial to distinguish between applications and admissions. Offa can oversee attempts to widen the pool of *applicants*, but it cannot interfere in the process that determines *which applicants are admitted*.

The 2011 White Paper indicated that the government intended to review Offa's powers, but any significant change would require primary legislation. It has however beefed up the quango – promising to up its budget and increasing its staffing to ten full-time employees.

It was in this charged context that a recent spat erupted. Offa's first Director, Martin Harris, retired in August 2012. In February 2012, BIS proposed Les Ebdon, former vice-chancellor of the University of Bedfordshire, as his replacement. In a small but central operation like Offa, the person in the director's seat makes an important difference to the judgements around satisfactory compliance. Ebdon had promised to use the 'nuclear option', if necessary, prompting fears from certain quarters of a shift towards 'social engineering'.

Against a backdrop of op-ed columns from Michael Gove's proxies (Melanie Phillips, Charles Moore and Dominic Lawson), the Conservative members of the BIS Select Committee sabotaged Ebdon's nomination only to be overruled by Vince Cable, the Secretary of State with ultimate responsibility for universities. Ebdon took up his post in September 2012.

FEE WAIVERS AND BURSARIES

There are two key measures in relation to widening participation initiatives. *Fee waivers* reduce the headline annual fees for particular individuals by a set amount while *bursaries* are paid out to students while studying to help with associated costs and living expenses. Fee waivers therefore reduce income for institutions while bursaries are expenditure.

Fee waivers and bursaries are considered equivalent under the terms of the access agreements higher education institutions draw up with Offa. BIS has directed Offa that a minimum bursary is no longer stipulated for the poorest students and would prefer to see fee waivers: 'A waiver has the effect of reducing the cost of borrowing to both the public purse and the student.'[16] With NSP funds, individual HEIs determine how it will be offered, but it will typically concentrate on fee waivers since the government *stipulates* that only up £1,000 can be provided as a *'cash* bursary'.[17] Despite this clear steer from the government, 'please help reduce the cost of HE', different institutions have made different decisions about the balance between fee waivers and bursaries.

The University of East London, for example, has offered *no* fee waivers in order to maximise bursaries, which have a more immediate effect. The vice-chancellor, Patrick McGhee, argues that fee waivers *only benefit the Treasury* (lowering its exposure on the growing borrowing used to create student loans), while bursaries support students while they are studying. His institution has developed a suite of distinct offers including a 'Progress Bursary' for which *all* students are eligible.

> Every student who successfully completes their first semester receives a progress bursary: a card loaded with £500, which can be spent on books, stationery, art materials, IT products, field trips, printing, and even nursery and accommodation costs. They get more when they complete further semesters, to a total value of £1,100, and parents and other sponsors can load money on to the card too.[18]

The available money can then be spent in certain shops on certain products. It seems to have had some success in encouraging retention. In relation to the NSP, UEL offers this scheme to students from local schools and colleges and sidesteps the limits on *cash* bursaries by using the Progress swipe card – credits of cash value of up to £2,000 are uploaded.[19]

The National Union of Students also favours bursaries. Based on the information contained in the access agreements submitted to Offa, they have calculated that spending overall on bursaries will be lower than it was *before the new higher fees came in.* The wealthier institutions have slightly increased the bursaries on offer, while the less well-off universities, despite the example of UEL, will have cut their bursaries from £230.5 million to £140.5 million.

PRICING DECISIONS

Having looked at costs and funding, we need to consider pricing decisions. This is a complex terrain and I will indicate a number of distinct, *basic* strategies. Setting aside questions concerning efficiencies, which a market approach with competitive pressures is meant to encourage, is the only consideration on price-setting how much each course costs?

There are a number of considerations, not least how accurate the methodologies used to produce estimated costs for individual subjects are. Initially used to prepare costing for research bids, their extension to cover teaching is unsuitable.[20]

In the short term, the market forces are sufficiently novel for the general dynamics to be unclear. When we combine this with the uncertainties that will be outlined in Chapter 5 on the market mechanisms governing recruitment, we will see that it is rational for institutions to set fees towards the top end so that they can compensate for any fall in numbers. Many institutions do not have the wealth or retained surpluses to have any alternative to setting higher fees.

Further, since the student sees nearly a doubling of fees, many institutions have rightly concluded that it is better to charge fees as high as possible so as to have some additional resource to *improve* facilities, contact hours, etc.

Such surpluses on some subjects can also be used to cross-subsidise other activities: an institution may continue to run prestigious courses or research activity at a loss. This may be particularly important for arts and humanities subjects: what guarantee is there that management will allow these departments to keep their surpluses? It is clear from the USA that science subjects and in particular science research is subsidised by tuition fees from humanities undergraduates.[21] Steve Smith, former president of Universities

UK, observes, 'Of course, institutions may want or need to cross-subsidise STEM [science, technology, engineering and mathematics] by top-slicing HASS [humanities, arts and social sciences] but then again many would argue that this has always happened.'[22]

Finally, a theme we will return to later: the current undergraduate set up is not a basic consumer market. Higher education offers positional goods determining future opportunities: setting low prices may send the wrong signal to potential applicants, who are using it

---

Coventry University

Coventry University has established Coventry University College.[23] It offers a stripped-back model of learning and tuition: classroom-only subjects with all learning materials provided as handouts or online. Students have no access to sports facilities and though they have access to the university's libraries they are not able to borrow books.

Aiming at a flexible provision, CUC organises its academic year into six blocks of six-weeks each (scheduled akin to half-terms) for which it charged £1,200 per block in 2012/13 when the college opened. Assessment is modular at the end of each block. A full-time student only needs to attend four of the six blocks available in a year. The normal annual fee is therefore £4,800. The second aspect of flexibility is the weekly timetabling: classes are available from 10 a.m., seven days per week, with classes continuing until 10 p.m. on weekdays. Lessons are repeated, enabling students to pick their way through a timetable to suit their other commitments much as one might choose different classes at a gym.

Coventry University validates the degrees offered in Accounting, Banking, Finance, Insurance, IT Legal Studies, Management and Tourism, while the college also offers a variety of Foundation, HNC and HND courses. The college is, however, a separate institution with its own building and staff, who are on weaker contracts than academics at its parent university. The college initially intends to recruit around 1,000 students.

A controversial 'no fail' clause which originally appeared on the institution's website has now been removed: 'We have total confidence in our teaching standards, in fact, we offer a guaranteed pass to you if you follow our recommended route through your study for professional awards – and if you don't we'll pay for you to have another go.'[24]

The University of Hertfordshire has recently announced a similar scheme using a for-profit subsidiary. Coventry University also runs a London campus based in the City 'offering a real business experience' with degrees in Law, Management, Finance and Accounting.[25]

to judge the prestige, status or the quality of education on offer: 'we are and always will be a £9,000 university', as I heard one Russell Group student representative declare in 2011.

With regard to this last point, a few universities did offer different fees for different subjects based on costing calculations. For 2012/13, the University of Derby kept to a maximum fee of £7,995, which it reserved for 'specialist courses' that included items such as field trips, but used two additional fee categories to reflect 'the true cost and individual characteristics'.[26] Specialist courses accounted for around 20 per cent of its provision, 'resource intensive' ones were priced at £7,495, 'classroom-based' at £6,995.

Derby may have suffered from the 'positional good' effect as its applications dropped by over 20 per cent for 2012/13 entry. In its access agreement for 2013/14, it has revised its prices upwards. It has introduced a maximum fee for its BEd, while fees for specialist courses are now £8,800, resource intensive come in at £8,250, and classroom-based have seen a similar increase of £800 to reach £7,700.[27]

A more radical strategy is to go cheap and to set up a 'no frills' subsidiary: the Ryanair model of provision (see box on Coventry University).

This rapid survey of fees and funding should indicate the depths that lurk beneath the headline fee figures. Universities have to make novel decisions about market positioning in the absence of central grants. The next chapter looks at the workings of the student loan scheme that funds fees and maintenance.

3
Student Loans: The Basics

Here, we will outline the basic operations of the relatively uncommon 'income contingent repayment' loans, which are generally misunderstood. We will return to the issue of student loans in more detail in Part 4 of the book. That later section will look at the macroeconomic impact of loans, the attempts to sell outstanding loan accounts to third parties, and the general issues that loans have for higher education policy.

WHAT DO LOANS COVER?

All full-time Home students studying for their first undergraduate course at a UK institution in receipt of public funding are eligible for maintenance loans and loans to cover tuition fees. Neither Home part-time students nor EU students are eligible for maintenance loans or grants, though they can access loans for fees.

The level of maintenance loans and grants available to students is means-tested against household income, which for the majority of students equates to that of their parent(s). This may seem a strange decision given that almost all students are over 18 and assumed to be independent adults for other purposes. But the government recently confirmed that, 'It has been a longstanding principle of student support that maintenance grants and loans are generally paid as a contribution towards living costs rather than to cover them in their entirety.'[1] The assumption is either that maintenance support is supplemented by families, even where the individual qualifies for the maximum grant, or that students *work* to supplement this support, or that they access other debt – such as credit cards, bank overdrafts or alternative loans.

When warning potential students not to fear the debt associated with government-backed loans, many commentators forget that this is not the only form of debt that students accrue. The repayment terms on overdrafts may be extremely tough – such as paying back a £2,000 overdraft within a year of graduation.

Figure 3.1 shows how the maintenance grants and loans available vary according to household income. It shows the level of loans available to those studying away from home outside of London. The maximum loan is £5,500 per year – it is for children of households earning up to £42,600. Such students studying away from home in London can receive up to £7,765 in loans.

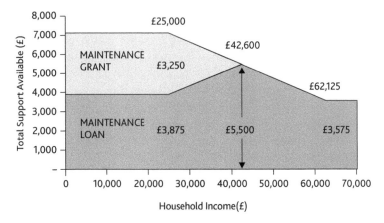

Figure 3.1   Student support – maintenance grants and loans

Source: BIS, *The Government Student and Graduate Finance Proposals* (BIS 10–1259)

Student loans are administered by the Student Loans Company (SLC), which has subsidiary operations for each part of the country (e.g., Student Finance England). It is a company limited by shares, wholly owned by the government. It serves over one million students annually and oversees the accounts of former students, though HMRC is responsible for collecting repayments through payroll deductions and tax returns.

In effect, the SLC acts as a factor overseeing repayments on behalf of the government. Eighty-five per cent of students take out loans to pay tuition fees to universities and colleges, but the relation of creditor and debtor is between the student and the SLC. This arrangement is extremely attractive to private and for-profit companies, who do not wish to have the burden of chasing repayments themselves or organising their own loan schemes through banks.

While eligible students attending the established, publicly funded institutions access loans by right, those attending 'private' institutions do not. In Chapter 7, we will look at the 'designation' scheme run by BIS which allows students on certain private courses to access maintenance loans and grants on the same terms as those at established universities and cover up to £6,000 of tuition fees from 2012/13.

INCOME CONTINGENT REPAYMENT LOANS

Since 1998, the UK has adopted an unusual kind of loan called 'income contingent repayment' loans, ICR loans for short. Monthly repayments are determined *by the current income of the borrower* not by the total amount borrowed. This means they are fundamentally different to the kinds of borrowing with which most people are familiar: such as mortgages or unsecured loans which have fixed periods of repayment and where the amount borrowed is meant to be repaid along with any interest that has accrued over the life of the loan. In addition, ICR loan balances are excluded from credit reference checks and will not be considered as debt in mortgage applications, although the impact on disposable income obviously will.

For the loans under discussion here, repayments commence in the April after graduating or leaving university. For the new scheme, the repayment threshold has been set at £21,000 for 2016. With ICR loans the threshold does not just determine when repayments begin, it also determines the level of repayments: in this case, 9 per cent of gross income over £21,000.

For example, if two former students both earn £25,000, they will repay £360 that year (9 per cent of £4,000), even though one might have graduated owing £40,000 and the other £20,000. ICR loans therefore are potentially *open-ended* – the period of repayment is determined by how long it takes the regular repayments to cover the initial amount borrowed (subject to interest rates). This represents the mandatory minimum repayment: borrowers have the option of making additional payments. Although an 'early repayment penalty' was considered that possibility was dropped after consultation.

With this in mind, from the perspective of graduates, it is very difficult to sustain comparisons with the issues that have arisen around fees and loans in countries such as Chile, the USA or, lately, Quebec. The tuition fee loans in these countries are traditional style loans, where borrowing must be repaid within a certain period and where sizeable repayments are demanded from recent graduates regardless of income.[2] Student debt is therefore experienced more punitively than in the UK where low earners are currently shielded. US Federal Student loan debt has reached $1 trillion and there are advocates there for moving to ICR loans, or 'smart' loans as Eliot Spitzer has tagged them.[3]

Part-time students

Numbering 500,000, Home or EU part-time students account for roughly one third of the undergraduate population, though provision across the country is patchy and not all higher education institutions provide extensive opportunity for students to choose this mode. Some 'pre-92' universities see a contradiction between part-time provision and pursuing research excellence and international prestige, choosing to focus exclusively on the market in full-time school-leavers.[4]

Part-time study had already been affected by reforms such as the last Labour administration's 'Equal and Lower Qualification' ruling. This policy stipulated that institutions could only receive direct funding for students who were studying for a qualification of a higher level than any they already possessed (see Table 6.1 in Chapter 6). £100 million of direct funding for part-time study was lost annually as a result. Fees were reported to have risen by as much as 25 per cent. Businesses were expected to pick up the costs by sponsoring employees to pursue relevant courses, but this funding did not materialise in the manner anticipated and enrolments shrank by 3.2 per cent following its implementation. Hardly a sensible policy, when retraining should be encouraged.

The current Coalition reforms also cut direct institutional funding for part-time study. Fees have therefore had to rise further. As a trade-off, access to the student loan book has been extended. From 2012, those beginning higher level study for the first time – 25 to 30 per cent of part-time students – can take out loans to cover tuition fees: these are now subject to a maximum cap of £6,750, 75 per cent of the full-time equivalent.

Part-time students' loan repayments will begin to fall due four and a half years after commencing the course: this therefore means that most will be eligible to repay before graduating. The repayment threshold is the same as for full-time students: £21,000.

Already a volatile market, part-time study appears to have been badly affected by the higher fees with some institutions apparently reporting a 30 per cent fall in accepted places.[5] The danger is akin to that espied by Milton Friedman: underinvestment (see Chapter 4 for more detail).

IS IT A LOAN OR A TAX?

The mechanism governing repayments on student loans resembles an additional level of tax with monthly repayments deducted at source from payroll or self-employment tax returns. We might therefore consider former students to have a marginal rate of tax of 41 per cent over £21,000: 20 per cent income tax, 12 per cent national insurance, and 9 per cent student loan. Or equivalent to 61 per cent at the higher band, c. £35,000, where income tax is 40 per cent.

The government and its supporters are keen to stress this resemblance. In particular, monthly repayments for borrowers will be *lower* on the new scheme owing to the higher repayment threshold. If the repayment threshold were still £15,000 as it is for those who took out ICR loans before 2012, then our two example graduates who earn £25,000 would be repaying £900 annually, not £360 – £75 per month, rather than £30.

Legally, though, the arrangement is a loan 'with the best features of a graduate tax'. One reason a loan scheme has been adopted is that loan debts can be pursued outside the British tax system. As already noted, EU students must be treated equitably with regard to university fees. Through a loan scheme, money can be recouped from those who leave the UK.

At 2010/11, there was £111 million outstanding on balances belonging to 18,000 EU students. Of those, 9 per cent were behind with repayments, while a further 33 per cent were either not currently repaying or not in contact with the SLC.[6] *The same issues would arise with Home students emigrating* and this is an issue that has troubled the ICR loan schemes in other countries, such as New Zealand. The government has increased the annual operating budget of the SLC by £10 million in order to improve their ability to collect debts from abroad.

In a second regard it is also not like a tax: there are individual balances and so *repayments stop* when the balance on the account is cleared. (This benefits the highest earners: under a graduate tax they would continue to pay and therefore make more contributions.) Although student loans are not dischargeable in bankruptcy, they are nullified in the event of death or disability.

Most importantly, it is government policy on new loans to write off any outstanding balance remaining 30 years after repayments first fall due.[7] The potentially open-ended nature of ICR loans is brought to a halt. In this way, the loans have a built-in subsidy to protect future low earners. As a result, between 20 and 30 per cent of graduates are modelled to be better off than before (they repay less overall), despite graduating with larger debts. I will discuss the distribution effect of the loans later: lower earners are better off but a significantly heavier burden falls on middle incomes.

There is much that is counter-intuitive and unfamiliar about the effects of ICR loans: they have certain merits but are complex and have drawbacks that will be discussed over the course of the book.

I will now move on to discuss the specific details of the scheme and its administration: interest rates, repayment rates and thresholds, and the 'write-off'.

INTEREST RATES

The newly issued loans will have 'real rates' of interest; that is, the rates will change annually and be tied to inflation, in this case the Retail Price Index (RPI). While studying, students will pay an interest rate of +3 on the preceding March's RPI. For loans issued in September 2012, this will be 6.6 per cent for the first year as RPI in March 2012 was 3.6 per cent.

From the April after they have left university, borrowers will pay a rate of interest determined by their earnings. Those earning below the repayment threshold will pay just RPI, a 'zero' real rate of interest, while those earning over £41,000 will pay RPI + 3. Those earning between those two limits will pay a rate between RPI and RPI + 3 as determined by a taper, which increases by 0.00015 per cent for each additional pound earned. These interest thresholds are expected to be uprated annually in line with the main repayment threshold (see below).

The real rates of interest will mean that many of those repaying will be making repayments that do not cover the accruing interest. This is the case for both our students from earlier who repay £360 in their first year. From April 2016, assuming interest rates of 3 per cent on their commencing balances of £40,000 and £20,000, they accrue interest of roughly £1,200 and £600 respectively, but are only paying £360 that year.

An important point to understand from the policy perspective is that governments have the executive power to vary interest rates on new loans. The Coalition announced its intention to set *real* rates of interest, i.e., above inflation. To do so it had to sneak passages into the 2011 Education Act overwriting the relevant clauses of primary legislation (interest rates on loans taken out before 2012 are prevented from going above RPI).

However, its new powers went further and extend to setting *commercial* rates of interest in line with those 'prevailing on the market'. Although governments may not seek to set rates this high, it does mean that there is *administrative leeway* to change interest rates within those parameters. Secondary legislation can be used so long as market rates are not exceeded.

REPAYMENT THRESHOLD AND REPAYMENT RATE

As already explained, the repayment threshold has been set at £21,000 for 2016 when the first repayments on the new loans fall due. The repayment *rate* will be 9 per cent of gross earnings above that threshold (this rate has been consistent across all the iterations of ICR loans). Again, as with interest rates, where the threshold is set is an administrative matter and only requires secondary legislation.

Chapter 1 explained how a concession to the Liberal Democrats meant that the threshold should be increased annually in line with average earnings from 2017. This adds another variable and another layer of complexity to the scheme, but also ties the threshold down and gives administrators less flexibility.

It is notable, however, that the regulations for the new loans, which were only 'made' in May 2012, do not mention any uprating and instead only set the level at £21,000.[8] Since no increase would need to happen before 2017, when those to whom the commitment was made are unlikely to be in government, it may be that we should expect the threshold to be frozen. Since the threshold is a convenient and effective mechanism for controlling the level of repayments, breaking the commitment to annual uprating has several advocates concerned with the sustainability of the scheme (see Part 4).

THE 'WRITE-OFF'

The loan scheme incorporates a commitment to write off the outstanding balances for individuals 30 years after their repayments first become due. The first significant write-offs on loans taken out in September 2012 will be seen in 2046. The write-off period on loans issued before 2012 is 25 years. In Scotland, it is 35 years, in Wales and Northern Ireland, 25. As with the other administrative details, the write-off can be changed using secondary legislation.

Repayments for Men and Women

Figures 3.2 and 3.3 and Table 3.1 come from the Institute for Fiscal Studies who have a sophisticated graduate 'population' built out of representative salary paths. They modelled a single cohort of 10,000 male students and 10,000 female who were assumed to enter higher education in September 2012.[9]

The chart shows the distribution of lifetime earnings distributions for men and women which underlies the simulated graduate population. There is a difference of £1 million in the median lifetime earnings for men (£2.6 million) and women (£1.6 million) according to the IFS.

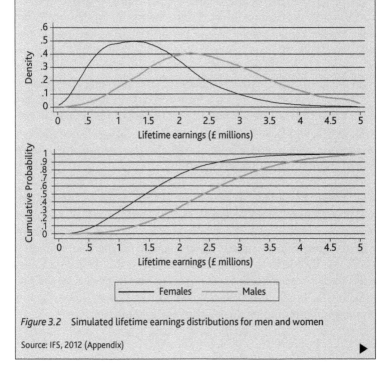

Figure 3.2   Simulated lifetime earnings distributions for men and women

Source: IFS, 2012 (Appendix)   ▶

This is in effect a subsidy offered to individuals who take out loans. The government underwrites the initial investment: if the individual's education does not result in higher earnings and sufficient repayments to repay the borrowing and interest, then the government picks up the tab. 'Public money' is now a subsidy to individuals, rather than expenditure through grants made directly to institutions.

The IFS tabulated the results of their simulations by lifetime earnings decile and by sex. Starting from a debt on graduation of around £40,000, we can see the 'Net Present Value' of graduate repayments and the percentage of the loan that is therefore repaid on NPV terms.[10] The bottom row summarises the average effect solely by sex: the IFS estimates that on average women will repay 53.8 per cent of the value of their loan, men 87.2 per cent. That is, 46.2 per cent of what is loaned to women will be written off.

Table 3.1   Projected graduate repayments by lifetime earnings

Decile of lifetime earnings	Total Repayments (Net Present Value)			Total Repayments as percentage of borrowing (NPV)		
	All	Women	Men	All	Women	Men
Poorest	£4,064	£3,920	£5,764	11.1%	10.7%	15.9%
2	£9,534	£9,155	£11,352	25.9%	24.9%	30.9%
3	£15,244	£14,481	£17,550	41.6%	39.4%	48.3%
4	£20,939	£19,994	£22,805	56.8%	54.2%	61.9%
5	£26,724	£25,833	£28,054	72.2%	69.9%	75.7%
6	£31,155	£30,418	£31,935	83.9%	82.0%	86.0%
7	£34,933	£34,978	£34,901	93.4%	92.9%	93.8%
8	£36,858	£37,166	£36,712	98.4%	98.9%	98.1%
9	£38,702	£38,815	£38,664	102.0%	102.3%	101.9%
Richest	£40,374	£40,560	£40,345	106.3%	106.5%	106.3%
All	£25,852	£20,032	£32,690	69.2%	53.8%	87.2%

Source: IFS, 2012

On current estimates, the government expects that just 68 per cent of what is lent will have been repaid by 2046. That is, for each £1 lent only 68p will return (in today's prices and factoring in the government's own costs of borrowing). The remainder will be lost with the write-off. There is a notable gender difference hidden within this figure. Owing to different patterns of lifetime earnings, around 90 per cent of what is lent to men is repaid, but around half of what is lent to women will be written off.

PHILOSOPHY OF THE SCHEME

The philosophy behind the scheme can be gauged from this David Willetts letter published in the *London Review of Books*. It summarises the main points covered so far in this chapter.

We are replacing the teaching grant with an alternative source of income from government in the form of student loans, with graduates only starting to repay once they are in well-paid jobs. We write off about 30 per cent of those loans because we recognise that there will be some people who cannot afford to pay them back. This offers the best features of a progressive income tax charged at a rate of 9 per cent on earnings above £21,000 per annum until graduates have paid off the cost of their university education. But as we are going to get back around 70 per cent of the money through these graduate repayments, the cost to the Exchequer is much less than it would be from an unconditional teaching grant. Some of the savings we make on the teaching grant will go into a more generous maintenance package for students so that students from poor backgrounds are not put off. It will also enable more income to reach universities than under the old system. Our estimate is that, in cash terms, the overall public support for universities in 2014–15 could be 10 per cent higher than in 2010–11.[11]

It is like an income tax; it is more progressive – relative to the earlier loans; more income gets to universities at a time of austerity; 30 per cent of what is loaned is to be written off beginning in 2046 (this has now been revised up to 32 per cent as of 2012).

The obvious point is elided: although monthly repayments are lowered, individuals will on average be repaying for longer and more in total. But is the scheme progressive? A progressive tax is one that takes an increasing proportion of the taxable base as that base increases. The key to this is then the repayment threshold which has been raised from £15,000 in 2011/12 to £21,000 in 2016.[12] Above that threshold the tax rate is *proportional* – it is fixed at 9 per cent – though the interest rate on outstanding balances varies according to income.

What this means is that those on the lowest incomes will pay less than under the previous scheme, both in terms of monthly repayments *and* in terms of total repayments. The loan scheme is less regressive than the previous scheme. However, in terms of a graduate tax or general taxation, the highest earners would continue to contribute, while under a loan scheme they stop repaying even before the 30 year policy write-off (see deciles nine and ten in Table 3.1).

Returning again to the IFS modelling, we can see in Figure 3.3 that under the new scheme the lowest quartile of earners repay less in total than under the previous system (in NPV terms), despite starting with higher debts. IFS assume roughly £40,000 of debt on graduation as compared to £15,000 on the previous scheme marked as 'current system'.

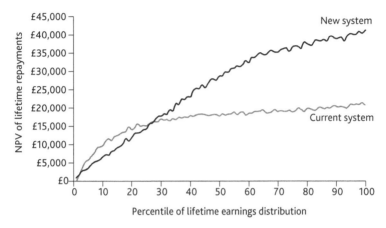

Figure 3.3   Repayments under the old and new schemes

Source: IFS, July 2012

A further point that Willetts has made is significant. From the charts above, we cannot see *when the repayments are made*, but this should also be considered as one of the merits of the new scheme.

> In the old system we inherited from Labour where the repayment threshold was £15,000, all the burden of paying back was paid by people in their 20s and early 30s just when the pressure is heaviest. ... The total amount of repayment goes up but we do spread it much more evenly across the lifecycle.[13]

The higher threshold shifts the distribution of repayments to later in the loan lifecycle with the majority of repayments falling in the second half of the 30 years. This is laudable in one regard. On the other hand, by shifting more repayments into the future the scheme becomes more volatile and less predictable. This will be the main theme of Part 4.

AMBIGUITIES

Here we should consider some of the ambiguities generated by the complexity of the scheme and the unfamiliar ICR loans.

First, Professor Nicholas Barr provides an important alternative perspective on the question above. Is the loan scheme progressive, if the expense of it means that many are excluded from higher education owing to the rationing of places?[14]

Second, the commitment to underwrite the loans means that the headline tuition fee offered by universities is not really a *price*. The cost to graduates is primarily determined by their future incomes not by their initial debt at graduation. For the average graduate, there will be no difference in terms of total repayments between taking out loans to cover fees of £6,000 per year or £9,000 per year.

Now the main point of a loan scheme over a graduate tax is to have a market where prices operate as a meaningful signal. That is, the intention is for different institutions to set different fees for different courses. This would not have happened with a graduate tax, since each graduate would be taxed the same rate whether they had been to the University of Oxford or the University of West London and whether they did astrophysics or accounting. The public subsidy distorts the market and unless it is removed there will be no proper price.

Third, the government has been sending out mixed messages. On the one hand, the scheme is meant to be progressive and affordable, but on the other, BIS has been encouraging *fee waivers* rather than bursaries (see Chapter 2). The design of the scheme means that it is like a tax and therefore one should not be put off by the headline fees; simultaneously, institutions are supposed to offer fee waivers to poorer students as part of access agreements *in preference to bursaries* which support them when they are studying (i.e., when they need it, before they benefit from their projected higher earnings).

Fourth, we are forced into the surreal situation of assessing the loan scheme and likely repayments by looking 30 years into the future. These loans are unsecured, there is no asset connected to them that can be cashed in, such as, say, a mortgage backed by property. We have to assume that there are no profound political or economic changes: that somehow *nothing happens* for the next 30 years, as if it were just empty time. Indeed, on the best models, most repayments begin to arrive in the final decade of the loan lifecycle, while the system as a whole begins to reach operational maturity only sometime in the mid 2030s. Our habits are not really up to thinking about ICR loans with this kind of design.

Fifth, loans are issued in a culture with a particular social psychology, or ideology, of debt: that one pays back what one owes.

In such a culture, having an individual loan account showing an outstanding balance may be subject to interpretations at odds with the *intentions* behind the design of the scheme. How will the public view graduates who have received an expensive education but who then choose to pursue less remunerative careers? What about people who emigrate and end up working in a country where the costs of living and salaries are much lower?

TERMS AND CONDITIONS

The question of distribution is different to the question of sustainability. The latter is determined by the level of repayments received in future. Estimates depend on both the general shape of the economy and graduate earnings for the next 30 years: for the most part, this means making assumptions that it will be similar to the last 30 years. If the economy stagnates and graduates struggle to find appropriate jobs, then repayments may be much lower than anticipated.

The broader implications for the management of higher education will be discussed in Part 4 but we need to focus on one implication here: the contractual situation of borrowers.

Assuming that future governments hold to the commitments made by this one, then it would seem that the risk of lower than expected repayments here falls on the Exchequer. But governments have the option of changing the terms and conditions offered to future cohorts.

Governments can also use executive powers, granted to them by the existing legislation, to alter the terms and conditions for *existing* or current borrowers. A clause on page eight of the 2012/13 'Student Loans – A Guide to Terms and Conditions' reads:

> You must agree to repay your loan in line with the regulations that apply at the time the repayments are due *and as they are amended*. The regulations may be replaced by later regulations.[15]

That is, it is not just that Parliament is 'omnicompetent' or that future governments cannot be bound by the decisions of earlier ones. Rather, it is that Parliament has used its legislative powers to give the executive leeway to alter all four administrative details, without its oversight. It is clear that the loans are now not merely income contingent, but *future-policy* contingent.

It is now too easy for governments to make such amendments: there is very little legislative or legal protection.[16] New Zealand, which operates an ICR loan scheme, used its May 2012 Budget to increase the repayment rate from 10 per cent to 12 *for existing borrowers*.[17] These borrowers have clauses similar to that cited above and so have no legal ability to challenge this decision.

Responding to a question on this matter put by the BIS Select Committee, David Willetts commented:

> in the letter that every student gets there are some words to the effect that Governments reserve the right to change the terms of the loans. That is a text that has always been there for students, but we have no plans to change the framework we have explained to the House of Commons and set before this Committee. ... We have set out our plans, but there is always that health warning that successive Governments have put on the letter the prospective student gets, and I would be irresponsible if I did not say that statement is there and always has been there.[18]

The function of that 'health warning' in the 'letter' changes as primary legislation changes, for example, with the removal of statutory clauses setting interest rates at RPI. Besides interest rates, repayment rates and the write-off, most likely is that the repayment threshold may be frozen.

Borrowers therefore face some uncertainty – especially if the current economic stagnation continues. Future governments could decide to exact higher rates of repayment. While it would be unprecedented for the terms on loans to be made less generous, we need to bear in mind that the new loans are much larger and involve a much greater outlay, and hence risk, for the government.

One potential solution to this issue of protection is to remove the clause cited above and write the terms and conditions into the agreements that individuals sign. This would provide some protection against the use of secondary instruments to change terms for existing borrowers. Of course, *primary* legislation could overwrite such contracts, but that would be much more difficult to implement. The strength of political will required to effect change is gauged by the impediments to be overcome.

To summarise the main points of this chapter: ICR loans are potentially more progressive than other loans, especially when combined with the write-off subsidy. But the scheme is complex and ambiguous, presenting difficulties for a full market owing to the lack of proper price and also leaving concerns about the sustainability of the scheme. However, this is the price the government is willing to pay to achieve a new market in undergraduate recruitment. Replacing grants with loans is the central plank of these reforms, and, politically, the prime objective.

Part 2
Marketisation

This section of the book provides a thorough account of the nascent market in undergraduate recruitment as the government seeks 'supply-side' reforms to change what is on offer to potential applicants: new institutions, changes to established ones, and regulatory overhaul.

I feel that the scale and ambition of these changes and their potential consequences have been underestimated largely because the reforms have been pursued in piecemeal fashion and because university vice-chancellors were confident of operating in the new terrain. September 2012's figures on recruitment may have changed some attitudes as new undergraduate numbers have dropped to levels last seen in 2007.

Chapter 4 examines the motivations, intentions and assumptions behind the new market initiatives, while Chapter 5 tracks the decisions implemented by the government in setting up new artificial recruitment mechanisms and shows why these changes contributed to a large drop in undergraduate recruitment in 2012.

Chapter 6 covers regulation. Without a scheduled higher education bill, we find ourselves partially in limbo while the market reforms continue apace. The focus of the chapter is on new 'risk-based' regulation of degrees as a central feature of the new market and what that means for current arrangements.

Chapter 7 examines the market entrants who benefit from the creation of a 'level playing field': this is the external privatisation, or 'marketisation', of the sector outlined in the Introduction. It looks at the entry of private equity through this route and provides a bridge to Part 3 on privatisation.

The general effect is clear. Elite institutions, the most selective at undergraduate recruitment, and certain kinds of *cheaper* provider (e.g., HE taught in further education colleges and private operations) benefit from the reforms: they are allowed and encouraged to expand. The majority of institutions previously in receipt of public money for undergraduate provision are being restricted – it is getting harder for them to maintain their numbers.

The strong market position of the established universities must be nullified if new providers are not to be driven out by normal competitive pressures. The government needs to ensure that aspiring providers are not squished in a freely competitive market. Instead we see the kind of intervention that was developed in the utility privatisation of the 1980s and 1990s: monopolies must be *broken up or restricted* so that market competition can flourish.

4
Why a Market?

Market solutions are a key plank of a general ideology that runs across all political parties. Many ministers and influential individuals in government today were junior ministers and advisors in the heyday of Thatcherism. For them the 'discipline of the market place, the power of the consumer and the engine of competition' was needed in education. But the stumbling blocks were profound since a proper pricing signal was necessary for choice to be effective. Nicholas Timmins recounts the prolonged efforts of Keith Joseph and the young Oliver Letwin to thrash out the problems with a voucher system for primary and secondary education; repeatedly hitting practical problems for want of technical knowledge.[1]

The market envisioned by the Conservatives in higher education, as a lightly regulated sector with a variety of providers, cannot appear fully formed. It has to be created. Therefore we need to see what is currently happening as transitional arrangements aimed at reconfiguring the sector, its institutions and what they offer (the 'supply side') prior to that new market. Some of the measures will be more restrictive in the short term.

I will suggest that the endeavour is misconceived. In two ways, the government misunderstands the kind of 'good' that education is:

1. The market is being set up as if undergraduate education were a normal consumer good: it is not. For better or ill, undergraduate higher education in England is a *positional* good: institutions are ranked in a hierarchy, and opportunities are restricted.
2. Its reforms treat it as solely of benefit to the private individual, missing the associated public benefits which are now at risk.

The market is often presented in simplistic fashion as a contrast to 'central planning'. What free market competition is meant to do – and we do not have it yet in higher education – is distribute scarce goods more efficiently, matching supply to demand through the pricing signal. Price is the 'single best indicator of quality' according

Friedman's 'The Role of Government in Education'

In education, the ideologues backing these changes have a clear icon. Milton Friedman's 1955 essay, 'The Role of Government in Education', lays out the terrain. Its ideas, though altered, are being realised through the use of modern financial instruments, administration and data-management techniques.[2]

Friedman's vision is clear: the state should not administer, let alone own, institutions of education but fund a 'voucher' to students who then take it to the institution of their choice – whether public or private, charity or for-profit. The voucher represents a fixed sum of public money which can be redeemed at any institution; where fees are higher, parents pay the difference.

A voucher has the advantage over direct funding of institutions since (a) the institutions would not be dependent directly on government, but on student choices, (b) the voucher would fund 'activities it is appropriate for the state to subsidize', (c) vouchers could be used at private institutions – (who are otherwise faced with 'unfair competition' from state-subsidised institutions able to charge much lower fees) – thereby promoting a diverse mix of providers, which would 'likely … be more efficient in meeting consumer demands'. (Friedman believes that vouchers should only be used

▶

to the Browne review, which advocated the abolition of tuition fee caps for that reason.

Beyond this principle, several others are offered. As Willetts put it in 2009: 'You couldn't win the argument for higher fees unless you could show what was in it for students and their parents.'[3] So what is in it for students and parents?

First, popular 'first-choice' institutions will be freed from current numbers restrictions and allowed to expand by accepting qualified students whom they would previously have rejected for lack of places. Willetts has been keen to encourage Oxford and Cambridge to follow his lead here, but instead it is the next tier down where such movement has been seen. More students will get their first or second choice institutions.

Second, the aim is to 'foster a more diverse sector that better reflects the numerous reasons why people enter higher education'.[4] In this way, applicants will be offered more choice. The key is diversity of institutions and courses. There is a diverse private

at 'approved' or 'qualified' institutions but does not develop an account of what regulation would be appropriate.)

This position on public funding through vouchers holds good for 'general education', where the 'gain accrues to other members of society', but for *professional and vocational training*, a loan is more appropriate. The latter is 'human capital investment', which only benefits the individual in so far as the training received increases productivity and boosts subsequent earnings.

We should note here the deviation of current UK government policy which has removed all direct funding to 'liberal arts' subjects: these boost citizenship and leadership according to Friedman, and so count as general education. Similarly, Friedman decries governmental funding for medical or dentistry training given the high salaries available afterwards, yet these are areas where large grants still remain.

While Friedman would prefer private insurance companies, or the like, to offer such human capital loans, he appreciates that there are worries about the lack of security on these loans and the 'factor' issue – the administrative challenge of keeping track of borrowers and repayments. In light of this market 'imperfection' and the risk of underinvestment it engenders, it is appropriate for government to intervene here to 'help people make productive investments in themselves'.

We can clearly see the central co-ordinates of the Coalition policy: removal of grants, supply-side reform, fee loans extended to students at all qualified providers.

education market in different kinds of training (yoga, IT, languages, etc.) offered via short courses. Should a three-year degree be treated any differently?

David Willett's credo was set before the vice-chancellors in a speech to Universities UK Spring conference in February 2011.

I have worked on many different areas of the public sector over the past 30 years. The biggest lesson I have learned is that the most powerful driver of reform is to let new providers into the system. They do things differently in ways none can predict. They drive reform across the sector. Research by Caroline Hoxby shows that admitting new schools causes existing schools to raise their game. It's the rising tide that lifts all boats – an insight which lies behind Michael Gove's recent school reforms. It also lies behind Andrew Lansley's proposals to empower GPs so they can choose providers in the best interests of patients.[5]

Beyond choice, the third point is that the general consumer pressures present in such a market will drive up quality. In response to this rising tide, Willetts suggests all universities will have to up their game and concentrate on offering an improved student experience. This is a 'bottom-up' reform raising standards of achievement through consumer pressure. This is the equivalent in education to the line that free markets are the best means towards increased prosperity for all. Chiefly, Willetts believes that the sector has had too little incentive to focus on teaching – students as consumers will rectify this.

However, it is not clear if this third point is not in some conflict with a fourth point. Will the market drive up standards or will it offer better *value*? Writing in the *London Review of Books* in response to Howard Hotson, Willetts states: 'This competition will be partly on price, especially through fee waivers and suchlike for students from lower income backgrounds. But, equally, it will be competition by quality.'[6] This is not so straightforward as Willetts imagines. Value is of course measured across two axes – quality and cost: both 'cheap and cheerful' and 'expensive but worth it' offer value in this sense.

Finally, a fifth point is that these reforms are about making the sector more responsive to other stakeholders and are aimed at breaking up the vested academic 'producer interest', which protects jobs and the status quo. Only competition between 'providers', and importantly 'price signals', can deliver a product of the quality desired by a broader community and not determined solely by the desires of academics. The Browne review, for example, reported that the higher education system did not seem to be responsive enough to the needs of business:

> 20% of businesses report having a skills gap of some kind in their existing workforce, up from 16% since 2007. The CBI found that 48% of employers were dissatisfied with the business awareness of the graduates they hired. *This evidence suggests there needs to be a closer fit between what is taught in higher education and the skills needed in the economy.*[7] (my emphasis)

Commercial pressures will encourage institutions to orient in this way. But this evidence can be read otherwise, as we will outline below.

WHAT MIGHT BE WRONG WITH MARKET REFORMS?

So we have five points in favour of market reforms: (i) the most selective institutions expand, (ii) new providers offer diversity, and consumer pressures drive up either (iii) quality or (iv) offer a better range of value options, and (v) university courses become more relevant as they are required to collaborate more with industry and employers. What are the problems with this vision?

Why Education is Not a Consumer Good and What This Means for Choice

Before looking at each of these claims, we should first reiterate what was pointed out in Chapter 3. Owing to the design of the loan scheme, there is no genuine pricing signal: the headline fee is not necessarily what a graduate pays. Moreover, unlike training and short courses, an undergraduate degree is not currently amenable to normal consumer experience. The kind of consumer testing through repeat purchase, with, for example, brands of baked beans or beer, is not generally available here. Higher education is for most a 'one-off' purchase, since as yet the mechanisms to transfer between institutions and courses with valid, recognised credit are either complex or not in place. Further, the benefits of the product often do not become clear during 'consumption' but only later, well after study has finished. For this reason, it is referred to by Roger Brown as a 'post-experience' good.[8]

At the heart of market-based solutions lies the figure of an informed, rational consumer. But if the normal consumer experience is not available, what alternatives are there? The government has promoted the importance of information provision by institutions. Writing to the *Guardian*, Willetts claimed that 'the prestige of institutions should be based on quality of teaching, not just research. So we will massively improve the information available about different courses at different institutions...'.[9] But it is not clear that information about courses can rectify this fundamental difference between education and other homogenised consumer goods, no matter how reliable and accessible such information is made.[10] While genuine information on costs, for example, is important, none of what is proposed is an objective measure of teaching quality nor capable of making statistically significant comparisons between subjects or institutions.[11]

The league tables popular with the press often concentrate on the 'inputs': the selectivity of the institution, the students who attend, or the wealth of the institution (the 'spend per student'), rather than the *pedagogical* experience. While other surveys tend towards measuring how 'satisfied' students are rather than offering any genuine measure of what they have learnt.

The argument in favour of competition was that institutions would have to focus on teaching quality, but, in practice, more resources may be diverted to data management and maintaining *statistics*. And it is far from clear that any such data will displace the general attitudes of employers and the public towards higher education qualifications.

The Browne review averred that 'students are best placed to judge what they want to get from participating in higher education'; but knowing what you want is not the same as the quality of the course on offer. In the new market with hundreds of potential higher education providers, the assumption that consumers can become well-informed about what is available appears misplaced, and many applicants may be mis-sold courses of study. It will be a saturated market where even the experts are unfamiliar with most institutions.

Students cannot try different courses repeatedly as they would with other consumer goods. Information cannot capture quality objectively. For these reasons, 'indirect or symbolic' proxies will operate as signals. Prestige will function strongly here. Owing to historical legacies and the composition of British society, higher education is a *positional* good in so far as there is a hierarchy of institutions and the value of a university place depends on its selectivity and relative scarcity (that is, it is not a consumer good in so far as it is *not available to anyone who wishes to purchase it*). Students who attend Oxford and Cambridge gain a huge advantage in subsequent employment opportunities. In 2012, some institutions tried to recreate prestige artificially by setting higher entry requirements. Many had to drop these requirements dramatically in 'clearing' in order to make up their numbers.

Popular Institutions May Not Expand

From such a perspective, one might see that the expansion of popular providers may not be in their own interest: ill-considered growth and loss of selectivity may undermine an institution's *position* in this regard.

Indeed, Oxford's submission to the Browne review indicates a different goal: altering its student demographic to increase the percentage of postgraduates and doctoral researchers – moving towards the 'shape' of Yale and Harvard. Though the submission emphasised the importance of tutorial-led undergraduate study, it was not clear that Oxford believed it *had* to be one of only two institutions to offer that mode. Recall also that both Oxbridge and Cambridge stated that the costs of its undergraduate tutorials are in excess of the £9,000 available. Expansion would entail further losses. Since the tutorial and weekly essay is what differentiates 'Oxbridge' provision it would make no sense to abandon this pedagogical mode in order to get more students in.

> It is not self-evident that popular courses should wish or need to expand. There may be greater market risk in so doing and highly-performing institutions may not wish to expose themselves to this. It is also unclear what incentive exists for highly-performing institutions to expand especially where the full costs of a course in such institutions are not covered by the combination of residual grant and tuition fee.[12]

David Willetts seems extremely confused on this matter, apparently believing it is the city of Oxford's planning approach that prevents expansion.

Diversity and Quality

Turning to diversity, the effects of which will be seen more clearly in Chapters 6 and 7, it is important to understand that this diversity will be encouraged whilst overall student numbers in the system remain largely capped. Diversity at the expense of established provision in a zero sum game is quite distinct from the expansion available in a market without such restrictions.

Moreover, questions of quality will be to the fore in the market. New entrants are encouraged by lowering existing barriers and safeguards, not least around quality of provision. This can be seen most clearly in the lowering of the eligibility criteria pertaining to university title and degree awarding powers, which we will examine in Chapter 6. Can a responsive market co-exist with the traditional quality and validation processes?

With recruitment to the fore in a market, indeed the primary aim for many institutions, we may see inefficiencies in so far as resources are oriented that way, rather than towards *instruction* (the third argument in favour of the reforms was that consumer pressure would improve *teaching* quality). Investment may instead go towards the *general student experience* or factors influencing the first impression made on those attending open days. We may therefore see bigger spend on prettifying the campus, building new leisure facilities and upgrading student accommodation and other areas. In the USA, this expenditure has become conspicuous and driven more by a need to outdo rivals publicly. Here is a phenomenon very close to the potlatch described by Georges Bataille.

In so far as these factors above combine with competition on price and *value for money*, we will see an increasingly polarised sector. All scenarios show resources increasingly flowing towards a small minority who already have the historically accumulated advantages of wealth and prestige. Very simply, under the previous funding system, a student studying sociology, for example, at whatever university, would pay the same fees at £3,375 and the government would provide an equivalent level of funding directly to the institution via a block grant – equal resourcing. This equality now disappears. (I am not suggesting that universities should not select on A level results. I am suggesting that additional resources – higher fees – should not follow those selection decisions. These are two different issues and again different aspects of competition.)

We are on the cusp of a new, more unequal terrain. Perhaps one comprising two leagues – a Premier League and a Conference where the vast majority of institutions scratch around for students and where there is no relegation or promotion between the two. Given the arguments offered in favour of value for money, this polarisation may be a *desirable outcome* for the market reformers.

Responsive to Consumers and Business

The fifth and final argument in favour of reforms is that the sector would become more responsive.

When much of the income of higher education institutions came from the block grant for undergraduate tuition, this was assumed to be a 'proxy measure' for activity.[13] But as Tristram Hunt noted in the *Guardian*, universities are being pulled between various demands: breadth of provision may not be sustainable in a market driven by undergraduate fee income.

> The real problem is that universities are expected to be all things to all people: agents of social mobility, drivers of urban regeneration, centres of fundamental research, partners in business, exemplars of teaching, hubs of inward investment. For our top-flight institutions this is all do-able but many middle-ranking universities, unable to compete on cost or quality, will suffer.[14]

From the Mandelson years onwards, universities have been encouraged to 'focus on their strengths' or to find an effective market niche. Allowing consumer choice to drive quality and frame the provision available seems to risk breadth and quality.

Becoming responsive to demand may see universities shedding subjects which could lead to lost capacity and a contraction in the breadth of what is on offer. A much circulated cliché amongst academics relates to how other factors such as popular television shows influence choices at degree level. Applications for Archaeology were boosted by *Time Team* in the 1990s, while Forensic Science received a huge boost from *CSI* and *Silent Witness*. Brian Cox's programmes on the Solar System and Universe have had a similar effect on Physics. Should a market in HE be able to absorb these shifts in demand? Or should we mothball or close courses as these trends wax and wane? The specialised training of research may be hard to revivify when trends shift again. (We may even see the problem of oversupply in certain subjects seen to be more professional or vocational – a potential glut of business and law graduates, for example.)

Given the associated debt and basic mechanics, of which more in subsequent chapters, a 'more responsive sector' might end up being one that is more oriented to training, whether vocational or professional. Are we only interested in an education system geared towards employment? Should the main point of the system be to conduct training for employers or indeed a large-scale *sift* on behalf of employers so that they are able to draw up recruitment short-lists by casting their eyes over a CV (effectively externalising recruitment costs)? Since the abolition of the Industrial Training Boards, funded by an industry levy, many costs have been passed on to the taxpayer or the individual. 'British businesses spend less than their overseas counterparts on training, far less on research, and – with a few exceptions – are not exactly world leaders when it comes to apprenticeships.'[15]

These concerns relate to the five motivations for a market-based initiative and put the onus on government not simply to rely on credulous ideology. Unfortunately, since this government wishes to see a certain amount of creative destruction, what would count as evidence for a change of course is not clear. As we will see in the next chapter, even a drop of 50,000 accepted places (15 per cent) is seen as 'modest' or 'acceptable' rather than the first evidence of market failure and underinvestment in Friedman's terms.

To conclude this chapter, I wish to stress the danger to broader public benefits.

PUBLIC BENEFIT

Hunt touched on the public benefits provided by universities and colleges. By encouraging a level playing field for private providers, some of them for-profit, the provision of training, whether vocational or professional, is privileged over other aspects of education, and any broader public benefits or goods are likely to be threatened as private providers have no obligation to promote such activities or achievements.

Similarly, market reforms intended to encourage efficiencies may mean the jettisoning of activities that do not produce revenue. Moreover, a consumer approach pushes the focus onto accreditation – the qualification awarded – rather than the overall experience, a tendency towards commodification: only the exchange value of the credential is presented. It effectively becomes a financial asset, an 'investment' that boosts future earnings, or a positional good in the job market. Universities are then judged by how well they provide training that increases graduate earnings profiles (see Chapter 13 for more detail).

Over the summer of 2011, a group of academics came together to produce an alternative approach to a market in higher education. They argued that public interest is not exhausted by demonstrating that public money is spent 'properly', and that the alternative to markets was to attempt to ensure that, *whatever students apply to do*, the provision meets a high standard delivered by a professional academic team who are research-active and engaged with the broader community of colleagues and practitioners. The document they produced, 'In Defence of Public Higher Education', aimed to account for the public goods neglected in the market-led vision of undergraduate study supported by the government and the Browne review.

Its opening paragraph states that documents produced by the Browne Review or BIS 'make no mention of the public value of higher education. The only benefits mentioned are the private benefits to individuals in the form of higher earnings deriving from investment in their human capital, and to the "knowledge economy" in terms of product development and contribution to economic growth.'[16] Its list of broader benefits included:

- 'Public universities are necessary to build and maintain confidence in public debate.'
- Universities promote a broader cultural life than economic return: creative arts, music, drama, etc.
- The brainpower and skills of a population is a national asset not merely private human capital investment.
- Universities produce professionals who play a key function within society – doctors, teachers, etc.
- Universities have an immediate economic impact in their locality, but also provide broader social and community benefits through use of facilities and cultural life.
- A recent report by New Economics Foundation was cited, which found that when considering higher education's benefits 'just three *social* outcomes – greater political interest, higher interpersonal trust and better health – contribute a benefit of £1.31 billion to UK society over and above the economic benefits'.[17]

The document concluded that these goods and benefits need to be preserved through direct public funding. The block grant was one way of achieving this.

We might add that it is unclear how the reproduction of academic and intellectual life more generally will be promoted if the system of reproduction based on *postgraduate and research degrees* breaks down owing to accumulated debt, consumer pressures and the absence of funding.

Having set out these aims and core concerns about the whole approach, we will now turn to particular features of the market: the numbers controls governing recruitment; the proposed regulatory framework; and the 'new providers' being encouraged to enter.

5
Market-making:
The Control of Student Numbers

Fashioning a new market in undergraduate recruitment requires direct government intervention at several stages. This chapter shows how the transitional arrangements for undergraduate recruitment at universities in receipt of public funding serve three ends. They are designed to drive down overall Exchequer costs, free the most selective universities to expand should they so choose, and create the conditions under which new private providers can enter the market.

With regard to the last point, the majority of institutions will find it more difficult to recruit than in previous years owing to the artificial restrictions first announced in the 2011 White Paper and implemented with instructions to the quango, Hefce. The creation of a 'level playing field' for private providers is achieved through *bias* against many established institutions, who in a free market would outcompete any newcomers.

The advantageous market position enjoyed by public universities first needs destabilising. Indeed, so restrictive are the imposed recruitment arrangements that only seven institutions charging over £7,500 appeared to be clear candidates for expansion and neither Oxford nor Cambridge intended to do so.

Although David Willetts is arguing that more applicants than previously got into their first choice university, this increase is a tiny number when compared to the tens of thousands who exercised their choice not to go at all in 2012. At the time of writing, undergraduate numbers entering in 2012 were estimated to be 50,000 down on 2011.

This chapter will show how the new numbers controls contributed to that decline and what it signifies given that the government is no longer committed to providing support for 'unviable' institutions. We will go through each component of the numbers controls in turn: the overall cap on students in higher education; the AAB+ policy; the manner in which the 'core' for each institution is calculated; and the margin pool of 20,000 places.

When the plans for higher education were announced late in 2010, loans were presented as a lesser evil compared to the forced reduction of undergraduate numbers (however temporary). Instead we now seem to have both: a loan scheme and a large fall in numbers which will please the Treasury.

OVERALL CAP ON NUMBERS

The government controls its loan outlay – for fees and maintenance – by controlling the overall numbers of Home and EU students starting each year. Undergraduate places are rationed. For September 2012 entry, this cap amounted to around 325,000 places at HEIs (with a further 25,000 HE places available at FE colleges).

The Browne review was concerned with the problem of how to lift this cap to *expand* provision and thereby meet the unmet demand evinced by each year's thousands of unsuccessful applicants. In contrast, the Coalition policy was to not only maintain an overall limit on numbers, but to remove 10,000 places which had been introduced by Labour for 2010. This fundamental difference between the intentions of Browne and that of the current policy makes a large difference to market dynamics.

That overall limit was previously constructed out of specific recruitment allocations assigned to each institution.[1] The White Paper proposed the managed 'liberalisation' of this central imposition on institutions, often 'spun' as 'quasi-Soviet', over the medium term. The result was new supply-side mechanisms to govern recruitment: the new AAB+ grouping, a special category of applicants, plus the 'core' and the 'margin'; we examine each in turn. These are artificial constraints and more complex than what went before.

Many institutions are hamstrung, encouraged to manage down their numbers; this allows for space for new providers, who benefit from direct intervention by the government.

'AAB+'

'AAB+' names a group of applicants who achieve A level results of A, A, B or better.[2] It was estimated that there would be 85,000 applicants in this category in 2012.

Each university and college can recruit *as many of these candidates as they are able to* (with the exception of medicine and dentistry which are still centrally controlled separately by Hefce on behalf of the NHS). High end institutions seeking to expand will look to pick up these candidates, but each candidate recruited deprives other institutions, creating a 'zero sum' sub-game within the overall numbers controls. This 'mini free market' thus produces unwanted 'threshold effects'. A volatile competition for a restricted grouping of students was made worse by the initial estimates being too high. I will explain the implications of this in more detail below.

From the applicant's perspective, this policy should offer more choice to those achieving AAB+ as institutions will be very keen to recruit them and some institutions may even offer blandishments, such as *merit scholarships*, common in the USA, in order to boost numbers. The University of Kent and Queen Mary offered fee waivers of £2,000 or £3,000 to students scoring AAA, while Goldsmiths has offered ten free places to the 'brightest and best students from Lewisham, our local borough'.[3]

The think tank, Higher Education Policy Institute, has warned of an 'arms race' developing, as institutions try to fight off rivals for these candidates: 'The upshot may be that there will not in reality be a large movement in AAB+ students between institutions, but these universities will pay a high price to maintain existing numbers.'[4] One potential problem here has been marked by the University of Cambridge: 'As others have pointed out, AAB+ students will not on the whole come from socially deprived groups. Allowing universities that can attract more students qualified in this way to expand may run counter to the desire of the White Paper to promote greater social inclusion in such universities.'[5]

The government intends to expand this pool incrementally each year and has confirmed that for 2013/14 the benchmark will be lowered one notch to ABB+ bringing roughly 40,000 further applicants into this class.

THE 'CORE'

Each institution still has an imposed cap on its annual recruitment. But these cores are smaller than previous allocations, since 'AAB+' students and the 'margin pool' of 20,000 (explanation to come) have been carved out of them. The core places are set for applicants with grades *below* AAB+, that is, equal or lower than ABB. Any AAB+ applicant is 'free', but each 'ABB-' applicant *costs*: each counts against the core.

Calculating the core is complex with several stages, but in brief, Hefce used data on the students recruited to each institution in previous years to compile the new numbers. Most importantly, past performance in AAB+ recruitment was the most important factor in determining the cores for 2012. An institution which had managed to recruit 1,000 AAB+ students in 2011 *had that number subtracted* from its central allocation. This means that institutions can only maintain their numbers by competing for AAB+ students and equalling or bettering their previous performance.

In order to address the concerns about widening participation raised by Cambridge above, the most selective universities were given a large advantage here: no core could be lower than 20 per cent of the previous year. For example, an institution which had 2,500 AAB+ students out of a first year complement of 3,000 would have its core reduced to 600 (20 per cent), rather than 500 (3,000 minus 2,500). Thus leaving it with greater potential to *expand* – its 'implied total', according to the official jargon, would be 3,100: the new core *plus* the 'implied' AAB+ students, resulting in a potential increase of 100.

Here is the first instance of what was set out in the introduction to this chapter: elite, selective institutions benefit, others are put under recruitment *pressure* despite the enormous unmet demand to go to university. Tables 5.1 and 5.2 show the early contours of the new polarisation created by government. These are the Premier league and the lower league mentioned in the previous chapter.

Table 5.1 shows those higher education institutions suffering the biggest loss of 'implied places' by percentage in 2012 (ranked by loss with largest at top). The columns show, in order from left to right: the core, anticipated AAB+ recruitment, implied total for 2012 entry, the 2011 numbers control (for comparison), followed by numerical and percentage differences.

Table 5.2 shows all higher education institutions which lost *fewer than 5* per cent of places (excluding specialist institutions which chose to 'opt out' and institutions which bid for margin places). It also demonstrates that there were only seven institutions 'implied' to gain from the policy. These are indicated in bold: Oxford, Cambridge, Bristol, Durham, Imperial, LSE and the very small Courtauld Institute of Art. University College London is on the cusp, but improved its recruitment to achieve expansion in 2012.

There are a couple of further implications of this policy to emphasise. First, less prestigious institutions are *unlikely to be able to recruit sufficient additional AAB+ students* to make up for their loss to the core. These institutions will therefore shrink.

Second, were the selective, prestigious institutions to decide to expand, then the others would struggle to maintain their past

Table 5.1 Biggest losers by percentage – 2011/12 numbers compared to 2012/13 number control

Institution	Core for 2012–13	AAB+	'Implied total' for 2012–13	2011–12 Student number control limit	Difference between 2012–13 & 2011–12	Implied percentage change
University of East London	4,055	263	4,318	4,940	-622	-12.6%
University of Bedfordshire	2,738	198	2,936	3,351	-415	-12.4%
Middlesex University	3,944	362	4,306	4,905	-599	-12.2%
University of Northampton	2,340	162	2,502	2,848	-346	-12.1%
Liverpool Hope University	1,206	105	1,311	1,490	-179	-12.0%
Edge Hill University	2,128	239	2,367	2,687	-320	-11.9%
University of Central Lancashire	4,997	929	5,926	6,711	-785	-11.7%
University of Lincoln	2,553	377	2,930	3,315	-385	-11.6%
University of Sunderland	2,234	288	2,522	2,852	-330	-11.6%
Leeds Metropolitan University	5,000	543	5,543	6,264	-721	-11.5%
Newman University College	404	41	445	502	-57	-11.4%
Sheffield Hallam University	4,942	536	5,478	6,176	-698	-11.3%
University of Greenwich	3,946	331	4,277	4,824	-547	-11.3%
University of Westminster	3,565	473	4,038	4,553	-515	-11.3%
De Montfort University	3,555	400	3,955	4,460	-505	-11.3%
Bath Spa University	1,512	230	1,742	1,964	-222	-11.3%
Manchester Metropolitan University	6,604	617	7,221	8,121	-900	-11.1%
Liverpool John Moores University	4,904	545	5,449	6,128	-679	-11.1%
University of the West of England, Bristol	4,601	600	5,201	5,849	-648	-11.1%
University of Essex	2,467	378	2,845	3,200	-355	-11.1%
University of Bradford	2,124	165	2,289	2,574	-285	-11.1%
Kingston University	4,685	443	5,128	5,764	-636	-11.0%

Source: Hefce, 2012

Table 5.2 Institutions with no 'margin places' losing fewer than 5% of allocations (excluding specialist arts institutions who opted out)

Institution	Core for 2012–13	AAB+	'Implied total' for 2012–13	2011–12 Student number control limit	Difference between 2012–13 & 2011–12	Implied percentage change
University of Oxford	588	3,030	3,618	3,171	447	14.1%
University of Cambridge	584	3,102	3,686	3,255	431	13.2%
London School of Economics	162	748	910	835	75	9.0%
Courtauld Institute of Art	10	44	54	51	3	5.9%
University of Bristol	602	2,933	3,535	3,410	125	3.7%
Imperial College London	281	1,622	1,903	1,836	67	3.6%
University of Durham	643	2,892	3,535	3,449	86	2.5%
University College London	580	2,439	3,019	3,042	–23	–0.8%
University of Warwick	703	2,488	3,191	3,259	–68	–2.1%
University of Exeter	950	3,125	4,075	4,176	–101	–2.4%
University of Bath	724	1,625	2,349	2,415	–66	–2.7%
King's College London	770	2,232	3,002	3,112	–110	–3.5%
Royal Veterinary College	113	183	296	307	–11	–3.6%
University of Sheffield	1,377	2,883	4,260	4,419	–159	–3.6%
University of Nottingham	2,005	3,470	5,475	5,697	–222	–3.9%
University of Birmingham	1,752	3,102	4,854	5,061	–207	–4.1%
University of York	1,255	1,959	3,214	3,358	–144	–4.3%
University of Southampton	1,558	2,592	4,150	4,342	–192	–4.4%
University of Manchester	2,875	3,883	6,758	7,085	–327	–4.6%
School of Oriental and African Studies	409	318	727	763	–36	–4.7%
University of Newcastle upon Tyne	1,658	2,203	3,861	4,061	–200	–4.9%

Source: Hefce, 2012

performance and therefore face even bigger losses than 'implied'. Institutions who previously picked up AAB+ candidates rejected by the top handful may find themselves exposed here: caught between the immovable object of the number of AAB+ applicants and the irresistible force of bullish institutions.

There is though an alternative for an institution not wishing to shrink: institutions can consider bidding for the new 'margin' of places.

THE 'MARGIN'

The margin is a second pool of 20,000: a pool of *places* as opposed to *applicants* (AAB+). Its 20,000 do not represent additional places in higher education; the margin was created by taking a percentage cut from each institution's core. Institutions were invited to bid for those places for specific courses. Any numbers gained through successful bids were in addition to the core and AAB+ recruitment. However, only those institutions charging under £7,501 on average *after fee waivers* were eligible. This is therefore an incentive for institutions to lower prices *or switch their 'spending' commitments in access agreements from bursaries to fee waivers so as to sneak under the qualifying average.*

When the White Paper announced the new margin pool in June 2011, universities had already set their 2012/13 fees and agreed their access initiatives with Offa in time for recruitment to begin in Autumn 2012. The 'margin' appeared to be a crude intervention to encourage institutions to revise their original decisions: they could then bid for some of the places they had lost from their core.

The message was clear: the less selective universities ought to lower their fees to £7,500. The difficulties of such a move were set out in Chapter 2, especially for the London institutions with higher overheads. Most universities decided to 'hold tight', preferring to lose places but maintain a higher fee.

Further bias can be seen in BIS's instruction to Hefce, which oversaw the first tendering process. Hefce was to 'pay attention to value for money and quality, particularly encouraging bids from FE Colleges and alternative providers with the capacity to introduce new, or grow existing, higher education provision'.[6]

HE courses taught in FE colleges are cheaper, with the average tuition fee in 2012/13 coming in at £6,989 per year (as compared to £8,100 in universities). The margin was aimed at taking places away from the established universities and distributing them to cheaper providers, many of whom were offering HNCs and HNDs, not full degrees, validated by the for-profit education conglomerate, Pearson. Here, lower level qualifications are replacing undergraduate degree places. The end result of the process was announced in February 2012: '9,643 places have been distributed between 35 higher education institutions (HEIs), and 10,354 places between 155 further education colleges (FECs).'

Assessing the full impact of this swing is a little complicated. Ten thousand places appear to have been transferred from HEIs to FE colleges, but some of the places awarded to FE colleges compensated for lost places previously *franchised* by higher education institutions (see Chapter 6 for more details). But the big winners amongst universities were Anglia Ruskin (569 places), London Metropolitan (564), Nottingham Trent (558) and Staffordshire (549). Amongst FE colleges, Hartpury (352), Newham (294), Newcastle (260), Norwich (249) and Mid Kent (214) picked up more than some universities.[7]

The 20,000 places allocated this way will be repeated in 2012/13 enabling the change to bed in. For 2013/14, however, only a further 5,000 places will be redistributed through the margin and it will operate in a different manner with the eligibility fee cap altered.[8]

WHAT ACTUALLY HAPPENED IN 2012?

So far I have treated the numbers controls separately from the question of successful recruitment. This enabled the demonstration of a systematic bias against a large group of English universities. The numbers controls made it more difficult to maintain numbers at many institutions, but this is different from their ability to recruit in the new terrain, which depends on a large and complex network of factors.

What did happen in the 2012 recruitment cycle and what might it further reveal about the future contours of this new market? As I write in September 2012, UCAS is reporting a drop in new Home/EU undergraduate enrolments of at least 50,000. The overall reduction in numbers was anticipated but not on such a scale: Hefce anticipated that HEIs would lose 19,500 places, while FE colleges would gain 8,570 directly funded places (a 48 per cent increase). Although authoritative analysis is not yet possible at the time of writing, we can suggest six further factors:

1. fewer deferrals from the 2011 entry cycle as applicants opted to avoid the imposition of higher fees;

Opt-outs and Exemptions for the Numbers Controls

Exemption
Specialist institutions offering creative arts, performing arts and design can apply for exemption from core, margin and 'AAB+'.

To be eligible, institutions must *recruit primarily via audition or portfolio*, not *qualifications*. Most have exercised this 'opt-out' and instead maintain their previous student numbers allocations, reduced only by the minimal cuts (around 3 per cent) needed to reflect reduction in overall student numbers. In return for exemption, they have no option to expand.

This opt-out will remain in place for at least three years beyond 2013/14. Such conservatoire and studio settings can often also attract direct funding through the 'small and specialist institution' funding.

This policy applies only to specialist *institutions*: the same *courses* offered within larger universities providing a diverse range of subjects cannot apply for exemption.

Since applications to such courses are often 'post-qualification' (the applicant will already have sat A levels or equivalent before embarking on a preparatory foundation course), whether a candidate is AAB+ or not is known in advance. Although opting out avoids the complications above,

---

2. a wariness from institutions around *over-recruitment* given new enhanced penalties and a less flexible scheme;
3. the mis-estimation of the 'AAB+' numbers, which reduced that pool by *at least* a further 6,000;
4. unfamiliar threshold effects caused by AAB+;
5. a reported failure on the part of the margin places to attract students;
6. and, perhaps most importantly, changed consumer behaviour.

Taking each point in turn, the 2012 entry cycle began with a base of deferred acceptances, which was lower by about 10,000 on previous years, as some of those applying in 2011 who instead may have opted for a gap year decided to avoid the new funding regime.

Second, institutions may have been reluctant to risk over-recruiting. The new measures looked to be more punitive – with a penalty of perhaps £10,000 per student and no margin for error. Such tight restrictions will present universities with difficulties in a system where offers are made before qualifications are known in the majority of cases, and where 'articulation arrangements'

selective institutions with canny management may have worked out how to exploit that situation. If popular courses in say, Fine Art, at Goldsmiths or UCL, where no opt-out is possible, decided to expand, then specialist art schools who have opted out may still struggle to recruit.

Overseas Students
Overseas, non-EU, students are not subject to any recruitment allocations, or fee caps, though the current issues with the UK Border Agency and Home Office, who are recording students in the net migration statistics, may limit this avenue (see Chapter 8).

Alternative Financing and Sponsorship
Overseas students are exempt from numbers controls because they cannot access the student loan scheme. One option mooted was to allow Home or EU students *who chose not to take out loans* to be treated similarly. This was rejected as benefiting richer students unfairly.

 While the possibility is excluded for individuals, where entire courses are sponsored by companies or charities, these *do fall outside the numbers controls* as all fees are covered and there is no 'draw on public funds'. Such 'closed' courses are 'off-quota'. Here we can see an incentive for universities to extend industry and business collaboration.

guarantee places to those who have succeeded on lower level, access or foundation courses run within the institution or at partners.

Third, earlier in 2012, Hefce had estimated that there would be 85,000 applicants with AAB+ or equivalent. This benchmark factored in an expected annual increase in those achieving the highest grades at A level. However, 2012 saw the first decline in numbers achieving top grades for 20 years. According to reports, the pool of AAB+ applicants *with A levels* was *10,000* below the estimate. An increase of 4,000 in applicants holding qualifications equivalent to those grades at A level partially offset this reduction.

In total, only 79,000 applicants were classed as AAB+ reducing the pool by 6,000. Overall numbers were therefore reduced by the same amount, because *core allocations at each institution had been reduced to accommodate the estimate*. The core was stable but the reduction in AAB+ meant competition at this level was tougher than anticipated. The new elite shown on Table 5.2 further disadvantaged themselves as they are less likely to accept some equivalent qualifications, such as distinctions in BTECs. The Russell

Group is reporting lost income totalling £80 million amongst its members and filled 11,500 fewer places than expected.[9]

With regard to the fourth point – expansion and 'threshold' effects – although Oxford and Cambridge opted not to expand (for reasons explained in Chapter 4), Bristol, Durham, King's College London, Imperial and UCL *were aiming to do so*. Bristol took an additional 600 and UCL, 300. As explained above, this leaves fewer AAB+ applicants for others to recruit, undermining their ability to match their past performance. As an example of a 'threshold effect', the University of Southampton reported that its numbers were down by 600, though its 'implied total' indicated that a par performance would see 192 fewer. They complained that they had qualified applicants who they would like to recruit, but were prevented from doing so by the restrictions on core recruitment. We may see here a polarising tendency *within the elite* as first and second choice institutions outcompete those who pick up applicants rejected by the very top.

Other reports indicate that some prestigious institutions dropped the normal grade requirements significantly in Clearing in order to maintain stable numbers. As their place in this market depends on their position as *selective* institutions, some of the new elite may retrench and reduce numbers rather than have to repeat such behaviour in future. From the elite perspective, the influence of other positional markets, such as research and global competition, provides a further set of considerations.

In the medium term, a few institutions have plans for serious expansion. UCL's designs for a new campus in Stratford have been approved by Newham council, while Imperial has just purchased the former BBC site in White City, to be known as Imperial West.

What this reveals is a level of complexity on the supply-side misjudged in government rhetoric about consumer choice. From the demand side, points five and six, we can see that consumers may have exercised their right not to buy the product on offer, judging it over-priced. David Willetts has claimed that more applicants than ever got into their first choice universities, but thousands opted not to take up offers made to them.

We need to emphasise one political advantage of a market. Willetts and members of BIS have described the fall as 'modest' or 'acceptable'. The market enables them to maintain 'clean hands' in a way they would not have managed had they imposed cuts of 50,000 centrally. Blame can be passed to institutions who misjudged the new market. But in policy terms the government does not have clean hands, and is pressing on with its gamble. By pushing on to move to ABB+ in 2013, the government is 'doubling up', hoping things will settle down despite the problems with the threshold effects described above.

We are moving forward very rapidly here and the consumer behaviour that is most noticeable is a mixture of debt aversion and doubts about whether higher education is worth it for 30 years of repayments.

VIABILITY

I conclude this chapter by emphasising how the numbers controls and the market have a further edge: financial viability. University finances are probably the best they have been in recent history, with large cash reserves and surpluses at most institutions; but there are also significant debts and few are immune to the problems that would come from a failure to recruit at their recent levels.

In the short term, it is possible to sit tight in the face of a small loss of income, but with the cumulative effects of shifting pools eating into the core, along with changing pressures on applicants, it is not clear that there is a 'do-nothing' scenario in the medium term. Many institutions will have to consider retrenchment – narrowing provision and concentrating on areas of particular strength. Other options include concentrating on postgraduate or short-course provision, or lowering fees to go for the market opened up to commercial providers.

But this market may also undermine the viability of established institutions. The government is sanguine about such a turn of events. Paragraph 6.9b of the 2011 White Paper states:

> Currently, HEFCE can take action in the public interest where an institution is at risk of getting into financial difficulties. Providers that perform poorly under the new funding arrangements will primarily be those that fail to recruit enough students. Like its predecessors, the Government does not guarantee to underwrite universities and colleges. They are independent, and it is not Government's role to protect an unviable institution. However, we see a continuing role for a public body to work with institutions at risk of financial difficulties.

Its proposal for a 'continuing role' is for Hefce to act as administrator and oversee an 'orderly wind-down of activity' that would protect the students (by finding them alternative institutions at which to complete their studies).[10]

Any 'failure to recruit' is going to owe much to the artificial supply-side impositions outlined above. There is large unmet demand which ought to increase as the compulsory school age is raised to 18, assuming potential students are not all dissuaded by the mess of a financing scheme. Institutions who through bad luck fare poorly in this new rigged game know the blame should be placed mainly on the government's reforms and their rushed implementation.

Mergers have been seen before in the sector, while management takeovers of 'unviable' hospitals are now occurring in the National Health Service. Late in 2012, the University of Bolton sought out staff opinion on an appropriate response to the 'imminent financial and sustainability risks' it faced. It offered three basic scenarios: redundancies, do nothing, or seek takeover by another university.[11]

One function of this instability is to ease the entry of new providers and private equity into the loan-funded sector, creating new outlets for value extraction. This will be the theme of Chapter 7, while the possibility of university 'buy-outs' is discussed in Chapter 9. In the next chapter we will see how the overhaul of the framework governing degree standards also serves to create a level playing field for private operations.

6
Risk, Deregulation and Deprofessionalisation

What kind of regulatory framework do you need for higher education? The route into this question is to consider that while it is perfectly possible to set up Crouch End College and award diplomas in coffee retail, the title 'university' and the power to award *degrees* of various kinds are legally protected.[1] In addition, there are laws and regulations governing the kind of institutions that can receive direct public funding (grants) and which students can access the loans provided by the SLC. At root is a question of standards and whether they are to be guaranteed, policed, monitored or left to market forces. The government wants to see a new, diverse range of experiments in provision, but can it avoid the associated risks with people's education and student experience?

A lower bar on 'market entry', to create a 'level playing field', allows more businesses into the sector but threatens the traditional approaches to quality assurance. If it becomes easier to gain the power to award degrees or to style a business as a 'university', how does the sector avoid a 'subprime crisis'? Concerns here arise around the deprofessionalisation of higher education.

THE DELAYED HE BILL

When the Higher Education White Paper was published in June 2011 it set out a proposed structure for a new three-tier regulatory framework. This would have been the centrepiece of the planned Higher Education Bill. With the Bill now delayed, perhaps indefinitely, as a result of Coalition politics and union-led opposition, we are therefore somewhat in regulatory limbo.

In June 2012, the government formally responded to consultations run off the back of the White Paper, and seemed to indicate that they were adopting a wait-and-see approach:

> The White Paper set out proposals for primary legislation to create a new regulatory framework. Many responses to the White

Paper stressed that we do not yet know the full effect of the new funding arrangements. Hence, *it cannot be clear what form of regulatory framework will be appropriate*. We will therefore not at this stage be seeking to introduce changes to primary legislation, but will move our reform agenda forward *primarily through non-legislative means*. We will keep this situation under review.[2] (my emphasis)

Responding to Howard Hotson in the London Review of Books, David Willetts had asserted that quality assurance depends on 'regulation and a clear legal framework'.[3] But now he apparently no longer holds to that position, since he is happy to see how things develop before legislating reactively.

In a blasé moment before the BIS Select Committee, when asked directly about the likely date for the appearance of a Bill, Willetts replied, 'Who knows?' The government intends to be 'ingenious' in using its existing powers to press on with a piecemeal recomposition of the higher education landscape. But there is one pressing issue to be resolved with primary legislation: Hefce needs to be given powers to control access to the student loan book. There will also be political pressure from universities as they demand clarity and begin to feel the competitive pressure from below. A late Bill, prepared in 2014 towards the end of this Parliament, could be one way to exploit that pressure – pushing through primary legislation under the cover of urgency, meaning that scrutiny is limited.

This chapter will look at the proposed regulatory framework which is primarily designed to integrate private operators into what was the publicly funded higher education sector. It will consider the implications of the proposed framework and its new 'risk-based approach' to quality (which is proceeding after instructions were given to Hefce).

THE REGULATOR: HEFCE

A lightly regulated market of private companies needs a regulator. The Browne review had proposed creating a superquango, HE Council, to act in this way. This would have required primary legislation as it involves the creation of a new body. Instead, the government is keeping the existing quangos, Hefce, QAA, OIA and Offa, and tweaking their functions. This enables it to effect piecemeal reforms more quickly, especially as the senior personnel in these existing organisations are supportive of the government's reforms.

Hefce has been nominated to act as the lead regulator. It is to be transformed from a funder which has some regulatory functions to the lead regulator which provides some (mostly research) funding. Its function will be analogous to Monitor in the NHS, or the regulators in the utility sector (Ofgem, Ofwat, etc.). That would seem to transform it at core, even though the name and personnel may remain the same. Hefce's chief executive Alan Langlands was formerly chief executive of the NHS executive (1994–2001), and recent board appointments have been of people with NHS experience.

Originally established in 1992 to oversee standards of provision, distribute grant funding, and monitor the use of that funding (and general financial stability), Hefce has gained several functions in the intervening years. For example, it now oversees the universities and charities which are exempt charities (the majority) on behalf of the Charity Commission. Responsibilities for promoting knowledge exchange and widening participation were also added more recently.

Under the new structure, Hefce would be tasked with promoting competition in the interests of students as consumers and overseeing qualified providers; it is meant to achieve a memorandum of understanding with the Office for Fair Trading and to concentrate on 'abuse of market position', price fixing and 'anti-competitive practices'. It is not clear at this stage how Hefce can oversee competition between private companies and hold some of them to additional requirements in respect of charitable status.

In so far as it needs to be given new powers, then primary legislation is required. The government's efforts to be 'ingenious' may have some effect, but instructions to quangos are in danger of exacerbating a democratic deficit, given that Hefce only appears to be accountable to the Secretary of State.

HEFCE AND PUBLIC FUNDING

Owing to the changes achieved without legislation, we may indeed hit some major snags if nothing is established before 2015. For example, Hefce's powers only relate to the bodies *it currently funds with grants*. It therefore has no current relationship with the private sector.

It ensures compliance with student numbers controls at established universities (the subject of Chapter 5) because it threatens to claw back *grant funding* in the event of over-recruitment. Over-recruitment was a viable strategy for publicly funded institutions because the institution would still receive *fee income* from students.

All eligible students have the *right* to access loans for tuition fees and maintenance. This now becomes a pressing problem. Once we hit 2014/15, when three cohorts of students will be on the new funding regime, Hefce will no longer be distributing *any* block grant for undergraduate teaching to many institutions (for example, those which do not teach medicine or the subjects that still attract some direct funding).

In such cases, there would no reason for the institution to comply with the imposed numbers controls – every student in the college would have the right to access loans and there would be no carrot or stick that Hefce could use to effect compliance. In a recent consultation, Hefce admits: 'Our current ultimate sanction is withdrawal of funding, which may not in the future be an effective mechanism.'[4]

Hefce would therefore have to be given the power to enter into binding contracts with providers as a condition for access to the loan book. This would underpin the basic sanction in the proposed regulatory framework. Paragraph 6.13 of the White Paper contains the following passage:

> HEFCE, as primary regulator, will be expected to monitor providers, address signs of failure and agree recovery arrangements. Should an institution fail to meet any of these requirements, despite having been given time to take remedial action, *their access to student support finance could be suspended or stopped.*

We should therefore expect to see some form of primary legislation even if it is not in the guise of a Higher Education Bill.

THE FRAMEWORK: WHAT WAS PROPOSED?

As already noted, the proposed framework was intended to integrate the private sector and what were the publicly funded HEIs. A three-tier system would see institutions positioning themselves at one of the indicated levels:[5]

1. *Bodies holding taught degree awarding powers (DAPs).* These institutions must comply with quality assurance measures and provide an independent dispute resolution arrangement for students (with the Office of the Independent Adjudicator).
2. *Institutions designated for student support.* 'Student support' covers maintenance grants and loans for fees and maintenance. Those seeking access to that money for their students must abide

by additional regulations. They would be obliged to set fees under the maximum tuition fee cap (currently £9,000) and be assessed by the regulator to ensure financial sustainability. They would have to comply with student numbers controls as per Chapter 5. Any institution seeking to charge over £6,000 per year would have to enter into an access agreement with Offa.
3. *Institutions seeking access to teaching grants.* These institutions would meet all of the requirements for 1 and 2, but in addition, must be not-for-profit and meet any conditions specific to the grant. This would cover subjects in Bands A, B and, from 2013, C1 (see Chapter 2 for details).

Established higher education institutions already in receipt of public grant funding would fall into tier 3. Tiers 1 and 2 primarily relate to private higher education providers which have decisions to make about how to position themselves, since this proposed framework alters the conditions under which they currently operate, especially in relation to access to student support. This is discussed in detail in Chapter 7.

Here we now look at 'degree awarding powers' (DAPs), which are crucial to quality regulation.

DEGREE AWARDING POWERS

Higher and further education in the UK currently operates under a framework that differentiates qualifications on a scheme determined by the amount of study required and different learning outcomes. This framework is shown in Table 6.1.

Table 6.1   Further and Higher Education Qualification (FHEQ) framework

Higher Education Qualification	FHEQ level
Doctorates	8
Master's Degrees (MSc, MA, MRes, MPhil, etc.) Postgraduate Diplomas Postgraduate Certificate in Education (PGCE)	7
Undergraduate Degrees Graduate Diplomas Graduate Certificates	6
Foundation Degrees (FdA, FdSc) Higher National Diplomas (HND) Diplomas of Higher Education (DipHE)	5
Higher National Certificates (HNC) Certificates of Higher Education (CertHE)	4

Source: QAA, Further and Higher Education Qualification framework, 2008

Under current regulations, undergraduate degrees are level 6. The institutions able to award degrees are restricted: it is a legally protected qualification. Level 4 corresponds to one full year of study at undergraduate level, level 5 to two years.

The majority of institutions that hold the power to award degrees do so by virtue of statute or Royal Charter. That is, they were granted the powers by the state. The former polytechnics, previously awarding Council for National Academic Awards (CNAA) degrees, were granted the power to award their own degrees under the 1992 Further and Higher Education Act: this was a crucial component of their transformation into autonomous *universities*. Exceptionally, Oxford, Cambridge and the Archbishop of Canterbury have the power to award degrees without having received that formal decree (in some ways this is a feudal legacy).

Since 1992, the Privy Council has overseen a process by which other institutions can apply for DAPs in accordance with regulations that were amended in 2004 for England and Wales.[6] As part of its deliberations, the Privy Council is advised by the Quality Assurance Agency and the appropriate minister. Bodies not in receipt of public funding only receive powers for six years, at which point they must be renewed.

At present, the assessment is dependent on staff and institutional set-up. Crucially, since degree awarding powers are given to 'autonomous' institutions, those applying must offer 'a well-founded, cohesive and self-critical academic community that demonstrates firm guardianship of its standards'. Staff must not only be 'competent to teach' but also be 'active and recognised participants in research and/or advanced scholarship'.[7]

Alongside this fundamental principle, the institution must have a track record in undergraduate teaching and clear and appropriate mechanisms for ensuring that academic judgement is safeguarded and promoted. An institution is responsible for *enabling* staff to maintain 'a close and professional understanding of current developments in research and scholarship in their subjects', as 'teaching for degree-level qualifications should reflect, in a careful, conscious and intellectually demanding manner, the latest developments in the subject of study'.

This point is perhaps underappreciated: academics are therefore responsible for standards, and institutions for ensuring that academics are supported in this regard. It rests on the sine qua non that a self-critical academic community exists.[8] The high bar set here is the key plank of current quality control.

The Quality Assurance Agency

The Quality Assurance Agency is an independent charity, and technically not a quango. It has a UK-wide remit: higher education institutions within the public framework are required to subscribe. These subscriptions generate one third of its annual income; the remainder comes from a contract with Hefce, on whose behalf it conducts audits of higher education institutions.

Because it relies on the self-critical community of academics, the QAA focuses on paper trails, handbooks, guidance manuals and assessing procedures. It is viewed dimly by many academics owing to these 'box-ticking exercises'. If it were clearer that the QAA's role here is supposed to be *complementary* to that of academics, such resentment might be avoided.

However, the QAA's attempts to colonise academic judgement through its 'benchmark' standards in different subjects is unhelpful here. Similarly, the recent initiative to establish QAA as a kitemark is probably misconceived given its dependence on academic communities and its own status as a subscription-based institution.[9]

Its other core function is to prepare independent reports for the Privy Council in relation to applicants for degree awarding powers. Comments by the chief executive, Anthony McClaran, in October 2012 seemed to indicate that QAA had begun to see its role as offering a 'gateway to new providers' as opposed to policing stringent requirements.

WHAT WAS PROPOSED IN THE REFORM OF DEGREE AWARDING POWERS?

The government has not yet prepared detailed or draft regulations on degree awarding powers. But it is keen to create supply-side reform in the interests of a more diverse market. Advocates of 'supply-side' reform may take different positions on what should be done here. Some promote online learning and two-year fast-track degrees, which involve students (and academics) eschewing the traditional timetable with three terms or two semesters and summer holidays and instead studying through without a break to create an extra term or semester.

Others are in favour of making the *content* of a degree more vocationally or professionally relevant. While still others believe that the government should be moving away from the traditional focus on level 6 – and the middle-class shibboleth or rite of passage of three years full-time study away from home. Many students may be better served by well-designed level 4 and level 5 qualifications where they can acquire higher level vocational and professional skills suited to the current shape of the labour market.[10]

These three developments appear to be happening simultaneously. This means that things are increasingly becoming blurred. What seems clear is that the government would like to reframe our current understanding and practices around degrees and what institutions can award them.

Pushing for alternative providers will involve lowering the current barrier to DAPs or making access to them through *partnerships* of one kind or another more easily available. We will look shortly at the new 'risk-based' quality assurance measures being implemented without legislative change, but we first need to consider the liberalisation that introduces new risks in the first place.

This is the crux: allow more operators to operate but react to any failings. For example, the White Paper indicated that the required track record of higher education provision would be reduced to just two years and, in addition, *overseas* activities would be considered. One might consider this in context: it took roughly 20 years for polytechnics to receive their own DAPs.

The basic idea is that more institutions will be allowed to award their degrees, but if concerns about quality are raised, the regulator will have the power to intervene and 'suspend or remove degree awarding powers, *however granted*, where there is clear evidence that quality or academic standards continue to be below the acceptable threshold and efforts to improve the position have proved unsuccessful'.[11]

BODIES THAT DO NO TEACHING: PEARSON DEGREES

A further idea strongly supported by Willetts was the radical suggestion that it should be possible to grant DAPs to institutions that *do no teaching*. The preferred recipient of these powers is Pearson plc, which owns the examination board, Edexcel, that awards HNCs and HNDs, level 4 and 5 qualifications. In 2011, Willetts wrote:

> In addition, we will end the fixed, yet illogical, link between degree-awarding powers and teaching. We have, perhaps unintentionally, created a regulatory system which says that awarding bodies must also teach students. That would be seen as absurd in

any other part of the education sector. It is also ahistorical, for the past growth of higher education in England was based on colleges teaching students for external degrees. The polytechnics, for example, taught degrees examined by the old Council for National Academic Awards. This is a model with much going for it because it means students at new institutions can obtain degrees or other qualifications from prestigious and well understood institutions. Employers, in particular, are likely to value such clear signals.[12]

Having seen the centrality of academics within the current quality control system, the reader may be surprised by the strength of this intention. But the idea was developed in the Technical Consultation where the government *committed* to 'removing the barriers' that prevented *non-teaching bodies* from gaining DAPs. To analyse the proffered argument critically:

1. There is nothing 'illogical' in the coupling of DAPs and teaching: according to current regulations, academic communities safeguard standards and represent 'professional integrity and judgement'.
2. It is not clear why Willetts believes we need to turn the clock back to the mid 1800s, given the infrastructure we now have available. To be 'ahistorical' is not to see the change that has occurred over the last two centuries: Willetts makes an opportunist appeal to history.
3. Higher education is not like any other part of the education system, even though Willetts and some in industry do see undergraduate study as 'more school', or merely training.
4. The polytechnics did *not* have its degrees *examined* by the CNAA. The CNAA validated programmes as being of degree level, it did not set or mark exams: it was not offering an external degree (see Box).
5. The CNAA was staffed by seconded senior *academics*. Non-teaching bodies may not have academics *at all*.
6. Note the importance of brand in 'prestigious and well understood institutions': Willett's intention was to extend DAPs to Pearson/Edexcel, which already awards HNCs and HNDs in England.

That said, this kind of change would have required primary legislation, so with the Bill postponed this idea is on hold.

Partnerships and External Degrees

External degrees are degrees where the examinations or assessment are open to anybody. One does not need to register for a degree *programme*, the candidate organises study towards the assessment themselves. The most significant of these is the University of London's International Programme (indeed this is what students at Anthony Grayling's ill-starred New College of the Humanities will sit, at an exorbitant mark-up). The London Programme is constructed from the courses and academic input of its constituent colleges and universities: the quality is meant to be guaranteed by those staff. It is therefore not like the division of responsibility we see in secondary education: examination boards (awards) and schools (teaching institutions).

Partnership arrangements between institutions are varied but typically refer to arrangements between a 'senior' institution holding degree awarding powers and a 'junior' which does not. Note that the junior partner would therefore be *outside* the three-tier regulatory framework. The senior partner is responsible for safeguarding standards. Partnership arrangements with overseas institutions are big business and make quality assessment even more difficult. Nearly 300,000 students were registered for a UK degree overseas in 2010/11. The main three modes are:

- Franchise arrangements: A course designed and assessed by the senior institution is delivered by a partner institution, commonly a further education college.
- Validation: A course designed, taught and assessed by the *junior* institution is *validated* by a higher education institution as being of degree level. The student receives a degree from the senior institution.
- Articulation arrangements: The senior institution agrees to guarantee places on, or offer fast track entry to, a higher level course for students achieving specific grades on a separate course offered by the junior partner.

As we will see, complex arrangements may combine more than one of these modes.

WHY IS THE GOVERNMENT KEEN ON PEARSON DEGREES?

Pearson's popularity with Willetts depends on a particular issue that has arisen with regard to partnership arrangements between universities and FE colleges offering HE level courses ('HE in FE').

Around 250 colleges offer HE in FE with around 25,000 places available through Hefce's number allocation in September 2012, and further places through franchise arrangements with HE institutions. The latest report on the topic calculates that 1 in 12 HE students is in a further education college: 177,000 students in 2009/10.[13]

Willetts is keen to extend this provision because it is cheaper than other options. It has been estimated by the Association of Colleges (AoC) that its members could offer a full degree programme (level 6) for £5,000 per year. However, current arrangements are threatened by the new numbers controls. FE colleges offering degree level courses currently have partnerships with HEIs who either *franchise* some of their places to FE colleges, or *validate* courses developed by the FE college (see Box). In franchise arrangements, the university passes places from its own student numbers allocation to the partner delivering the course (see Chapter 5). With recruitment tightening, a rational response would be to claw back such places to protect core provision and bring back 'in house' places previously run at a partner.

Martin Doel, Chair of the AoC, has described the relationship as 'feudal', and both Willetts and Vince Cable warned back in 2011 that 'Universities should not impede cost-effective provision of HE by colleges.' Cable twice explicitly referenced reports of 'anti-competitive practices' by universities in this context, stating on one occasion:

> If there is substance in these suggestions, then this must end. As I've repeatedly emphasised, the intention is for student choice to drive supply, not Government intervention. But it is a legitimate role for Government to examine options for intervention in markets which are not operating to best effect – and to support fair competition, for example between FE colleges and universities. Where we see barriers to entry, or uneven playing fields, we will take steps to address them.[14]

The proposed requirement for Hefce to police anti-competitive practices and abuse of market position has direct pertinence here.

Though the margin provided places directly to FE colleges, these courses would also require a partner, in this case to *validate* what is on offer. Cable later condemned the suggestion that universities might increase their fees here. He warned that any loss of FE provision would be a 'backwards step'.[15]

The University Title

In June, Willetts announced 'ingeniously' that he had lowered the current eligibility criterion to the legally protected 'university' title with immediate effect. Previously, those seeking university status would have needed 4,000 full-time students; now the government will consider applications from those which only have 1,000 'full-time equivalent' higher education students, 'of which at least 750 are studying for a degree', and where this represents more than 55 per cent of the total student body.[16] The College of Law became the first institution to benefit from these changes, announcing in November 2012 that it would be known as The *University* of Law. Given its purchase by private equity (see Chapter 9), it is the first for-profit university in the UK. Around the same time, ten 'university colleges' were cleared to apply for the full title.

Universities were formerly seen as distinct institutions or societies concerned with the pursuit of knowledge and the advancement of learning *for its own sake* and distinct from institutions offering technical higher education. Importantly, universities were understood to be communities of *scholars* – 'A corporation or society which devotes itself to a search after knowledge for the sake of its intrinsic value.'[17] It is this form of corporatism which is being replaced by a different understanding of 'corporations'.

Now, however, when allied with changes to DAPs, the difference between a university and a training provider, however specialist, is being eroded, as the title is now open to small institutions, indeed *mono*technics. Since 2004, in England and Wales, there has been no requirement that institutions offer a broad range of subjects, nor that they offer higher degrees or pursue research.[18]

What then does the university title signify? Does this change in meaning help consumers or merely boost the brand of providers?

This is where Pearson/Edexcel degrees would come in. Pearson plc is a publicly quoted, UK-based multinational specialising in education and publishing. Pearson has a market capitalisation of roughly \$10 billion. In the UK, it owns the *Financial Times*, Penguin Books and the examination board, Edexcel, through which it already offers its own BTECs, HNCs and HNDs, in partnerships with FE colleges.

Willetts indicated that he had been approached by education providers who wanted access to an 'externally validated' degree so as to extricate themselves from the problems FE colleges currently experience. The key point is that Pearson/Edexcel has no students of its own, hence no numbers controls to worry about, and so would not face the conflicts of interest described above. Were Pearson/Edexcel to gain full DAPs, the attractions to colleges and government are clear: the infrastructure exists at the local level, while Pearson obviously has the capacity through Edexcel to roll out cheap mass provision. Willetts enthused: 'The combination of a local FE college, regional employers and an awarding body could be an important embodiment of the Big Society. So these challenges have to be addressed to open up the system.'[19]

But because Pearson/Edexcel does no teaching itself and therefore has no academics, it does not qualify for degree awarding powers under current legislation. With no Higher Education Bill in the offing, the government cannot proceed directly with its intention to remove legislative barriers here.

RISK-BASED QUALITY ASSURANCE

Despite not having the three-tier framework in place to regulate all institutions with degree awarding powers, the government has instructed Hefce to push ahead with plans for a new 'risk-based approach to quality assurance', which should be introduced by January 2014. As Roger King explains, there are two dimensions to such an approach:

> In competitive market-like systems, such as that proposed in the White Paper for higher education in England, risk is regarded as two-dimensional: it provides the basis for consumer protection on the one hand (protecting against risk), while encouraging enterprise on the other (encouraging and managing risk-taking).[20]

Hefce as regulator wishes to uphold the interests of students *and taxpayers* in a competitive environment and 'support efficiency and effectiveness in institutional management and governance'.[21] A risk-based approach attempts to balance these two potentially conflicting demands.

By relaxing the barriers to participation, the government seeks the benefits of 'enterprise'. But in so far as lowering the barriers removes one of the main controls for quality, then there is a risk to the 'consumer'. The fundamental deregulation concerns the place of academics and their professional practice and judgement within the system.

The market envisioned by the government involves removing this criterion: a risk-based approach is designed to allow quality to be monitored but for provision to respond to consumer demand. That is, instead of professionals upholding an agreed standard, customers will drive the process and determine what standards are or are not acceptable. In many of the 'new providers', the teaching staff are not academics as defined in the current regulations in so far as they are not 'recognised' as active scholars or researchers (see above).

In concrete terms, Hefce proposes lightening the audit burden on established universities and colleges by 'visiting' less frequently (or invasively) than the current six-year cycle. For newer institutions and first-time entrants, the burden would be greater until they had built up a successful track record. On top of this two-tiered audit cycle and a complaints procedure, there are a series of potential 'triggers'. These might include very low scores in key aspects of information provision and certain events such as 'changes of ownership, actual or proposed' and 'significant variations in provision', such as course closures or growth in collaborations and partnerships.[22] (A clause inserted into the November 2012 consultation on designation stated that any such change would automatically trigger a re-assessment.[23])

There is a need to come up with robust regulation to cover changes of ownership, but our key group, academics, are largely absent from the discussion: 'triggers', many initiated by students, and audits by regulatory bodies are here replacing professional practice. It is not clear how Hefce proposes to protect whistleblowers or how they intend to ensure that competitive pressures are not distorting the safeguarding function that rests on academic judgement.

I do not wish to mystify academics. Even prior to the new market, the 'self-critical community of scholars' had been eroded to a large extent by an expansionist executive and managerial class. Roger Brown indicates that it has been in nobody's interests to properly assess what has been happening to standards and student achievement: 'Equally depressing has been the failure of any national body to take responsibility and ownership of the problem. Too often, when presented with evidence of these detriments, the sector's response has been tardy and defensive.'[24] Further, there does appear to be growing evidence that fewer hours of study are required to gain an honours degree. A Hefce report from 2009 reported that the UK (roughly 30 hours per week) now compared unfavourably with France (42).[25] Earlier research by Hepi in this area was cited in the 2011 White Paper to underscore 'legitimate concerns about the variation in student workload' across subjects and institutions (for example, varying between 19 and 45 hours per week for Law).[26]

But the question of what *higher* education is does depend on addressing the question clearly: whose responsibility is quality and who is in a position to assess it? A combination of regulatory and market reform could serve to *deprofessionalise* the sector, removing one of the potential, though currently neglected, bulwarks against declining standards. The trends of the last two decades would have to be reversed to make this effective.

RISK AND PARTNERSHIPS

Those questions lead on to partnership arrangements. I have no doubt that many partnerships are productive, but quality assurance measures have become extremely attenuated here and we have had one recent scandal (see below). Since partnerships are potentially lucrative for many institutions, there are pressures on quality assurance. Since these arrangements can often deliver cheaper courses, the government has been supporting their expansion by enabling students on more of these courses to access loans. Unfortunately, there now appears to be the potential for a large-scale problem with subprime degrees.

The QAA is revising its guidance on collaborations and wishes to set out principles 'capable of embracing any form of collaboration, including potentially those not yet existing'. The 'diverse portfolio of activities' to be encompassed currently includes arrangements with 'non-academic providers and employers', such as the *Guardian*'s proposed MA in Journalism (to be franchised from Cardiff University). The facts on the ground have already moved beyond traditional partnerships to become complex nests involving more than two organisations and modes. As the QAA note: 'Historically, degree-awarding bodies have collaborated with partner organisations but higher education providers who do not have degree-awarding powers may themselves be involved in *managing collaborative arrangements* with other organizations' (my emphasis).

For example, Icon College of Technology and Management in London offers a BSc in Business Administration which is built from a HND offered by Edexcel, and an articulation agreement with a separate company called MDP. MDP specialises in offering the 'top-up' third year necessary to transform the HND (level 5) into a BSc (level 6).[27] MDP does not have its own DAPs, what it offers is validated by the University of the West of England.[28] There are *four* organisations involved here: Icon College is doing the teaching, but the qualification is initially Edexcel's, which *articulates* into MDP's top-up as *validated* by UWE.

Pearson's new venture, Pearson College, will utilise a similar structure. It is offering a BSc in Business and Entrepreneurship.[29] Pearson makes use of Edexcel to award a HND for the first two years of the course, with the third year validated by Royal Holloway University of London. Royal Holloway 'tops up' the diploma into a full undergraduate degree. The added dimension here is that Pearson's degree has been designed in collaboration with industry (BT, Atos and Cisco) and it itself is a non-teaching body. So which 'community' is Royal Holloway assessing? What role do self-critical academic communities play here, *if any*?

It is here that we truly see how a risk-based approach has been extended – both the above schemes are 'enterprising', but responsibility for the quality of the degree ultimately rests with UWE and Royal Holloway. How can such supply chains with multiple partner organisations fit into the current audit and assessment scheme?

One might be inclined to argue 'caveat emptor', but students at Icon can access the publicly backed loan scheme: there is a taxpayer interest here as well as the need to consider whether such access to student support is considered to signify approval for the programme.

The University of Wales fell foul of such arrangements. It generated two thirds of its annual revenue of £15 million through partnership fees. A BBC Wales documentary uncovered that its validation processes were being exploited by unscrupulous college managers down the chain. The QAA had already expressed 'no confidence' in its international partnerships and this further disclosure proved to be the undoing of the institution. It will be dissolved into a new body operating under the original charter of Trinity Saint David.[30]

The attraction of extending degree awarding powers to Pearson is also clear in this context: it would eliminate the need for the complex 'top-up' year in these cases. However, beyond the concerns about having degrees awarded by non-teaching bodies, there is also the question of Pearson's corporate status. As mentioned above, it is a public limited company with a market capitalisation of approximately $10 billion. It runs education at all levels as a profit-making enterprise.

With Hefce now proposing a separate audit cycle for partnership arrangements and other forms of non-standard provision (including distance learning programmes, branch campuses and joint ventures),[31] it may be better to consider creating a *not-for-profit* body to oversee partnerships along the lines of the old Council for National Academic Awards. Partnerships may be the rot in the system that is most open to commercial abuse: validation is the 'Achilles heel' in quality assurance, according to Roger Brown.

The reforms proceeding without a Higher Education Bill are designed to diversify the market by encouraging collaborations and partnerships, but in doing so risk is introduced into what was the public system. Although there are some sound proposals coming from Hefce, by downplaying the role of academics in ensuring quality a deprofessionalisation is perpetuated that is intimately connected with deregulation and risks to quality. The problem of quality has been neglected despite the resources put into the quangos. The chief reform needed is to support academics in resisting commercial and direct management pressures when necessary. Currently, senior quango staff are too keen to facilitate both of these forces.

Willetts's enthusiasm for extending degree awarding powers to Pearson, a for-profit multinational that does no teaching, exemplifies the government's approach. A cheap mass system can be offered through such provision, but will it better serve students and the nation than what we have at present?

7
'New Providers', For-profits and Private Equity

Following on from the previous chapter's discussion of regulation, here we look at how opening up public funding to private providers is already under way and will provide the gateway for large for-profit companies and private equity to establish themselves in competition against the established, charitable sector and to extract profits through state-supported loans. According to the schema set out in the Introduction, this chapter therefore addresses the *external* privatisation of the sector. It provides a bridge between the discussion of current markets and Part 3's concern with various other forms of privatisation, including 'buyout' – the potential for private equity to purchase an established university.

Writing in his book on intergenerational public policy, *The Pinch*, David Willetts managed to avoid dealing explicitly with higher education, but on schools he was clear:

> It is the failure to open up the supply side which is the reason why, despite years of ambitious attempts at education reform, Britain now lags behind many other advanced Western countries. We have already got parents who want to choose and a significant amount of public money that would follow them. ... But we have not created the mechanisms to provide more of the good schools that they want to choose. We must make it easier for people, including parents themselves, to set up new schools. New school providers must be able to enter the maintained sector.[1]

A parallel passage in the White Paper reads: '§4.1 Better information will enable students to make informed choices about where to study. But that will not be enough unless popular higher education institutions and courses can expand, and new providers, including those who offer different models of higher education, can enter the market.' *Real* choice requires not just information but a diversity of providers. 'Free universities' has come to mean something distinct from 'free schools': Willetts has not yet called for parents to set up their own universities, but integrating the diverse private sector into the public is the core goal of the reforms.

Such integration requires the creation of the level playing field, best exemplified by the massive reduction in direct public funding going to established institutions and the extension of the loan scheme to private providers through the 'designation' process outlined below.

As we saw in Chapter 5, the short-term restrictions on the majority of institutions are a deliberate step in a process designed to destabilise them prior to the entrance and expansion of the alternative providers, who in contrast will be nurtured into the new terrain. The established universities are unable to retaliate or even defend their numbers as the government is instituting complex submarkets in which they must first compete with each other.

This is the prime lesson from the privatisation of the UK nationalised utility companies in the 1980s and 1990s: the national monopoly must be broken up or hamstrung so that it does not simply eat up the new competition using its established market position in the early days. In such a circumstance, the public institutions would simply re-establish themselves in the dominant position. To think like some in government, you must see publicly funded higher education as just such a monopoly – this is why 'abuse of market position' is one of the anti-competitive practices that Hefce is to police with the aid of the Office for Fair Trading.

The clear advantage of new providers from the perspective of 'supply-side reform' is that they look very different to the current established sector. They are more flexible with regard to timetabling, open to online learning, two-year and 'no frill' degrees. They are likely to be closer to industry and more interested in preparing 'job-ready' graduates. As one advocate of for-profit providers argues: 'Prospective adults and a modest number of recent high school graduates are attracted to post-secondary institutions that quickly lead to employment. Their curricula are tailored to employer needs without the multitude of frills found in other sectors.'[2] New operations may even be offshoots of particular companies.

They will offer novel study experiences, more choice to the consumer and, effectively, stimulate the market by giving a kick up the backside to the inert, complacent publicly funded institutions. Willetts states that he would like to see new liberal arts colleges and specialist providers, but the diverse range of operators about to move in is much broader than that: 'The biggest lesson I have learned is that the most powerful driver of reform is to let new providers into the system. They do things differently in ways none can predict.'[3]

DESIGNATION FOR STUDENT SUPPORT

So keen is the government on private provision that it has been expanding a shadow finance scheme allowing private providers to seek 'designation' for specific courses using powers granted to the Secretary of State by the 1998 Teaching and Higher Education Act.[4] Students on these designated courses can access maintenance loans and grants to support living costs in the same way as those at universities in receipt of public funding.[5]

In 2011/12 such students were able to access up to £3,375 to put towards the cost of their tuition fees. This was equivalent to the cost of tuition fees at publicly funded universities. From 2012/13 that amount has been increased to £6,000. However, the private institutions might have been charging much higher than that. Designated courses are not subject to numbers controls – neither on recruitment nor on the number of students who can access loans or grants.

Regulation and funding demarcates the public and private sectors in UK higher education, not corporate form per se (see Chapter 9). All universities in receipt of public funding are private institutions established as charities. This distinction is eroded by the current reforms which will make access to the loans the prime source of public support. By using existing powers *quietly* to achieve this expansion, the private sector is being nurtured and the invitation has been accepted: there are designated courses now at over 150 private institutions. Approval was recently given to 98 Edexcel courses at London College UCK within four days of their application being received.[6]

In 2010/11, students on these courses accessed over £40 million in loans and grants. Since rapid expansion of the scheme followed the formation of the Coalition government that figure leapt to £100 million in 2011/12. This could double again in 2012/13. At this point, recruitment will be boosted by the higher tuition fee loan available and because many of these courses will be charging fees that are now competitive when compared to the established universities and colleges.

The main criterion for designation is that the particular course leads to a valid higher education qualification: for example HNC or HND overseen by Edexcel/Pearson, or an undergraduate degree. Six private institutions have their own taught degree awarding powers: BPP university college, Regent's College, The College of Law, ifs School of Finance, Ashridge Business College and University of Buckingham. Designated degree courses at other private institutions will therefore be *validated* by institutions that do hold degree awarding powers.

If one looks at the list of 'designated' courses, then besides missionary and theological colleges and alternative health centres, one can see Burnley Football Club, museums, theatre companies and other institutions which one would not normally associate with higher education. It is such small operations that will rapidly begin to fill the sector, creating the saturated market noted earlier. As an example of the new risk-based approach, in October 2012, Guildhall College had designation status removed from two courses *following student complaints*, the first instance of this kind (in 2011/12 its students received £1.7 million).

The proposed regulatory framework outlined in the 2011 White Paper (and above, Chapter 6) was supposed to *replace* the designation scheme and cement the place of private providers allowing them to register at Tier 2. Access to student support would continue, but in return for those private providers giving up some of their independence by agreeing to regulations governing student numbers, tuition fee caps, information provision and access arrangements.

Delay to any higher education legislation suits these operations: with regard to numbers controls, the longer new legislation can be delayed, the stronger the position of the private providers who can currently *expand*. It will be difficult to force them to reduce numbers at the time of integration. A working group formed between Hefce and SLC is considering how this might be possible even without a Bill: a consultation was published in November 2012.[7] However, numbers controls would only apply to full-time undergraduate degrees, leaving courses based on other qualifications and modes of study free to expand.

MULTINATIONALS AND PRIVATE EQUITY

Beyond the small operations described above, the government has its owns ideas about some larger fauna gracing the sector. Pearson plc has been mentioned, but other multinationals and transnational private equity also figure:

> The global higher education providers that operate in many countries from India to Spain to the USA need to know that

BPP University College of Professional Studies

BPP is viewed favourably within higher education reform circles. It is often referred to as the only 'for-profit' with degree awarding powers (granted in 2007), although technically the degree level courses are run by a non-profit distributing subsidiary of BPP Holdings.

Upon assuming his office in May 2010, David Willetts granted the subsidiary the use of the protected title, 'university college'. John Browne made his first public appearance after the publication of his 2010 review at BPP and commented:

> I was particularly pleased to deliver my first speech on our review here at the BPP Business School. This School is exactly the type of private provider which our report sees becoming more important in the future. Ours is a system which loosens controls on what type of institution can teach what. Instead, it forces institutions to think more clearly about their mission and how they can best serve their students.[8]

In 2010, its parent, the publicly limited company BPP Holdings, was taken off the stock exchange when purchased outright for £368 million by Apollo Global (a $1 billion private equity joint venture between Apollo Group which owns the University of Phoenix and the Carlyle Group, which held a stake until October 2012 when the Apollo Group assumed outright control).[9]

BPP offers a clear example of how designation has offered the opportunity for private providers to expand. In preparation for the arrival in 2012/13 of the new loan fee limit of £6,000, BPP divided its undergraduate operation into four schools: Business, Law, English and a new school of Health covering psychology, nursing and chiropractic (BPP also owns McTimoney College of Chiropractic). It now has offices in Bristol, Swindon, Manchester, Leeds, Newcastle and Birmingham, along with three sites in London.

In 2009/10, 70 of its students accessed student support amounting to £0.5 million; by 2010/11 that had increased to 300 students and £2.5 million (£730,000 was loans for fees). In 2011/12, there were over 1000 students accessing £9.3 million (£2.65 million for fees), and BPP's designated courses had expanded to over 100, with each of its sites registered separately. Undergraduate applications were up 125 per cent for September 2012 entry and with the reforms discussed in the previous chapter, it is preparing to use the name BPP University.

we will be removing the barriers that stop them operating as universities here as part of our system – provided, of course, that they meet high standards which are a key feature of our higher education system.[10]

This commitment to help overseas institutions operate within the UK regulatory framework was augmented by an announcement from Willetts in January 2012, inviting ideas on new kinds of privately financed science and technology 'universities', concentrating on postgraduates and research, and joint ventures. International partners are prominent in this announcement, which should be read alongside recent efforts to have NHS trusts operate overseas.

> Globalisation is still at its early stages when it comes to Higher Education. The next round of new institutions may well link existing British universities with international partners. The surge in international investment in science and technology would make this a key part of the mission of a new foundation. It might be that today's institutions propose a new campus or a new international partnership. Or it might be new providers wanting to enter with different models. Today I can announce therefore that the Coalition is inviting proposals for a new type of university with a focus on *science and technology* and on postgraduates. Local economic partnerships, universities, businesses and international partners can come together to put forward proposals for new institutions.[11]

No government money is available, but Willetts pledged to remove any specific obstacles to the scheme, 'including by legislation where necessary'. Effectively the government plans to operate as a broker here, putting together finance with existing HE expertise.

Private equity, which has already boosted its presence in post-16 education through the acquisition of training providers, is well-placed to enter HE.[12] What is private equity? It is an alternative mode of capitalist activity whereby private funds run by investors purchase existing companies in part or outright. Companies are typically taken off the public equity (share) markets, hence the 'private', and a management team is put in place by the fund. This approach is seen by advocates to overcome the traditional conflict of interests in a publicly limited company between managers (agents) and owners (shareholders).

Private equity extracts value for the fund investors largely by levying management fees on the companies purchased and by making a profit on the subsequent resale or public offering of the company, typically within three to seven years of initial takeover.[13] Reforms to the funding of English HE make it easier for private equity to acquire a private education company and take advantage of the government's enthusiasm for change. Easy access to student loans, essentially risk-free money, may even make the sector more lucrative for a longer game than normally played.

For example, Greenwich School of Management and Brighton Institute of Modern Music are both owned by Sovereign Capital. In 2010/11, students at these two schools received a quarter of all funding that went to those studying on 'designated courses' – nearly £12 million (£3.7 million in tuition fee loans). The following year, those two colleges had over 3,000 students who were responsible for £28 million in student support (almost one third of the total issued to private providers in 2011/12).[14] The Parthenon Group, eager market consultants, have now described the sector as 'treasure island'.[15]

As we noted in the introduction, the backers of the Conservative Party have an interest in opening up the HE sector to private equity. In addition to the meetings described there, David Willetts has met with representatives of Apollo Group, the European and UK operations of Kaplan, Education Management Corporation, Laureate and Pearson. Twelve meetings in all. At the same time, John Nash, the founder of Sovereign Capital was invited to join the 'Red team' set up by the Chancellor, George Osborne, to advise on public sector reform by 'thinking the unthinkable'. Nash 'has donated more than £200,000 to the Conservative Party and more than £20,000 to Andrew Lansley'.[16] When he was in opposition, Willetts received direct, personal sponsorship in 2007 from an investor, Peter Hall, who believes 'it's corrosive poison for this country to have public enterprises so deeply involved in providing services'.[17]

CONCERNS REGARDING FOR-PROFIT PROVIDERS

At this point, it is important to distinguish private providers, which may be not-for-profit and even charities, from the *for-profits*. As explained throughout, the meaning of private and privatisation changes depending on the context. Here, it may simply mean *independence* from regulatory frameworks and the absence of *direct public funding*. A good example is the University of Buckingham, which has its own degree awarding powers and is a charity, but has always positioned itself as an independent liberal arts college so as to be free from bureaucratic burdens: it enters the National Student Satisfaction survey *voluntarily*. Such private providers are distinct from commercial, for-profit enterprises, also private, but which are primarily oriented towards making a return for investors and owners.

In principle, there is the question as to whether students at profit-distributing enterprises should have access to publicly backed student loans *and maintenance grants*. Even the collection of loan repayments provides an attractive free service to private providers, who would otherwise have to organise their own loan schemes. However, more importantly, the public system also has a built-in subsidy. This kind of boost to revenue generation is appropriate for charitable activities, but not for profitable, commercial activities. At a minimum, the latter should be charged for access to student loans to cover the associated costs of their students to the state.

However, beyond this general point, there is now extensive evidence from the USA of malpractice, attributable to the distortion in the educational setting of the profit-motive and, in the case of publicly quoted companies, share price. US for-profit universities have been implicated in various scandals involving aggressive 'boiler room' recruitment and the mis-selling of unaccredited 'professional' qualifications. These problems are seen to be intimately connected with the profit-motive and returns to investors.

The *Huffington Post* website ran an excellent exposé of 'predatory' recruitment practices at Education Management Corporation after it was taken over by Goldman Sachs, complete with the scripts used by recruiters, which instructed them to find potential applicants' 'pain' so as to convince them that college might be a solution to their struggles.[18] The company is now subject to an $11 billion federal lawsuit alleging fraud.

PBS's documentary *College Inc.* covered the manner in which for-profit operations offer 'subprime' degrees.[19] In the USA, these colleges spend more on recruitment and marketing than instruction, have miserable completion rates (under 20 per cent of students graduate within six years of enrolment), while their graduates rack up the worst default rates. The programme focused on the University of Phoenix owned by Apollo, who in the UK have acquired BPP.

A two-year US Senate Committee investigation led by Tom Harkin reported at the end of July 2012.[20] It found that profit distribution on average accounted for nearly 20 per cent of annual revenue, lower than marketing and recruitment (22 per cent) with *both higher than instruction* (17.4 per cent). Bridgepoint Education, described as a 'scam' by Harkin, had drop-out rates above 84 per cent while still making profits. Traded companies were open to most criticism, indicating the pressure to provide returns to investors and owners at the expense of the quality of education.

The Harkin report was concerned that these companies financed their expansion and profit extraction on the back of access to federal money through aid and student loans. Access to loans is precisely the issue here, but David Willetts has taken time to rebut those who claim he is opening up the sector to these kinds of abuse. In the *Guardian*, his letter stated: 'Peter Wilby claims we are seeking to emulate the US, but that misunderstands our reforms. America does not have the quality assurance, student support or widening access measures that we have and which our reforms will strengthen.'[21]

First, it is not clear that England does have a sufficiently robust quality assurance regime to deal with entities such as Education Management Corporation. The Harkin report is about the failure to regulate and protect the consumer interest when confronted with organisations that are within primarily profit-distributing structures. A regulator that promotes competition and student choice is insufficient. Second, in so far as they can charge less than £6,000 per year, for-profit institutions would also be exempt from 'student support or widening access measures' under the proposed three-tier regulatory framework. Moreover, subprime degrees, like subprime mortgages, are sold to communities relatively unfamiliar with the product. As such, institutions operating in that manner would superficially resemble institutions promoting widening participation.

Malpractice is not unpredictable. It is important to note, however, that the private and for-profit operations in the USA are *more expensive* than public alternatives. In the UK, the intention is quite different – they are supposed to undercut established provision. The government wishes to drive down the cost of mass higher education – they will therefore encourage competition on price, which is much easier to effect in higher education than it is in the NHS, where it proved a stumbling block that delayed the passage of the Health and Social Care Bill.[22] This puts a different complexion on things and explains the government's lack of support for the New College of the Humanities (see below).

Lowering the entry barriers is a risk, however, and there may be a lot of collateral damage. Their introduction into a zero sum game with the established universities may provide 'creative destruction'. The University of Cambridge, one of the institutions immune to the threat, made an official submission to the government in September warning of the dangers here:

> There is a serious long-term risk that new providers will be prepared to operate initially at a loss to take market share from some universities that will then become unviable. In many cases, this would be to the detriment of local and regional communities who would then lose the wider benefits that a local university with its diverse range of activities can provide (and which new operators without the same roots in local communities are unlikely or unwilling to provide).
>
> This effect would be gravely exacerbated if the new operators were to close because they had misjudged their financial models or withdrew their services locally as market conditions changed or their attention was drawn elsewhere. We could then be left with a depleted university sector and damaged communities.[23]

Private equity funds and multinationals have the deep pockets to position themselves in this way initially. Cambridge's warning about lack of local commitment can be seen in the University of Phoenix's recent decision to close 115 sites after falling enrolments: a public system committed to localities does not operate in this way.

Further confirmation of Cambridge's fears is seen in a striking finding of the Harkin report, which noted the extremely rapid growth of for-profits over the last decade. Enrolments were up over 200 per cent between 1998 and 2008,[24] with Ashford University expanding from 300 to 77,000 (mostly online) students following purchase by Bridgepoint Education Inc. The for-profit field was very small originally, with most colleges private companies in the hands of individuals. But in the late 1990s investors got involved. Federally backed student loans for fees removed the debt collection risk and Wall Street moved in. For-profit education in the US is now dominated by large multinational conglomerates backed by private equity and investment banks. This order of growth can be seen here in the colleges owned by Sovereign Capital.

Opening up the English market to these operators is therefore a gamble that we might not be able to undo. While the political parties may concentrate on whether the maximum fee cap should be £9,000 or £6,000, or whether the Liberal Democrats will go into the 2015 election still pledging to abolish them, the forms of privatisation outlined here may not be reversible.

OPPOSITION

Delay to the proposed Higher Education Bill can be attributed to a few causes. First, there is little appetite within the Coalition for any primary legislation involving higher education. Nick Clegg's apology for making a pledge to vote against tuition fees felt like an attempt to draw a line under the issue prior to the 2015 election. But it is primarily the organised opposition to the profiteering agenda that has forced the government to operate without a Bill. The University and College Union took a strong decision to focus their campaigning here, and Early Day Motion 1999 opposing 'for-profit universities' has the support of over 130 MPs.[25]

Over the Christmas 2011 break, after the publication of the White Paper, the government rushed out a tender inviting teams to survey UK private higher education, looking at their student make-up and graduation rates. Such evidence might have been better marshalled before drawing up policy, but this survey was intended as a means to rebut some of the arguments against the influx of private equity and provision, and perhaps to construct a rationale for its plan to grant the massive commercial conglomerate Pearson the power to award degrees. Concerns over quality and profit incentives in education converge in that particular instance.

It is therefore welcome that Hefce have proposed that any 'substantive change' in university ownership should be the trigger for a quality review. The *Huffington Post* exposé of Education Management Corporation emphasised how the culture of the organisation changed following its purchase by Goldman Sachs. But a reapplication for degree awarding powers would be a stronger measure, clearly framing the accepted point that degree awarding powers are not a tradeable asset. This would remove some of the confusion we currently see in the UK which will be discussed in Chapter 9.

LEGAL AND REGULATORY ARBITRAGE: THE NOT-FOR-PROFIT FORM

Having laid out the concerns relating to private equity and the presence of for-profits within the regulated framework as currently proposed, we need to be clear that concentrating only on the status of the corporate entity that delivers training or teaching is inadequate.

Profit-distributing group structures can use not-for-profit subsidiaries to 'game' the regulations or legislation. At present, this mainly relates to matters such as VAT exemption and access to public grants, but it could be used to circumvent any potential prohibition on students at for-profit providers accessing student support (or fees potentially charged to the institution for such access).[26] Since for most readers this will be complex and unfamiliar terrain, I will use a simple and high profile example. The structures explicated will reappear in Chapter 9, as this form of arbitrage could also facilitate the buyout of established universities.

NEW COLLEGE OF THE HUMANITIES

Although it has garnered the headlines and boosted the profile of its founder, Anthony Grayling, New College of the Humanities may turn out to be something of a sideshow.[27] NCH is not a university and does not have its own degree awarding powers. It will offer its own diploma while its students will also sit the external degrees available through the University of London's International Programme. It is technically a 'crammer', with students receiving intensive one-to-one tuition and a general liberal arts curriculum.

It opened its doors to 60 undergraduates in September 2012, only a third of its initial target after it was unable to secure 'Trusted sponsor' status from the UK Border Agency and so is unable to bring in students from outside Europe. Its fees of £18,000 per year are only competitive in that overseas market and a majority of its intake were on half-price or full fee waivers.

The College is unviable but for the deep pockets of its private equity backers. By far the largest shareholder, over 30 per cent of the company, is the Swiss family Ebstein, who run the venture capital firm Meru AG based in Lucerne. Grayling, other NCH Directors and some of its professoriate have also taken an equity stake in the parent company, a private company limited by share. Given its corporate form, it is potentially profit-making. A separate charitable trust, NCH Trust, has bursaries available for its students from a fund of £250,000.

Alongside the high headline fees, the profit-distributing nature of the company attracted criticism from those who think educational establishments that aspire to be 'Oxbridge colleges in London' should be charities.[28] Perhaps in response to such criticisms, but more likely to benefit from the same tax status as BPP University College, NCH changed its corporate structure in January 2012. A third company, limited by share and a wholly owned subsidiary of New College of the Humanities Limited, was established. It was *non-profit-distributing* and called Tertiary Education Services

Limited. In a further development, the parent and the subsidiary switched names that March. The parent is now called Tertiary Education Services Limited and the subsidiary is called New College of the Humanities Limited. The charitable trust was unchanged.

Grayling explained the new structure in an interview with *New Humanist* describing Tertiary Education Services as a 'service company ... a profit-making arm'.[29] This was not strictly accurate as TES is the parent company, which owns all assets and provides administrative and catering services to the subsidiary college. Money moves out of the college operation through payment for these services, rent on its Bedford Square building, and fees to directors 'for their service to the company as directors' and 'for any other service which they undertake for the company'. That is, although it is not allowed to distribute profits to shareholders, there are plenty of ways for money to move out of the subsidiary to the profit-distributing parent and directly to the significant shareholders in TES, who are also directors of NCH.

The interview with *New Humanist* continues as Grayling attempts to justify the for-profit angle:

> Though we think of them as public institutions, all universities are independent private corporations – given subsidies by the government to teach our children – and all of them, he says, have 'third leg' spin-off money making businesses: 'Everyone knows Oxford and Cambridge earn hundreds of millions from their publishing operations and science development, UCL owns 11 or 12 companies, one of them manufactures compression socks, designed by one of their staff, they sell millions.' His argument in a nutshell is that NCH in this respect is really no different from any other university.

But as TES is not a 'third leg' but the controlling company in the group, TES/NCH is distinct from the established public universities: their *subsidiaries* distribute any surplus or profit up the chain to the parent, *the charitable teaching institution*. NCH/TES works the other way: from *the teaching institution* to *the profit-distributing company*. The money moves in the opposite direction (see Figure 7.1). Indeed, because of its monopoly relation to its subsidiary, the parent could make a profit even if NCH loses money.

This kind of regulatory or legal arbitrage means that the group *structure*, not the individual corporate entity, must be assessed. Most of the proposed regulation discussed in Chapter 6 is weak when viewed from this perspective: not-for-profits can access VAT exemption and become eligible for receipt of *grants* (Tier 3 institutions on the proposed framework). But not-for-profit *subsidiaries* need to be viewed differently.

What we also see is that recent proposals to extend VAT exemption to for-profit entities, announced by George Osborne in the 2012 Budget statement, are not about 'fairness' or ensuring that different models of provision can proliferate, as claimed in the HMRC consultation.[30] Both NCH and BPP show that there is no real disincentive to new provision under current tax regulations. New exemptions are purely about facilitating the extraction of profits in the manner decried by Senator Harkin.

Again, we see intervention to favour private provision and private equity, not to ensure the quality of higher education or improve the student experience. There appears to be no good reason to extend access to student loans to students at for-profits and several reasons not to. A level playing field for profit-oriented private providers is not needed, but it lies at the heart of market reforms.

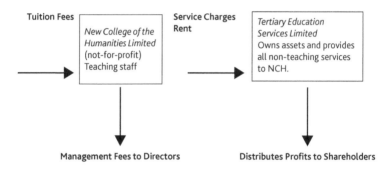

Figure 7.1   How money moves out of the not-for-profit subsidiary

Part 3
Privatisation

As noted in the Introduction, some commentators baulk at the use of the term 'privatisation' in the context of English higher education, since it is normally used to refer to the sale of publicly owned assets or the break-up of a state monopoly. Neither seems appropriate to describe universities and colleges which are already private institutions.

This section endeavours to overturn that narrow view of the process and fills out some of the trends already identified. The previous section on markets focused on issues such as *independence* from the regulatory framework, the commodification of education, and the 'external' privatisation of the higher education sector by changing the funding streams and encouraging the entry of 'alternative' providers. All of these issues can be understood as part of a broader process of privatisation – particularly the replacement of direct public funding to institutions.

In the chapters grouped together in this section we will examine the other forms of privatisation listed in the Introduction, beginning with 'internal privatisation': how the nature of funding streams alters institutions from within. Chapter 8 concentrates on how commercial imperatives come to the fore and uses overseas income as its main example.

Chapter 9 looks at the legal form of universities and considers the government's plans to make it easier for HEIs to adopt alternative corporate structures the better to access private finance. In this chapter, I will also look at the potential for private buyouts of established universities, joint ventures, and outsourcing. Chapter 10 surveys the recent moves towards university bond issues as a way of raising investment capital: I look at how this changes further the institutions in the sector. Finally, Chapter 11 considers issues of governance: how are universities run? How far are their 'boards' adequate to this new terrain where decisions about corporate strategy are raised to a new level?

8
University Finances and Overseas Income

The sector overall in England is at its healthiest for many years. The number of institutions making significant operating surpluses has climbed to nearly 70; the number reporting deficits dropped from 25 to 10 between 2010 and 2011. Cash and near-cash reserves have also been rising: to £6.5 billion (as at 31 July 2011). Simultaneously, the sector is looking at ways to further diversify its revenue base and seek out new commercial opportunities that make a return and so support their main activity. Again, *positioning* in these markets is complex and depends on different standings, largely determined in relation to *research* strengths.

When I interviewed Chris Hearn from Barclays Capital for *Research Fortnight* in September 2011, he told me: 'The last couple of years have been probably the best years that universities have ever had if you measure it in terms of income, surplus and the cash buffer that they have been able to build up.'[1] These reserves may provide contingency funds for the coming uncertainty of the new market conditions.

With direct state funding to institutions cut, the balance of private to public income in most higher education institutions will be shifted accordingly: 'internal privatisation'. The government therefore believes its reforms to undergraduate funding will move the balance between public and private income from 60:40 in favour of public to 40:60 in favour of private money across the sector, exempting universities from EU procurement law governing *public* institutions.[2] Many will welcome this shift as it removes universities from the aegis of a policy designed to open up the public sector away from protectionist national policies.

Private sources include industrial sponsorship, commercial operations such as short courses, partnership fees, spin-offs using university patents to create commercial products and, of course, *tuition fees* (home and overseas). For arts, humanities, business, law and social science undergraduate degrees, all income will be tuition fee income from 2012.

Additional private income runs in parallel with the interpenetration of values and practices of business and commerce into universities. In her farewell speech as Chair of the Charity Commission, Suzi Leather discussed the significant internal transformations charities undergo as finances change:

> But what really concerns me is a less tangible, less visible and longer-term challenge to charities' future. Namely whether [C]harities will continue to be able to demonstrate that they are fundamentally different from other types of organisations. ... charities themselves are becoming ever more similar to other types of organisations. Charities are encouraged to become business-like, including by collaborating with corporations, and many charities have trading arms that operate much like businesses. Charities are also entering into new areas of public service provision, including by joining consortia with other charities and organisations to provide services say in the criminal justice system. None of these developments are necessarily problematic per se. But, collectively, they contribute to a perceived blurring of boundaries.[3]

As she clearly states, public benefit is the legal *raison d'être* for charities. But as alternatives to direct state funding are sought, the commercial bottom line may increasingly win out. A.C. Grayling's complaints about the commercial activities of the established universities are perhaps accurate. As these private revenue resources proliferate, what happens to the functioning of the institution? How are those parts of the business seen that generate surpluses as compared to those which are propped up?

This plays across the ambiguities of the terrain. The 1988 Bologna Declaration, titled The Magna Charta Universitatum was adopted by the EU Ministers of Education in 1999. It reads:

> To meet the needs of the world around it, [a university's] research and teaching must be morally and intellectually independent of all political authority and intellectually independent of all political authority and economic power.

The UK has a strong tradition of defending academic freedom and institutional autonomy from direct political interference. Autonomy is normally conceived of as a negative freedom from a particular interest group. Making institutions increasingly private may further inure some from government meddling.

Many may be keen for increased independence from government but what relations do alternative sources of income require? There has been much less discussion of the influence of 'economic power' or market pressures on the institution (beyond the benefits consumerism is meant to bring). The movement of money may present a more profound challenge – it may be harder to resist. Individual partnerships will be seen as positive, mutually beneficial relations, but in each case it will be hard to assess the contribution to broader public benefit. Vice-chancellors champion institutional autonomy, but are they really seeking the freedom to act as the chief executives of corporate entities, who wish to be free of ties to the public however attenuated?

This chapter will consider a particular case to illustrate some of the strategies at work: income from non-EU students and overseas campuses.

FINANCES

Total annual income for UK HEIs is over £27.5 billion, of which roughly £23 billion comes in to English institutions. It breaks down as shown in Figure 8.1. The majority of income, a little over 50 per cent, came through teaching, whether tuition fees or recurrent block grants to institutions. The government's proposals for England will shift the balance here between tuition fees and grants, but the overall income from Home and EU students is likely to remain roughly constant in 2012. Overseas tuition fees are self-explanatory and will be viewed more closely shortly. They account for £3 billion: over 10 per cent of total income.

There are four other main categories here. 'Other income' can include the partnership fees and income from commercial subsidiaries, but one third of it is related to student accommodation, catering and earnings from conferences. 'Funding body grants', excluding teaching, covers mainly Hefce's research funding based on the research assessment exercises, while 'Research grants and contracts' includes grants made by the research councils.

The sliver at the top of the pie chart represents endowment and investment *income*. Endowments are funds provided by specific donations often with particular terms: whether funding a professorial chair, a research centre or library, or providing bursaries for students. Typically, a small percentage of the fund is released each year (whatever can be matched by income on management of

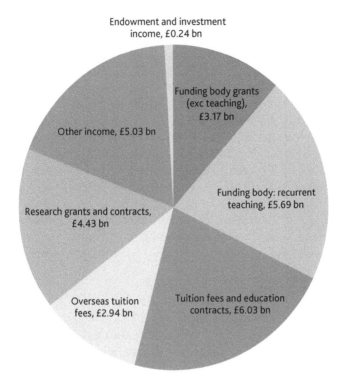

Endowment and investment
income, £0.24 bn

Funding body grants
(exc teaching),
£3.17 bn

Other income, £5.03 bn

Funding body: recurrent
teaching, £5.69 bn

Research grants and contracts,
£4.43 bn

Overseas tuition
fees, £2.94 bn

Tuition fees and education
contracts, £6.03 bn

Figure 8.1   UK HEI income by source 2010/11 (thousands)

Source: HESA, Press Release 174, 'Finances of UK Higher Education Institutions 2010/11', 8 March 2012.

the fund as an investment) – this is what is recorded as income in the chart above.

While endowment income in the USA accounts for 25 per cent of income, here it is tiny. Only the Universities of Oxford and Cambridge have significant holdings. According to a *Financial Times* report in October 2011, Cambridge now has endowments estimated at £4.5 billion after a ten-year fund-raising drive produced £1.2 billion. Oxford's stand at £3.3 billion. The rest of the sector *combined* has endowments amounting to £2 billion.

It is worth noting that efforts to increase charitable fund-raising through donations or endowments is less likely to produce dividends in the new funding terrain. The match-funding scheme run by Hefce between 2008–12 is unlikely to be continued. Indeed, the Russell Group have been looking at alternatives such as alternative investment products (see the discussion of 'mini-bonds' in Chapter 10).

The sector figures cited above mask the disparities in income that we noted in the Introduction (Figure 0.1). That showed the wealthiest institution, Cambridge, generating six times the mean annual income of £170 million.

The Russell Group shows the greatest diversity in revenue sources, dominating research funding and with less reliance on teaching and central funding. Now that Exeter, Durham, Queen Mary and York have joined the group, expanding its members to 24, it will also take close to 50 per cent of the total income illustrated above.

OVERSEAS STUDENT INCOME

We concentrate on overseas income here as the contours are diverse, complex and contested, involving every university or college in the country. Many investors see the sector on the cusp of a new globalised market which would allow 'degree awarding powers', particularly those based in the UK and the USA, to be 'monetised' in new form through online learning. We are not quite there yet, but overseas partnerships and campuses are expanding, while tuition fees from 'overseas students' – students from outside the EU – already play a vital role in income for all higher education institutions. For those outside the Russell Group and the 1994 Group, the proportion of overseas income is often *higher*. UK universities have been encouraged to pursue this money as export income. It is therefore possible to assess it as a general phenomenon.

Institutions are not bound by the same restrictions with respect to overseas students as they are with Home and EU students: there is no maximum fee cap (some fees rise to as much as £30,000 per year for specialist courses) and institutions are able to recruit as many students as they are able (though immigration rules apply – see below).

Figure 8.2 shows the origin of all non-Home students at UK institutions, including EU, who make up 5.2 per cent of the student body. By far the largest group now comprises students from China – 67,000. In the last decade, numbers of overseas students have climbed from under 175,000 to nearly 300,000: they now make up one in six of full-time students (overseas students are not eligible to study part-time).

This expansion has coincided with universities being moved out of the Department for Education to the Department for Business,

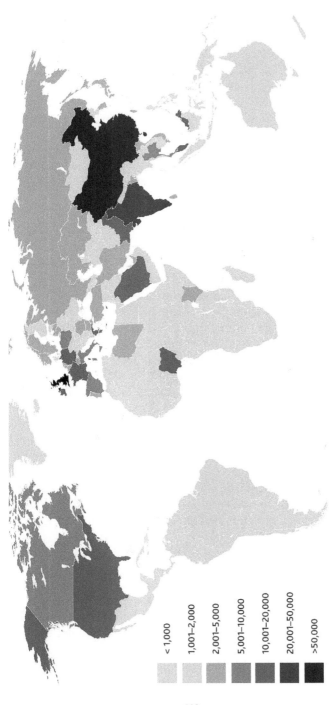

	< 1,000
	1,001–2,000
	2,001–5,000
	5,001–10,000
	10,001–20,000
	20,001–50,000
	>50,000

Figure 8.2 Non-UK domicile students at UK HEIs by country of domicile 2010/11

Source: HESA, 2010/11. Reproduced by permission of the Higher Education Statistics Agency Limited

Innovation and Skills (and its predecessor, DIUS). Higher education is seen as an important export industry (it is now the seventh largest such industry) as students spend not only fees but in the surrounding economy (estimated at another £8 billion per year).

HE has been identified by Vince Cable as one of our key 'traded services' with a central place in rebalancing Britain's economy and addressing the record current account deficit (the difference between imports and exports). New HE markets are emerging in Indonesia, Turkey and Brazil. These countries are developing with a young demographic and weak HE infrastructure. UK universities have been encouraged by BIS to cultivate and pursue this market, especially the Brazilian 'Science without Borders' initiative which will see 100,000 students sent worldwide for graduate studies.

However, there is a problem. Overseas students across all sectors, including those coming to the country for English language courses, account for nearly 50 per cent of all visas issued for entry into the UK. At its peak in 2009, 400,000 student visas were being issued, but the rules have since been tightened and the current government has declared a target to reduce *net* migration (immigration minus emigration) to below 100,000 per year by 2015. This is obviously difficult without reducing student visas and the government launched a crackdown on private tuition colleges (and some FE colleges) over the course of 2011.

In the year to June 2012, 280,000 student visas were issued: a reduction of 70,000 on the previous year. But net migration remained at 216,000, well above the government's target. Many, including David Willetts, have argued that HE student visas should be taken out of this count as students tend to return home after studying and the incentive to stay has been reduced by recent changes: students no longer have the right to work in the country for two years after graduation.[4] But the Home Office has refused to budge, as it still sees student visas as a route of entry for those who want to come in to the country to work. In fact, Theresa May, the Home Secretary, used her speech at October 2012's Conservative annual conference to attack the 'vested interests' opposing her approach.

They argue that more immigration means more economic growth. But what they mean is more immigration means a bigger population – there isn't a shred of evidence that uncontrolled, mass immigration makes us better off. ... They argue, too, that we need evermore students because education is our greatest export product. I agree that we need to support our best colleges and

London Metropolitan University

At the time of writing, London Metropolitan University had just won the right to have a judicial review conducted of the UK Border Agency's decision to strip it of its licence to sponsor non-EU students. LMU was the first university to be put in such a position (only a few weeks before the 2012 term was to begin). Previously Glasgow Caledonian and Teeside were two universities to have had their licences temporarily suspended, while several private tuition colleges had had their licences revoked.

Late in August 2012, the news broke that UKBA had revoked LMU's 'Highly Trusted Sponsor' status. LMU was therefore no longer able to offer places to students from outside the EU and in addition all its current overseas students, numbering at least 2,000, would have their visas withdrawn within 60 days of individual notification. Their only alternative was to find another university willing to offer them a place to complete their studies: a 'task force' was set up by Hefce and Universities UK to oversee and aid this process for 'genuine' students. However, following the review hearing at the Royal Courts of Justice, the UKBA has allowed LMU's existing students to remain for the 2012/13 academic year.

Theresa May took the final decision, the 'nuclear option', over-ruling BIS. It sent a clear message to universities and voters. Even if the 2015 net migration target is missed, it would not be for failure to take tough decisions. The reputational damage to UK higher education and the blanket condemnation from the sector appear only to reinforce this political stance.

LMU's problems are administrative and long-standing, 'seriously deficient' according to Damien Green, the Immigration Minister at the time of the decision. They stretch back to its formation as a merger between the University of North London and Guildhall ten years ago.

Reports from LMU staff suggest that the management were distracted by a lucrative validation deal with the private college, London School of Business and Finance (which triggered the 'aggressive' UKBA investigation in the first place), and a 'shared services initiative' involving a private firm to manage its administration (see Chapter 10 for details). The contract with LSBF involved LMU sponsoring 5,000 students at the private college, more than it was planning to recruit itself. This deal originally had the approval of the UKBA but then became the pretext for the second audit.

universities and encourage the best students to come here – but to say importing more and more immigrants is our best export product is nothing but the counsel of despair.[5]

Universities are therefore, to put it mildly, receiving mixed messages. BIS, their 'home' department, encourages them to diversify income streams and bring in more foreign students. The Home Office, meanwhile, is working to a very different political agenda and imposing restrictive administrative demands on adult students.

Universities hold 'Highly Trusted Sponsor' status which enables them to bring in overseas students on visas – but they must comply with an onerous administrative system based on record-keeping initiated in 2010: evidence of students' minimum English standards and attendance at lectures and seminars once in the country. The UK Border Agency's complex regulations run to several pages and changed 14 times in the three years following their introduction. If significant numbers of students fail to enrol or drop out without completing the course, UKBA can suspend sponsor status. Simeon Underwood, a registrar at the London School of Economics wrote in *Times Higher Education* of the impact at his institution:

> Our costs have grown. Between staff costs in admissions, staff costs in advice to students who are already here, management time, IT development and *fees to the UKBA*, the London School of Economics is spending at least a quarter of a million pounds a year to run this area.[6] (my emphasis)

The threat and power residing in the UKBA means that universities recruiting overseas students are probably taking more effort to comply with the UKBA than with Hefce or QAA, the main regulatory bodies in the UK.

OVERSEAS CAMPUSES

One possible to solution to this damaging political, interdepartmental impasse involves expansion overseas. This could be through validation partnerships as discussed in Chapter 6; though, however lucrative, these may involve reputational risk since the home institution has little control over what is happening abroad.

Alternatively, if the students have difficulties coming into the country, then let's take the universities to them. BIS has identified two parties interested in funding such ventures: Goldman Sachs and the Ontario Teachers Pension Fund, who may be looking to invest between £150 and £200 million at a time.

A new unit has been launched, UK Education Services (UKES), which will provide the support in this area as well as helping to sell other education services abroad. John Elledge, of *Education*

Middlesex University

The majority of Middlesex University's 1,000 students on overseas campuses are in Dubai. It has another much smaller campus in Mauritius: a joint venture via a subsidiary company registered in Dubai's free trade zone and an Indian-based partner. Middlesex University's attempts to open a third overseas campus in Delhi, India, through the Mauritius set-up, collapsed only two months before the scheduled opening, in circumstances that have not been made public.[7]

Middlesex has long had an international orientation, opening its first overseas offices in 1995 and gaining two Queen's Awards for Enterprise subsequently. Its distinct vision of its future priorities has led it to pursue an ambitious overseas strategy focused on South Asia, while using the powers it gained on becoming a university to validate and franchise degrees amongst international and domestic partners.

Capitalising on existing market advantages has its complement in reviewing departments which do not fit in with such vistas. In a very public dispute in 2010, Middlesex threatened to close, and then transferred to Kingston, its highest rated research centre: Modern European Philosophy has little appeal in overseas markets. Philosophy's mode of teaching, modes of assessment (essays) and dependence on libraries resist quantified, uniform approaches that are more amenable to mass roll-out through partnership and franchise agreements. Even in the case of Nottingham,

▶

Investor, describes what is on offer as a 'flat-pack campus': a single package of finance, expertise and construction. It might be better to see UKES as a 'one-stop shop', though Elledge also reports a 'speed-dating' event 'at which British and Brazilian universities could meet each other with a view to finding research partners'.[8] This office is also available to advise foreign governments looking to roll out higher education cheaply.

Overseas campus operations have been a bit of mixed bag, with only the University of Nottingham offering a real success story here through their campuses in Ningbo (China) and Malaysia. While Nottingham and University College of London may emphasise the strategic and research angle of their endeavours, the main aim of such campuses is to provide an alternative, *cheaper* route to access the populations of developing countries like India, China and Indonesia. It is reported that there are now more than 200

what is taken abroad are courses in business, commerce and, in some places, engineering, not the arts, humanities and social sciences.

To justify the closure of Philosophy, managers at Middlesex claimed that it was unviable and only continued owing to cross-subsidy from other departments. This claim was based upon an internal accounting method with a particular benchmark: a department was deemed to be 'loss-making' if it failed to contribute at least 55 per cent of income to central administration. To quote the Save Middlesex Philosophy website: 'It is not possible to say how – if at all – the [55 per cent contribution] relates to the university's actual central expenditure on facilities for teaching and research.'[9]

Philosophy was grouped with Religious Studies for this exercise. In 2009/10, the target was missed by two percentage points (53 per cent), but for the following year the contribution was estimated to be 59 per cent. Such opportunist use of figures, and the paroxysms of middle or junior management, masks the broader strategy.

The loss of such subject provision needs to be considered alongside another phenomenon at Middlesex: it shed all of its North London campuses bar one in Hendon while expanding overseas. When such commercial logic is evidenced at the expense of public interest (there is now no higher education in Tottenham or indeed Haringey) what recourse does the public have? In 2010, the Office for Fair Access identified Middlesex as the university which spent the smallest proportion, just 7.7 per cent, of its additional fee income on bursaries, scholarships and outreach initiatives.[10]

overseas branch campuses, with the UK, USA and Australia the most prominent players.[11]

The most recent developments with English universities involve campuses in Cyprus for the University of Central Lancashire and the University of East London. These seem to offer a different model as they are also being advertised to Home students – the £9,000 fee at UCLan's campus near Larnacka includes accommodation and some flights to and from the UK.[12] UEL Nicosia offers degrees in Business and Accounting; UCLan, mathematics and computer science. UCLan also has plans to open in Bangkok and Sri Lanka.

This strategy is not without its difficulties. High-profile US universities have opened branch campuses abroad only to have to close them when the business model failed. In UAE, George Mason University closed its Ras Al Khaimah campus without getting a single student through to graduation, while Michigan State in Dubai managed to operate for two years.[13] Although *Times*

Higher Education states that the UK is unique in not having seen an operation close down, this ignores Middlesex's Delhi campus which had the plug pulled two months before opening.[14]

The pension funds and financiers interested in backing overseas campuses are reported to be dissatisfied with the management teams in place at English universities. They want a more commercially oriented approach. How does this tally with a public education system?

The point of this chapter is to illustrate the pressures brought to bear on UK universities in the pursuit of alternative sources of income. The pursuit of overseas income has received encouragement from certain parts of government over the last few years and exemplifies the belief at the top that the UK is well-placed to benefit from a post-industrial knowledge economy.

Large operations such as Nottingham have been able to expand abroad without significant alteration to their home campus. The same cannot be said for Middlesex, which has seen a transformation in both its subject provision and its physical presence in North London. The pursuit of revenue-generating activities and new markets may come at the expense of what the public might see as core activities: this is why privatisation is the appropriate term. Public interest may be sacrificed for revenue streams, or 'demand-led' decision-making.

In the case of London Metropolitan, certain risks were run in order to access a lucrative contract. It is not clear how the public interest is served if academics, students and the local community are punished for the over-reaching ambition of senior management and the wrong-headed decisions of the UKBA.

9
Corporate Form, Joint Ventures and Outsourcing

The opening sentences of the Foreword to the 2011 Higher Education White Paper illustrate the government's understanding of the place of universities and colleges within society: 'Our university sector has a proud history and a world-class reputation, attracting students from across the world. Higher education is a successful public-private partnership: Government funding and institutional autonomy.'

What the government is keen to stress here is that higher education institutions are *private* corporations in receipt of (diminishing) *public* money. The basic unit of these reforms is the corporate entity, to be made more private in terms of revenue streams and to be placed within a regulated market. To this end, most of the discussion and consultation has been with vice-chancellors, the company heads, and the sector bodies, such as the regulators. Academics and the public have generally been bypassed.

WHAT KIND OF COMPANY IS A UNIVERSITY?

As pointed out by Peter Williams, the university system has grown from a small number of private self-governing communities of scholars into a mass system which plays a key role in the reproduction of our democracy.[1] At the same time, new institutions have become part of the system and some have grown into large enterprises with a global span. But does a system amounting to the aggregation of 100 private companies add up to a public higher education system? What kinds of companies are universities?

In 2008, David Watson approached this issue by asking, 'who owns the university?', or, in the parlance popular in the 1990s: 'who are the stakeholders?' He highlighted the 'hybrid, ambiguous public-private world' of higher education' by arguing that HEIs are closer to companies like BAe Systems, than their public sector counterparts, hospitals or schools. With the advent of primary care trusts and academy schools, this may no longer be accurate, but his answer was probably too simple even in 2008: a university is 'a private company with a majority of public contracts'.[2]

The legal forms of universities are varied reflecting their historical development over time. Amongst more than 100 higher education institutions in the UK, we find charitable trusts, companies limited by guarantee, chartered corporations, statutory corporations, not to mention the various anomalies such as Oxford and Cambridge and the three Scottish universities founded by Papal Bull: Aberdeen, Glasgow and St Andrews. Watson concludes that it is the members of the corporation or the governing council that 'own' the university, but the question of members, governance and owners is more complicated and varies with the form.

A further issue is transformation: government plans to make it easier for universities to *change form* 'the better to access private finance' were floated in the 2011 White Paper. Meanwhile private equity buyouts have become more likely: purchasing an established university outright would be an alternative route to the market to that outlined in Chapter 7. From this perspective, here we will also consider joint ventures, more forms of outsourcing, and 'shared service initiatives'.

CORPORATE FORMS

The traditional understanding of a university is of an independent community of scholars pursuing knowledge and advancing learning. Unlike their counterparts in some European countries, UK HEIs are not state institutions, their academics are not civil servants (as they are in Italy or Spain, for example). They are legally independent corporate institutions with charitable status (the majority are 'exempt charities'). Therefore, as already noted, care must be taken in the use of the term 'privatisation'.

In England, we can identify six general categories, along with some anomalies:

Oxbridge and Cambridge are *civil corporations*. Older than the modern British state, their constituent colleges are communities and separate registered charities.

The universities founded prior to 1992, numbering around 50, are *chartered corporations* in receipt of a Royal Charter.[3] As such have the legal status of a person and are not bound by ultra vires (see below) but changes to constitutions and any relinquishing of the charter, may require primary legislation or its equivalent. For Oxford, Cambridge and the chartered corporations (all in one sense *membership* organisations), the distinct legal status was exemplified in the figure of the Visitor, a representative of the Crown, who has the power to arbitrate disputes between the institution and its members.[4]

Higher education corporations (HECs), numbering around 45, are statutory corporations formed under the terms of the 1988 Education Reform Act.[5] The ex-polytechnics, excluding those formerly within the aegis of the Inner London Education Authority, have this status, along with other institutions which later took advantage of the same legislation to become HEIs.

These institutions were in public ownership but now have a *quasi-public status*. Chiefly, HECs do not have the full rights of private ownership associated with independent companies: they are unable to *dissolve themselves*. That power rests with the relevant Secretary of State, who may exercise it after consultation. Any assets are protected and must be preserved solely for charitable use in a successor company constituted as a company limited by guarantee.[6] HECs are also bound by ultra vires: they can only do what they have been given powers explicitly to do in the statutes that created them (or whatever is necessarily implied by those powers).

Companies limited by guarantee are distinct from the forms above in that they are entirely private companies and are able to alter their constitutions freely. Twenty-five universities have this form, comprising several post-2000 universities but also the London School of Economics and the ex-polytechnics formerly within the Inner London Education Authority: these institutions were always constituted as companies limited by guarantee. London Metropolitan University, which was formed from the merger of two of the latter, has the same form.

The anomalies: Three smaller universities and colleges are *trusts*: University of Chester; Bishop Grosseteste University College, Lincoln; Harper Adams College. Guildhall School of Music and Drama is a Department of the Corporation of London (and not a charity).

Our taxonomy is completed by considering *companies limited by share*. These are potentially for-profit entities providing returns to their shareholders. According to the lawyers Eversheds, a normal company limited by share, that is, one which has not adopted articles preventing the distribution of assets and profits, has 'all the benefits of a company limited by guarantee plus an ability to raise capital and make distributions which are not available to a company limited by guarantee'.[7]

This latter point is extremely significant for the new financial terrain of higher education. However, not all companies limited by share are profit-distributing. The Royal Agricultural College is even registered as a charity, while both BPP University College and New College of the Humanities (discussed in Chapter 7) are non-profit distributing bodies. NCH is wholly owned by Tertiary Education Services Limited. BPP is owned by BPP Holdings Limited.

Pearson, to which the government is keen to grant degree awarding powers, is a *public limited company (plc)* a distinct form of company limited by shares, where shares are freely traded (unlike the companies mentioned above which are *private*: their shares are not offered to the public). As an illustration of the investment advantages available to these forms, Pearson raised over £1 *billion* through a rights issue a decade ago. A further advantage, not mentioned by Eversheds, gives pause for thought here. When sanctions were introduced against the Gaddafi regime in Libya, Pearson simply suspended trading in the $200 million of shares owned by the Libyan sovereign investment fund. It saw none of the fallout that shook the London School of Economics over the *donations and contracts* signed with the regime, worth barely one hundredth of the traded shares.[8]

CHANGING CORPORATE FORM

The 2011 White Paper proposed new legislation easing the ability of universities to change corporate form so as to better access private investment (§§4.35–4.36). Such simplifying *primary* legislation would have been a keystone of the delayed HE Bill and largely aimed at allowing higher education corporations to become companies limited by guarantee without having to go through the Secretary of State.[9] The 2011 Education Act passed legislation allowing the analogous *further education corporations* the freedom to make such a move.

By giving higher education corporations the power to dissolve themselves or change to an alternative form, they would no longer be quasi-public. A similar process could be proposed for chartered corporations who wish to alter their constitutions that would take Parliament and politicians out of the process.

Currently statutory corporations and institutions holding Royal Charters require primary legislation (or its Privy Council equivalent: orders of council) to change their constitutions or amend articles. This is one way in which democratic oversight of higher education occurs. In the recent Charities Act Review conducted by Lord Hodgson, this oversight was simply interpreted as a *burden on parliamentary time and administrators*.[10] It instead suggested delegating the power to approve constitutional changes to the Charity Commission and leaving the trustees (governors) to concern themselves with changes to articles.

Further, it may or may not have been the government's intention to facilitate the ability of universities to shed their charitable status and take on a profit-making form.

CHARITABLE STATUS

Education is one of the four charitable activities, and institutions providing education can apply for charitable status even if they charge fees for tuition. Seventeen HEIs are registered with and regulated by the Charity Commission, as are the constituent colleges of Oxford, Cambridge and Durham (and all student unions). Owing to their place within group structures, neither BPP nor NCH qualify as charities, though NCH has an associated Trust.

The majority of established universities are 'exempt' charities. They are not registered with the Charity Commission but are overseen by Hefce with regard to their public benefit objectives. Farrington and Palfreyman's *The Law of Higher Education* offers the following explanation: 'The rationale for the exemption ... is that parliament has been satisfied that acceptable and appropriate arrangements already exist for carrying out the objects of HEIs and safeguarding their property.'[11] Financially, the main significance for exempt charities is that they do not require permission from Hefce to conduct sales or enter mortgages.

Given that the tenor of the proposed changes was to 'make it easier to attract private finance', we need to consider the main impediment facing charities. This is the point raised by Eversheds above: charities are unable to raise equity investment by issuing shares.

Faced with competition from new, potentially profit-making vehicles with access to private equity, established universities may prefer to ditch their charitable status and ape the legal form of the new competitors, whether as private companies limited by share or as publicly limited companies (potentially quoted on the stock exchange). This competitive pressure will be exacerbated if the VAT exemption for not-for-profit providers is extended to commercial operations – removing one competitive advantage from charities (setting aside the uneven distribution of donations and endowments with the sector).

THE 'SALE' OF THE COLLEGE OF LAW

Over the course of 2012, an example of such a change was seen. The College of Law, a rival to BPP in legal courses, announced that it was being sold to Montagu Private Equity, formerly part of HSBC, for around £200 million.[12]

A basic 'two-step' structured the deal. A profit-distributing subsidiary of Montagu was created before all staff, assets and undertakings associated with College of Law were transferred across. The new entity was called The College of Law Limited. In effect, the charity and the education and training business have been split – with the business transferring to the new entity. The charity, now renamed The Legal Education Foundation receives the £200 million and uses it to fund a trust supporting the original charitable objectives. (This could translate into funding students to study at The College of Law Limited.)

The teaching business will build on its sites at Chester, Guildford, London, Birmingham, York, Bristol, London Moorgate and Manchester. Now that it is a company limited by share and profit-distributing it may look to exploit its degree awarding powers in new markets, such as the new 'strategic collaboration' with Singapore Institute of Legal Education. Needless to say, Willetts was enthusiastic: 'With the new funding invested in the college, it will be able to build its brand, take its trusted degrees into other countries, and boost British education exports. It's an excellent outcome for everyone.'[13]

This is the standard route by which a charity is 'sold'. A similar move was seen in the sale of the University for Industry. It is the responsibility of the trustees to determine that the charity is receiving full value for its assets and that this is the best option to pursue the charitable objectives. Note that a charity cannot just decide to 'stop' being a charity.

I imagine most people find this process more than a little unsatisfactory. Trustees are meant to ensure that there are no conflicts of interest, but in the case of The College of Law the senior management team will transfer over to lead the new enterprise.

This obscure process has been conducted without any wider accountability to the public. The reasoning the trustees followed to approve the decision is not clear: The College of Law does provide some FAQs, but these are extremely vague on the technicalities and even the issue of profit distribution.[14] One issue seems particularly murky: what happens to the degree awarding powers granted to The College of Law in 2006? These are significant for the whole sector and not just private matters.

Legal Education Foundation maintains the Royal Charter, which cannot simply be discarded as it is the entity which was awarded DAPs. Technically, degree awarding powers cannot be sold or transferred from one entity to another. They were due for renewal this summer, but with no academics, the charitable trust would no longer be eligible.

BIS and the College are attempting to argue that the teaching business represents a continuing 'institution', which can be separated from the legal entity, and that DAPs were not granted by charter but by statute (through a process governed by the 1992 Further and Higher Education Act). But such a separation should not be possible for a chartered corporation for the reasons set out earlier – the whole entity is the corporation. Bypassing the ban on transfer of powers by claiming to transfer the 'college' bit of the corporation is therefore dubious, but would set a precedent for all HEI's whose degree awarding powers depend on statute rather than their original charter. In November 2012, the College was upgraded to full university status becoming The University of Law.

COULD A 'PUBLIC' UNIVERSITY BE BOUGHT OUT IN THIS WAY?

What would we say if several major universities began to follow the example of The College of Law as commercial pressures come to the fore?

Companies limited by guarantee are able to make such decisions without all the Privy Council palaver over the Royal Charter. Established universities with this form would need to negotiate two impediments – degree awarding powers (awarded in perpetuity in this instance) and continued access to grants as a not-for-profit. As less and less grant becomes available this latter point may not be such a problem.

A model for a buyout that would work for such companies was proposed by Eversheds in a 2009 report for Universities UK (Figure 9.1).[15] This is meant to be feasible under current legislation but would require government approval. It represents a similar form of legal arbitrage to that seen in Chapter 7. It enables the distribution of profits to investors by exploiting a group structure.

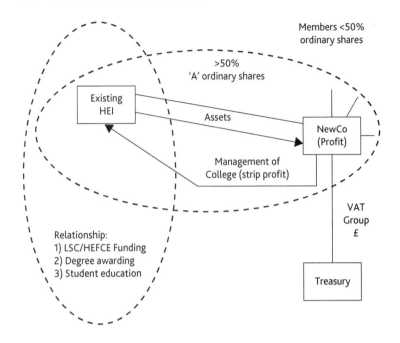

Figure 9.1   'A model for a university buyout'

Source: Reproduced as it originally appeared in Universities UK, 2009

To interpret this diagram: The existing HEI is on the left. It maintains degree awarding powers, not-for-profit status, and is responsible for teaching. (This is distinct from The College of Law sale where the teaching business and staff were transferred to the new company.) As the report explains in paragraph 3.12: 'Under this model, the existing higher education institution will retain its position as a designated institution for the receipt of funding council grant and any Learning and Skills Council funding (if relevant), as well as its own degree-awarding powers.' As such, the issues in relation to The College of Law's powers do not arise.

'NewCo' is a company limited by share. It is established with two classes of shares so that majority voting rights remain with the HEI. However, some of the other shares may be 'preference' shares entitling investors in NewCo guaranteed or superior dividends in return for waiving voting rights. All physical assets are transferred to NewCo. It generates returns because the HEI must pay rent and fees for services – this depends on a monopoly relation. Helpfully, the diagram shows the intention: NewCo 'strips profit' through *charging for the management* of the college or university. The main function, however, is to allow equity capital in NewCo to be invested in the operation of the institution. A clear example of a corporate structure designed to give access to private finance.

The Eversheds model is also meant to apply to higher education corporations, though chartered corporations are likely too big to need to consider this option. In this case, the Treasury would receive 'the capital value of the higher education institution' (§3.15). However, the current statutory 'asset lock' attaching to higher education corporations may present an impediment. If the HEC is dissolved, assets can only be transferred to a successor company, a company limited by guarantee, and assets must be used purely for charitable purposes.

This is much stronger protection than that indicated in the White Paper which promised only to ensure that 'the wider public interest will be protected in any such change of status' (§4.36). This phrasing became even weaker in the accompanying Technical Consultation: '[we will] *balance the potential benefits against the concern* that ... there is a wider social interest which *may* need to be protected' (my emphasis). One way in which the public interest may be protected is simply by having the purchaser also pay a sum to the Treasury in recognition of the public investment that has gone into these establishments over the years.

Hostile takeovers are not possible given the absence of shareholders. But the majority of higher education institutions face new commercial pressures. From this perspective, we need to reconsider the issue of institutional viability. If no merger is available, then private takeover, involving a change of corporate form, may be presented as preferable to institutional collapse. As I write, the future and financial viability of London Metropolitan is murky. Given that it is a company limited by guarantee, the likelihood of private purchase must be high.

Private equity firms in the USA have specialised in taking over struggling colleges before pursuing expansion. Any legislative changes proposed to corporate form may be less about making it easier for institutions to attract finance and more about making it easier for private equity to purchase a mainstream university by removing the current impediments: DAPs, 'asset locks', charters, and all.

Chiefly, the government would prefer to be in a position where such decisions do not have to be approved by the Secretary of State or Parliament, but are transformed into private matters for the board of governors or equivalent.

OUTSOURCING, JOINT VENTURES, PARTNERSHIPS, ETC.

Besides the outright purchase of universities or colleges, the 'cleanest solution' according to Eversheds, two other approaches exist for 'privatising' the university.

Outsourcing is familiar to most; it removes staff from the employ of the university and uses an agency to provide the service (this agency will be private and mostly likely for-profit). The government would like to help universities reduce costs by moving outsourcing further. It has now legislated (2012 Finance Act) to offer VAT exemptions on services shared between two VAT-exempt operations.

This clears a previous obstacle to pooling 'back room' services (administrative, IT, catering, maintenance, library and other 'support'): 'shared services' will in theory allow partners to access larger economies of scale if they keep provision 'in house' or offer greater leverage in new tenders. As I wrote for *Radical Philosophy* in 2012: 'This could accelerate the outsourcing already seen in the sector and indeed produce further outsourcing on already outsourced services.'[16]

Although described as outsourcing in some of the press coverage, developments at London Metropolitan University over the summer of 2012 pointed to something closer to the buyout model illustrated above. A tender document published in March 2012 advertised for a 'strategic partner', effectively a management consultant on a contract worth £74 million over five years.[17] What was being advertised was a three-stage plan:

1. The consultant would help to review and augment the administrative set up at the university.
2. The consultant would help develop a 'shared service partnership' aimed at making savings.
3. LMU would open up this 'backroom' service provision to other higher education providers so as to produce a 'high quality cost-effective' service.

Advertising for a management consultancy to take over the running of administration may have been the envisaged solution to the ongoing administrative problems which came to a head with the revocation of LMU's 'Highly Trusted Sponsor' status (see Chapter 8).

The difference from outsourcing is that the private operation is not providing the services to replace university posts. Instead, at stage 3, a 'special purpose vehicle' may be set up into which staff are then transferred. All services and operations were to be considered for this move, with the exception of teaching staff and the vice-chancellor. It is for this reason that it resembles the Eversheds proposal for a buyout (Figure 9.1): the subsidiary could well be a profit-making enterprise like 'NewCo' and a vehicle for investment.

However, the UKBA acted before the tender could be awarded and the contract was not awarded in September as planned. London Metropolitan will instruct its consultant to conduct stage 1, but this will now be an 'extensive and rapid Business Re-engineering exercise', an attempt to establish the institution as an ongoing concern.

Joint ventures take many forms but at root they involve either setting up a new enterprise or separating off part of an institution's existing activity. Such initiatives have focused on peripheral academic provision such as access degree courses, English language classes and distance learning provision. There is great interest from investors in spinning off online course provision. Joint ventures with private backers or delivery partners will be profit-making ventures – with both partners taking a share of revenues. Eversheds, again, outlines its ideas for likely future developments: 'research commercialization projects, revenues from overseas campuses and from selling access to the institution's degree-awarding powers in the private sector'.[18]

Joint ventures also figure in the government's plans for a new form of private funded 'university' and an expansion of UK HEIs operating overseas campuses (see Chapter 8). Attracting inward science and technology investment and boosting education as an export industry is a key goal for all political parties. These ventures will involve private finance and an existing institution, with the government providing logistical support and pledging to remove any legislative barriers. Education Services UK, a new unit of BIS, will effectively operate as a broker or match-maker here.

CONCLUSION

From this brief outline of joint ventures, partnerships, and outsourcing we can see that commercial operations and partnerships are already proliferating and creating a complex terrain in which democratic accountability is becoming more and more attenuated. The complexity of corporate forms, group structures and joint ventures make it difficult for the public to be aware of what is happening here. There is a need for a new branch of public interest business journalism.

Legislation is likely to be presented to Parliament as a 'streamlining' measure seeking to rationalise baroque procedures or to give more autonomy to institutions. But in the absence of strong regulatory frameworks, the function of Parliament or the Secretary of State in providing oversight of the sector will be eroded. We will turn to the issue of governance in Chapter 11, but at the heart of these matters is a push to make it easier for private equity to enter the sector through buyouts and ventures, while keeping democracy out of it.

10
University Bonds and Other Credit Products

Although the new market mechanisms generate uncertainty, conversely this may represent a window of opportunity for smart investment. With students facing higher fees, they may expect a better 'experience': money is needed to improve facilities and secure recruitment levels. Equally, as a small elite looks set to pull away, many may feel that now is the time to borrow so as to break into that group or indeed for the peripheral elite to cement their place. Such a prize could launch several ambitious strategies.

The sector's debts currently amount to about £5 billion: roughly 20 per cent of annual income. As we move to a more corporate model, we should expect this ratio to move. Chris Hearn of Barclays Capital believes the sector is 'underleveraged' and could take on an additional £4 to £5 billion of borrowing to finance investment. Combine that figure with cash reserves of around £5 billion and we could see sizeable movement.

Initially, such investment will only secure a larger share of the market, the market itself cannot grow owing to government controls. The influx of additional money would raise the stakes. In a zero sum game, investment is potentially destructive. There are therefore likely to be some winners and some high-profile losers. Overambitious or unlucky strategies may contribute to institutional implosion in a sector where the government is no longer committed to being the backer of last resort.

LENDING

In previous years, mortgaging assets or accessing unsecured banking lending through overdrafts or revolving credit facilities may have been more usual. But the financial crisis has led to a general contraction in traditional bank lending, while capital grants to universities from Hefce have also become much scarcer.

HE has been seen as a safe sector for lending, but this was largely due to large-scale public funding and a belief that governments would intervene to protect institutions that ran into difficulties. This view may be shifting as polarisation commences. *Times Higher Education* reported that this new thinking is revealed in an 'interest rate spread' between different institutions with banks charging more interest to institutions seen as less secure.[1]

It is in this context that there has been a renewed enthusiasm for bond issues by English universities. It is the common source of investment financing in the USA. Because it is debt, rather than equity, it represents an option for universities that wish to maintain their charitable status. Indeed, the government has been keen to encourage Housing Associations to go down this route and in recent years we saw the Wellcome Trust make a multi-million pound issue.

The history of bond issues by universities is relatively unknown. Although there have been a handful of recent 'private placements' by Russell Group universities, in 2012 we saw the first two university 'public offerings' since the late 1990s. De Montfort University issued £90 million of bonds with a further £20 million in reserve (issued but purchased by DMU). The University of Cambridge went for £350 million.

These are likely to be the first of several, as according to Barclays 'demand would be enormous' and it is irrelevant to their calculations about 'leveraging' whether universities use traditional bank lending or bond issues. I will therefore spend some time explaining bonds.[2]

BONDS: THE BASICS

Bonds are the building blocks for many more complex financial products, but at their simplest are tradeable IOU notes. They are issued by governments (Treasury 'gilts') and by companies and are increasingly common in the 'third sector'. Bonds are unsecured lending: they are not backed by assets, though in the case of bankruptcy, bondholders will normally be the 'senior' creditors and hence get first call on any assets that can be liquidated. There are three key components to the basic bond:

- The 'principal' is the amount borrowed.
- The 'coupon' is an annual interest payment normally defined as a percentage of the value of the bonds held – it can be fixed or indexed to, e.g., inflation. An important factor to appreciate is that the interest rate does not 'amortise' the debt: the annual payments are 'interest only'.

- The 'maturity' is a defined period at the end of which the principal must be repaid in full. The principal is not affected by the annual repayments made.

Universities will be offering longer maturities than is typical for corporate bonds. While the latter mature between 7 to 10 years, university bond issues will be at least 30 years and possibly up to 40. In 2006, Imperial issued £50 million on bonds that will not mature until 2056. With interest rates at historic lows, it is a great attraction to lock down borrowing for such periods.

For universities there is another attraction: one to do with institutional autonomy. As things currently stand, the financial memorandum each university signs with Hefce includes a clause relating to the annual costs of servicing borrowing. Universities must seek permission from Hefce if those costs go above four per cent of total annual income. What this means is that universities and colleges have more autonomy in relation to bonds. Since bonds are effectively 'interest only', annual repayments are smaller relative to the amount borrowed. They can therefore borrow higher amounts without going through Hefce.

Pension funds and insurance companies are keen on university issues, because the longer maturities on these bonds are a good match for the lifetimes of their liabilities. They are not necessarily looking for high returns but secure, long-term assets. Purchasing such bonds would also enable them to diversify their existing portfolios. Scottish Widows, M&G and Legal & General purchased the DMU bonds.

In terms of security, all universities looking at this avenue would need to pay for a rating from a credit ratings agency. Lancaster, Bristol, Nottingham, King's College London and Sheffield are all rated by Standard & Poor's, while Moody's covers De Montfort, Brunel, Keele and Cambridge (to whom it has awarded its highest rating Aaa/stable – better than its rating for the Bank of England).

RECENT EXAMPLES

In recent years, King's College London, Imperial, Manchester, Liverpool, Edinburgh and York have made *private* placements of between £50 and £100 million (Manchester) of bonds. The coupons were around 5 per cent. At such large universities, a bond issue is one way of 'hedging' an investment portfolio.

Cambridge's bond is the biggest issue in English university history, but it has such strong finances that it probably prefers to raise £350 million through this route than by disposing of other assets. In contrast, the recent £110 million public offering by De Montfort University (DMU) is a very different matter. For a start, its coupon of 5.375 per cent is much higher than Cambridge's (3.75 per cent), reflecting the different assessments of risk involved for bond purchasers. Although smaller, DMU's bond represents over 70 per cent of its annual income of around £150 million.

One final point concerns the *public* offering. The size of the Cambridge issue meant it was unsuitable for the private market. But DMU *had* to go to the market because its investors want the guarantee of a *tradeable* bond with sufficient liquidity to cash in the asset if needed: those taking on the private placements are convinced of the security of their investment and do not need such guarantees. DMU did not have the option of a private placement and it may have had to access more borrowing than it needs: the principal (£90/110 million) is a long way below the typical lower limit for a public offering of £200 million.

While economists such as David Blanchflower have extolled the virtues of using bonds for capital investment in important projects, it is not clear that DMU's issue will generate additional revenues. It appears to be a defensive measure designed to protect its place in the new market by overhauling existing facilities, pedestrianising its campus and buying its way out of a more onerous lending facility with Lloyds Bank.

The precursors for public offerings by English universities are not great, as they have been typically pursued by institutions with weaker finances. In 2009, Lancaster University used a new loan from RBS to pay off its bondholders 15 years before its 1995 bonds were due to mature. It was due to repay £35 million at that later date but gave out nearly £16 million extra in penalties and termination fees to escape early from an 'onerous' covenant that gave third parties a veto on further capital expenditure.

Bonds issued by the University of Greenwich in 1998 to finance the refurbishment of the former Royal Naval College (where it was unable to achieve secured lending against the buildings owing to their status as part of a Unesco World Heritage Site) have been withdrawn from public listings following the collapse of the specialist insurance company guaranteeing the bond. £30 million, the principal, is due to be repaid in 2028.

RESPONSIBLE DECISIONS

The two cases above point to potential problems with bonds. At 5.375 per cent on £110 million DMU will have to find around £5.9 million each year to pay its coupons. In recent years it has been making a *deficit* so just meeting annual costs is a challenge in itself, likely to involve cuts to staffing. But how will it also find the principal it needs in 2042? If additional revenue is not generated, and surpluses retained, then one has to consider where the money will come from. Although DMU's principal at £110 million may be worth around £35 million in today's prices (allowing for inflation), that is still nearly a quarter of De Montfort's current annual turnover.

Lancaster required additional borrowing to pay off its bondholders. This is known as 'refinancing'. Alternatively, the bonds may need to be 'rolled over': new bonds are issued to repay the principal on the maturing ones. One might see this debt dynamic as kicking a problem down the road. As yet, there is no mature bond market for UK universities, so we can only speculate that DMU will be able to rollover any debts in 2042. One well-placed financier told me that the market for university bond issues may not be as large, or as liquid, as estimated by Barclays. Does good governance equate to leaving a problem for a future set of governors to resolve in 30 years' time?

The economist Hyman Minsky developed a scheme to analyse this situation. There are three positions for a debtor: hedge, speculative and Ponzi borrowing.

Hedge borrowers are able to pay the annual interest from their income and reserve a surplus so as to pay off the principal (or they have sufficient liquid assets which can be realised if needed). They are therefore accessing borrowing as a way to best manage their investments – the University of Cambridge would be in this position with its borrowing.

Speculative borrowers can meet their annual costs of borrowing but not the principal borrowed and so will need to refinance. DMU would be in this position if it can reduce expenditure to meet the coupon.

The *Ponzi position* applies to those who are borrowing to ride asset bubbles. They can pay neither the interest nor the principal and are dependent on increases in asset values to cover their costs of borrowing. Let us hope that no English universities enter this position since their only asset bubble may be their tuition fee income stream.

Further, we need to consider the *pliancy* of the indebted beyond the need to meet interest payments and repay the principal.

Bonds have covenants that stipulate the conditions which must be met by the issuers or specify 'events' which may trigger changes such as requiring the principal to be repaid immediately. Bond covenants are now much less onerous than those seen in the 1990s, but DMU's still runs to over 100 pages and makes US Bank Trustees Limited the bond 'trustee' – an arbiter which determines whether certain defined events have or have not occurred.

One item in the covenant relates to the need to *maintain an investment grade credit rating*. Failure to achieve this is termed a 'negative rating event'. There is a further 'regulatory event' which is triggered if Hefce ceases to be the regulatory body responsible for DMU. In both cases, the bondholders may require DMU to buy back the bonds or redeem them immediately.

Recent events at London Metropolitan (see Chapters 8 and 9) may create a problem here. Both Moody's and Standard & Poor's base their university ratings on the 'likelihood of extraordinary support from the UK government' in the event of 'acute liquidity stress'. For Moody's this likelihood is 'very high', for Standard & Poor's, 'moderately high'. But following the decision of the UKBA, London Metropolitan has been holed below the waterline. If it does not win its judicial review it is likely to face acute liquidity stress as *a result of government agency action*. This is likely to have knock-on implications for DMU who may now find it harder to maintain its investment grade rating.

Is DMU a brave pioneer for bond issues by smaller institutions or is it taking some pretty hefty risks to avoid being stuck in a bad market position? Either way it has certainly abrogated some of its institutional autonomy to a dynamic that we do not yet fully understand.

THE FUTURE? BONDS IN THE USA

In the USA, there is a mature bond market. Issues represent the main method of raising investment. But there is an intimate relation between debt financing and tuition fee increases, since the ability of universities to raise tuition fees at will is well-regarded by credit rating agencies. This is largely neglected in commentary about the student debt crisis over there.

To take one example, the University of California is a useful proxy for the UK higher education sector since its budget is comparable, it

was previously largely state-funded, and it has several internationally regarded universities including UCLA, UC Berkeley, UC San
Diego and UC Davis. UC has an annual income of around $20
billion, comparable to the UK sector as a whole which was £27
billion in 2010/11.[3] One caveat: UK universities are not as diversified
as in the USA, where universities run sports stadia and hospitals.

UC uses several flavours of bond. However, its main 'general
purpose bond' is directly tied to tuition fee income, which is paid
into an account held by Bank of New York Mellon, the bond trustee.
Bondholders have first call on that income stream to service their
coupon if needed.[4] California State Auditors reported that 'pledging
tuition and fee revenue enables the university to obtain financing
under more favourable terms' but also that bondholders had not
yet needed to access that pool.[5] The pledged pool itself amounted
to $8.7 *billion* in 2010/11. Given that UC has issued total bond
debts of $14.3 billion (at 31 December 2011), concerns are natural.[6]
UC's debt to income ratio is now close to 70 per cent – much, much
higher than is generally seen in the UK, although DMU will take
that step in one bound.

Bob Meister has argued that the primary aim of the university
is now to protect its borrowing power in capital markets. The
university issued $1.7 billion of bonds in 2011 alone and believes
it can issue a further $3 to $5 billion in the next five years without
affecting its credit rating. Were it to risk downgrading a notch it
could access a further $5 billion on top of that.

The numbers are staggering. Across the US, higher education has
become increasingly debt-financed with individual students taking
out personal loans to pay the ballooning fees. Fees at some private
colleges, such as Vassar and Wesleyan, are over $40,000 a year. Total
student debt recently went beyond what its citizens owe on credit
cards and is somewhere around $1 *trillion* (one thousand billion
dollars). Any collapse in demand could have severe consequences
for the sector given the debt propping up its institutions.

The bond craze in California went so far that *San Diego district
educational authorities* issued bonds to replace investment that was
not forthcoming from the State. As Gillian Tett observes, 'Though
these bonds shield taxpayers (and politicians) ... today, they create
a headache later. At best this is a case of kicking the can down the
road; at worst, a case of the government dancing with loan sharks.'[7]

Something similar may happen here if a raft of bonds is issued
that do not have to be paid off until 2040 and beyond, while the
cap on tuition fees may hamper the development of a mature, liquid

market. (I stress the ambiguity of that final clause to refer back to questions about the developing debt dynamic.)

Whichever way one looks at it, the movement into bonds is undoubtedly a new phase of privatisation. Gambles such as DMU are taking may only be assessed in hindsight: having got in early it may limit its rivals' ability to match investment, but if the market fails to develop and it cannot generate higher revenues there may be extremely difficult times ahead. DMU has gone 'all in' as they say in poker.

ALTERNATIVE FLAVOURS OF BOND

The bonds described above are 'vanilla' bonds – there is nothing fancy about them except for some variations in covenants. As noted, these are the basic building blocks of financial products and other spicier flavours are available. As the market for university issues matures, new products will be developed. What follows is a brief guide to some of the main possibilities, which may be attractive to institutions unable or unwilling to go for the full-blown public offering or to those looking to boost borrowing capacity. We will briefly outline some newer initiatives and possibilities: social impact bonds, mini-bonds, and 'securitisation'. The latter is particularly important and will crop up again in relation to the government's attempts to sell the portfolio of graduate loan balances.

Social Investment or Social Impact Bonds

The government's vision of a Big Society depends on the development of new financial products. Rather than administering public services itself, the government, or proxies such as the Big Society bank, will act as a broker putting together private finance with local initiatives.

Social impact bonds differ from the basic kind so far discussed in that the return on the bond is not fixed. The coupon terms on bonds can be 'structured' to link payments (rather than just defaults) to events or options. They are at root a kind of derivative. Derivatives need not involve the buying or selling of stocks, commodities or currency; instead, they can involve *bets* on the changing prices of said items or agreements about other *outcomes*. They are second-order dealings.

With social impact bonds, the two parties – the government and the investor – form a contract with a set of conditions specified to determine levels and rates of payment in relation to a particular service. Neither party need *provide the service*. They are speculating on an objectively determined and agreed outcome: the performance of third parties against targets *whom the government has funded with the investor's money.*

In a pilot scheme run in Peterborough, a £5 million bond issue raised funds to provide accommodation and support to 3,000 ex-offenders. If the reoffending rate falls by 7.5 per cent after six years, then the bond purchasers will get £8 million back (from the savings made by the success of the scheme – i.e., fewer probation officers will be needed). Should it go the other way the entire bond stake could be lost.

The Office for Civil Society is offering to tailor such bond issues to individual schemes. The idea is similar to that behind PFI, in that the risk of the innovative approach to a social problem is financed privately. New 'early years' initiatives could also take this form: successful intervention would keep children out of care or prison with the savings made again going to the bond purchasers.

Such schemes could translate into research projects that otherwise fail to find research council or other support. The funding, and the risk, would be provided by private backers with any outcomes that are amenable to quantified or monetised solutions being the objective of the bet. The university itself could be the party to the bet rather than the government.

Securitisation

Securitisation involves turning illiquid assets and their associated future income streams into tradeable bonds ('securities'). Securitisation can take many forms but in general the performance of the bond is tied to the performance of the asset: for example, the coupon could vary and there may be no principal repayment when the bond matures. In this way, the bond may also be isolated from the general performance of the issuer.

Originally developed in relation to the repackaging of mortgage and other loan debt, securitisation has extended into other areas. David Bowie raised over $50 million in 1997 by selling ten-year bonds against the future royalties on his pre-1990 back catalogue (25 albums and over 280 songs). The return to investors was tied to the return on sales of Bowie's music. The income stream had been isolated from him personally and he was not required to meet any shortfall if income was lower than predicted (say, owing to the advent of file sharing). Prudential insurance company paid $55 million for the entire issue on a 7.9 per cent coupon. It was downgraded a number of times, finally hitting junk status in May 2003.

Football clubs have securitised their future gate receipts and season ticket sales. In return for cash to invest today, this was seen as a good gamble in the late 1990s. Tempted by the money available to Premiership teams through television rights and the riches of European competition, clubs adopted ambitious strategies to break into the small group of elite clubs.

Securitisation has already been seen in the higher education sector through the private finance initiatives and other off-balance-sheet solutions used in student accommodation. In such arrangements a specially created company, typically a joint venture between a bank and a construction company, will raise the capital needed for the project through bond issues securitised against the future revenue generated by rents. The contracts may be what are termed DBFO contracts – the third party designs, builds, finances and operates the rooms, which revert to university ownership after a period of 30 or 40 years (often the estimated lifetimes of the new-builds). Some contracts may stipulate that students be placed in the DBFO buildings before other accommodation is filled.

There is an exceptionally active market in student accommodation with several types of 'solution' including leaseback. The money involved is larger than the direct bond issues mentioned above: the University of Sheffield has a 'student village' on the back of which nearly £160 million of bonds was issued.

Mini-bonds

There is a current vogue for 'mini-bonds'. Here companies have designed boutique products to be sold to individual rather than institutional investors. These are much smaller offerings – under £5 million in some cases – while the coupon may be replaced with offers of the company's products, such as the debenture seats at Wimbledon or the gift vouchers to the value of 2 per cent offered by John Lewis on top of its 4.5 per cent coupon. Mini-bonds are not traded and may have a much shorter maturity. The John Lewis bond is five years.

Such offerings depend on customer loyalty. This has its equivalent in the university sector. Indeed, such an option was presented to the Browne review into university funding by the Russell Group. 'Graduate linked bonds' were meant to allow prestigious universities to set fees above the maximum tuition fee: the difference between £9,000 and whatever higher fee was set would be covered by issuing bonds to private investors:

Universities would then generate additional up-front investment by leveraging the future contributions of their graduates to secure funding from private investors. This could either be through issuing bonds directly linked to the income stream received from graduate repayments, or through the university itself selling annuities.[8]

As to the potential market for such products, the report suggested that alumni, loyal to their alma mater, might be encouraged to buy bonds '[with a lower coupon] than market rates, on the basis that they would be investing to support their own institution and its graduates'.[9] If charitable donations are threatened by the new terrain of high fees, then ironically that terrain offers a replacement. Investment rather than giving. Such markets could offer something more lucrative than direct fund-raising and without the unpleasant connotations of glad-handing wealthy and potentially embarrassing patrons.

CONCLUSION

As an alternative to borrowing from banks, borrowing through the bond markets appears to have advantages. But those advantages are most apparent for the wealthier universities with more robust cash-flows. We do not yet have a mature market in university paper and it is therefore hard to assess DMU's decision to issue around £100 million in this way.

In the USA such a mature market is intimately bound up with rapidly rising tuition fees: even the finances of a world-renowned institution such as the University of California are vulnerable to a shift in demand for higher education. Bond issues are not a sure-fire way to replace state funding and involve decisions which our universities and colleges may lack the capacity to assess. While corporate bonds tend to have short lives, university bonds do not mature until 30 years later. What do such temporalities mean for responsible governance? We will address this theme in the next chapter.

11
Governance and Public Accountability

The preceding chapters in Part 3 have set out the increasing complexity of the financing of universities and the decisions facing their managers. This chapter considers how universities are governed: that is, how senior executives are overseen and how that function allows for wider transparency and accountability, or not.

The government's intentions here are twofold: it wishes to treat universities as private companies and students as consumers. By giving the latter more power, universities will become more responsive to wider society. This is an alienated model of accountability and one that exacerbates the potential conflict between charitable objectives and commercial imperatives. Similarly, this approach contributes to a 'democratic deficit' in so far as the consultations surrounding higher education reform are limited to vice-chancellors and mission groups, as if the former were business leaders and owners, or representatives of the Confederation of British Industry or the Institute of Directors.

As outlined in Chapter 9, vice-chancellors are in most cases neither the owners of universities nor the agents of owners. Questions of management and governance are intimately related to the question of corporate form. While calls for institutional autonomy make sense in resisting direct political interference, we must be wary of allowing vice-chancellors to act as autocratic chief executives with even fewer checks on their decisions. What differentiates universities from most private companies is their relation to a board or equivalent and their charitable status. Almost all HEIs have their roots in local communities. How can we protect that legacy?

Since HEIs, as charities, are largely funded through donations and public funding, we expect their trustees to represent the varied interests of society, the public whose benefit these charities are meant to serve. But now these charities face unstable incomes and large-scale decisions about borrowing and investment, including even the decision (outlined in Chapter 9) as whether to sell the institution. In a commercial world can governors really play two roles, ensuring the pursuit of charitable objects and acting as a corporate board? Deciding how to direct received public funding in such a manner as to serve a constituency of varying stakeholders is very different from setting out to generate revenue.

We can identify clear issues here: the composition of boards of governors; commercial pressures; the channel for academic scrutiny of managerial decision-making; and wider public accountability. This chapter will treat each in turn.

GOVERNANCE STRUCTURES AND COMMERCIAL PRESSURES

Senior management, the executive, has operational responsibility, but a board or 'Council' in the pre-92 universities is responsible for setting the mission of the institution, approving corporate strategy and ensuring continued financial solvency. They must also comply with the relevant regulations and act as the equivalent of trustees with regard to charitable objectives.

Although the composition of boards varies, most university boards have a majority of 'lay' or independent members, neither academics nor students, who have shown, for example in the case of higher education corporations, 'capacity in industrial, commercial or employment matters or professional practice'. This reflects a desire for vocational or professional relevance to the local community. In an age of private funding and international reach these members of the board have a transformed role.

Representatives of the internal constituency, staff and students, have only a small presence. Owing to the corporate form of boards, responsibility for decisions is jointly taken. For this reason, staff and students on the board are *not* understood to be delegates or representatives, but are expected to use their independent judgement to make decisions in the interest of the corporate body.

For higher education corporations (see Chapter 9), it is important to recognise an important difference. With chartered corporations, the university as a whole is the corporation and is effectively an organisation of members: their complex governance statutes reflect this status. With HECs, only *the board* is the corporation. The board 'conducts' the university. As a result, the vice-chancellor, or equivalent, is more powerful; the board of governors is less representative for staff and students, with unions excluded at some places; the academic board has more of an advisory status: the 'educational character and mission' are determined by the governors. The set-up at companies limited by guarantee is similar.

COMMERCIAL PRESSURES

New commercial pressures in the market for undergraduate recruitment will increasingly mean that maintaining solvency and managing risk are the overriding objectives. We must not forget that the market solution depends on there being the real risk of failure for universities. The White Paper declared the intention not to act as backer of last resort stating that 'it is not Government's role to protect an unviable institution' (paragraph 6.9b).

Without large-scale public funding, self-preservation, the 'iron law of oligarchy', will mean that the primary aim of the organisation is the bottom-line of revenue generation with public benefit objectives following on later if, indeed, they do not conflict with the former. After the bottom-line, the main 'stakeholder' to corporate eyes is probably the unaccountable quango, Hefce, or indeed, in light of the London Metropolitan debacle, the UK Border Agency (see Chapter 8).

As universities become more commercially oriented, their management structures mimic commercial operations and come closer and closer to that model, intensifying previous tendencies. 'Command and control' executives may move away from collegial set-ups to hierarchical management structures. Performance indicators suit the professional practices and targets of managers rather than academics.

Certainly the proposed reforms about 'changing corporate form' may also have been intended to make it easier to rationalise statutes and streamline boards so as to become more 'corporate', with governors acting more as 'non-executive directors'. As John Holmwood notes, the line coming from vice-chancellors is that they need the power to operate 'quickly and flexibly'.[1] The changes at University of Central Lancashire, where the university will become part of an overarching group structure framed by a private company, are officially justified from this angle. The Chair of its Board of Governors announced:

> The University operates in a highly dynamic landscape and we need to become more agile, both in terms of future challenges and the opportunities presented to us. Becoming a Company Limited by Guarantee will provide us with much greater flexibility to respond to the constantly shifting political and regulatory landscape in which we operate in the UK and to take advantage of the opportunities around the globe.[2]

It is clear that any further shift from charitable status to a company owned by individuals, other companies or shareholders entails changes to the running of the organisation, especially if owners seek the distribution of profits or dividends. But even without such a development, increasing commercialisation generates similar effects: boards become less taxed by the need to represent various constituencies and more concerned with whether frontline delivery staff are meeting the expectations of customers.

From this perspective, we need to be wary of strident demands for institutional autonomy from vice-chancellors. The danger today is not direct political interference challenging academic freedom, but vice-chancellors increasingly acting as chief executives who in the absence of any clear owners have even fewer limits on their powers than their equivalents in other sectors. (At University of Central Lancashire, its new structure will see the vice-chancellor reporting in to the more senior 'group' Chief Executive from August 2013.) Institutional autonomy may translate into the freedom to act autocratically without regard to the constituencies the organisation originally set out to serve. Senior levels are increasingly populated by career professionals tied neither to the institution *nor the sector*. Regulatory frameworks are one way to limit the short-term perspectives of such individuals.

ACADEMICS AND GOVERNANCE

There is a chronic under-representation of staff and students on boards. Similarly, the various structures through which academics are represented internally have, in the words of Alberto Toscano, become 'monopolised in opaque and pernicious ways by senior management'.[3] While academics are meant to be responsible for safeguarding quality and standards, vital functions are increasingly being taken over by administrators and managers.

Audit cultures are part and parcel of the new managerialism oriented to revenue raising, tendering exercises such as the Research Excellence Framework, and compliance with government data collection. This is a consistent theme of both recent studies and academic complaints: with time eaten up by research, teaching and administration, academics are no longer able to be involved with even the limited democratic structures of the institution. Excess workloads have serious implications for the sector.

More worryingly, management pressures to improve examination results may also be eroding independent academic judgement and the key role of protecting standards.[4] An institution only has degree awarding powers if it can demonstrate that it is supporting academics to perform this role. But there is little scope for academics as a 'self-critical community' to review management decisions about course closures, which are often wrapped up in dismal consultation procedures. Recent trends at the chartered universities include attempting to remove Council (governing body) oversight of academic redundancies: in effect, delegating that procedure to management. Academics thereby would be relegated from members to employees: the situation experienced at the non-chartered universities.

WIDER ACCOUNTABILITY

Companies limited by shares and publicly limited companies are responsible to their owners – their shareholders. How do the owners (shareholders) ensure that the agents (management) act in the interests of the owners? With universities, what is equivalent relation? Increasingly it appears as if vice-chancellors believe they are agents *and* owners.

Throughout recent developments, the government has privileged discussions with vice-chancellors, their lobbying body Universities UK, and 'mission groups' which represent different subsets of vice-chancellors. This is in addition to meeting privateers, private equity managers and other profit-making interests. It is a national issue but how does the nation get a say especially if its representatives are denied the opportunity to debate primary legislation in Parliament?

In terms of public accountability, we can see that there is very little structural inclusion of a broader public, who have been largely kept in the dark as we creep towards a corporatised marketplace. As government funding disappears and the finances come from private sources, what transformation does this effect upon management? In one sense, the accountability that comes through public money is eroded, while board meetings are closed to the public and there is no requirement for any elected political representatives to be on university boards.

So what would be the alternative to promote a democratic, transparent and accountable system which protects and promotes mass participation beyond a consumerist approach? It is with such issues to mind that the recent von Prondzynski review into the governance of Scottish universities has developed the very different model of an *independent public body*.[5] Its recommendations on improving transparency and accountability through public meetings and elected chairs of governing boards now appear to have the support of the Scottish National Party. Along with having board meetings in public, it recommends that the position of lay members should be advertised externally and that the chair of the board should be directly elected. It also seeks to guarantee union representation (staff and student) along with a 'rector', again elected, whose responsibility would be to safeguard student interests.

In continuing to refuse to charge students resident in Scotland any tuition fees, the system north of the border is diverging. The possibilities for such alternative structures in England seem to be diminishing. The proposals in the recent Higher Education White Paper 'to make it easier to change corporate form' were not intended to midwife the first co-operatives or 'John Lewis' ownership models within the sector.

What seems lacking in the debate here is any notion of a participative institution. In his excellent 'biography' of the welfare state, Nicholas Timmins writes the following of the transformation of the polytechnics effected by legislation of 1988 and 1992:

> It was a revolution which happened so fast and so silently ... that it was almost invisible, barely debated in public at all. Universities found themselves made accountable in new and sometimes painful ways, their dons rated for research, with some under pressure to become 'teaching only' institutions. Almost all were desperately searching for ways to enhance their income.[6]

As originally conceived, the polytechnics, in contract to *autonomous* universities, were the *public* sector of higher education designed to serve local communities. This notion has been lost and needs to be recreated – not by turning back the clock to the 1980s but by recasting universities as independent *public* bodies.

Opening up board meetings to press and public might be one small step towards introducing a check against corporatism, but an alternative would be to give people more say in the processes at the institutions that determine the mode and content of education.

Institutions which see their primary responsibilities as the pursuit of truth and the advancement of learning may not see themselves as public institutions. Indeed, Cambridge wrote in response to the White Paper: 'Universities are not solely or in any strict governance sense accountable to their students. ... Universities serve many other interests, including society (through discharging public benefit obligations for example), research funders, donors, alumni, partners from across the public and private sectors and central Government.'[7]

Oxford and Cambridge may be the only two institutions immune to market pressures – they have the wealth and prestige to ride out whatever comes. But they serve only a small proportion of the undergraduate population. In order to safeguard a mass system strongly based in local communities and regions, we may need to move away from adherence to a unitary funding or market system and direct public money in a more targeted fashion, possibly even allowing the big beasts further independence.

The current government like the last is keen to encourage a diversified market of institutions offering different choices to prospective students. But in the event of market failure, where a local community can be largely ignored or abandoned in favour of more lucrative markets, what recourse do we have? How can the current governance structures mitigate against such possibilities?

The trends of privatisation lead to a corporate sensibility that maintains little broader responsibility other than corporate self-preservation or maximising market share. There is a broader question for democracy here. Reliance on private corporations to make decisions in the public interest – 'the market will sort it out' – is risky. Institutional autonomy is a principle that should override neither democratic accountability nor interventions by government. A market system of lightly regulated individual companies is unsatisfactory, particularly if democratic functions are passed to unrepresentative quangos.

Part 4
Financialisation

This final part of the book leaves behind institutions to take a different perspective: the impact of the new funding regime on public sector finances.

Loans behave in very different ways to grants and accordingly are registered differently in departmental budgets and national accounts. These accounting conventions have long-term implications for higher education policy, while in so far as loans generate information, the government is provided with a means to maintain certain forms of control over the privatised sector.

I will use the term 'financialisation' in this context to describe how policy will become determined in accordance with the risk associated with a growing student loan 'book'. Managing this risk will be the first priority of those subsequently responsible for universities and colleges. Financialisation names the process by which knowledge becomes enclosed by a system of accounting.

Chapter 12 will set out the main issues: in particular, how the government estimates and accounts for loan repayment and *non-repayment* and how this impacts upon departmental expenditure and the headline public sector finance statistics central to the current political narrative: the deficit and the debt.

Future governments may be faced with an unsustainable scheme and be required to make adjustments. Chapter 13 outlines some of the policy options available including the development of new institutional performance measures based on graduate earnings profiles and the ongoing attempts to 'sell' the portfolio of outstanding ICR loan accounts.

12
Loans: The Government's Perspective

The main intention of this chapter is to cast a critical eye over the suggestion that the new funding regime was a reaction to temporary budgetary pressures. As the previous chapters have shown, the new funding regime, especially the removal of significant levels of block funding, was central to creating a new market in higher education.

The Comprehensive Spending Review of 2010 was the *occasion* on which to launch this initiative. While the new regime does reduce BIS's expenditure, it is important to understand the accounting convention *through which* this is achieved and that the reduction in expenditure is accompanied by a sizeable increase in loan outlay. The bottom line is that the overarching narrative of 'deficit reduction' does not work in the context of student loans: the growth of debt is not slowed, it is rather *increased* in the short term. This is prima facie perplexing but the overall implications are central to understanding the policy terrain of the next few years.

As mentioned in Chapter 3, there is something surreal about the character of discussions concerning the new funding regime for higher education. Even to discuss the new loans issued to the cohort in 2012, we are obliged to assume that the scheme is allowed to run for 34 years without any alteration. The first '30 year' write-offs will be recorded in the national accounts in 2046. Politics is, however, likely to intervene, and this chapter will outline why.

First, we need to distinguish the *sustainability* of the scheme from its *distributional* effects as outlined in Chapter 3. Whether the loans are or are not progressive is a distinct question from whether the estimates of repayments between now and 2046 will prove accurate. If not enough of the money loaned returns, then the burden of meeting such a shortfall will be left to future higher education budgets.

One impact of the attempt to manage this risk is already apparent: tighter controls on, and indeed reductions in, overall numbers. Student places for September 2012 were reduced by 10,000 initially (additional places introduced in 2010/11 were not 'consolidated'), then by a further 5,000 to allow for a projected A level grade inflation that did not materialise. In addition, margin places were distributed to cheaper provision: FE colleges and non-degree courses.

A second impact can be seen in the decision to freeze the maximum tuition fee at £9,000 for 2013/14, i.e., it was not increased in line with inflation. Maintaining a tight control on numbers and fees is one way to restrict the Exchequer's exposure, but it is probably not politically sustainable in the longer term. Maintaining artificial 'supply-side' restrictions of this kind is difficult for ministers who believe in free markets; they may be hoping that within a few years their competition measures will begin to drive down price.

THE SAVING IN THE FUNDING REGIME

In order to understand the medium and long term issues, it helps to begin with the savings that are meant to be generated by the new funding regime. This regime depends on moving from grant expenditure (paid direct to institutions) to a set-up that involves higher tuition fees backed for the most part by student loans. This saves money because most of what is lent as loans is meant to come back as repayments, but it does not do so very quickly and this means that *estimates* for repayment rates play a key part in the accounts.

Although we have had no official statement on the savings expected to be achieved, we can piece together a figure of roughly £1 billion annually. The 2010 Comprehensive Spending Review announced that the grants made for higher education (excluding the research budget) would be reduced from £7.1 billion to £4.2 billion by 2014/15.[1] The entirety of this cut was to come out of the undergraduate teaching budget: spending on maintenance grants and access support, including the National Scholarship Programme, was actually increased.

In February 2011, David Willetts told the assembled vice-chancellors at the Universities UK annual conference that by 2014/15, when three cohorts are on the new funding regime, annual outlay would look as follows:

Hefce grant	£2 billion
Maintenance grants & scholarships	£2 billion
Tuition fee loans	£6.5 billion
Maintenance loans	£3.5 billion

There is therefore a total annual outlay of £14 *billion* of which £4 billion is the grants noted above and £10 *billion is loans*.[2] Tuition fee loans are much higher than before. Indeed, Willetts has estimated that owing to higher tuition fees, the sector overall will be roughly 10 per cent *better off* as a result of these changes.

So where is the saving to government if the funds needed to finance higher loans exceeds the savings to grants? The saving is realised through what some regard as an 'accounting trick' determining what does and does not count as *expenditure* when dealing with *loans*. (The specifics of accounting for such 'policy lending' may have contributed to an argument against a graduate contribution scheme.[3])

Grants paid to institutions are expenditure. A £3 billion cut to grants is a £3 billion cut to expenditure. Loans work differently. The money loaned is *expected to come back* – therefore it is not straight-forwardly expenditure. Initially, only the *estimated loss* on loans counts as expenditure. For example, if the government expected all of the money loaned to come back, then *nothing* would be recorded as spending: the loans would be revenue neutral. The government is however expecting to lose 32 per cent of what has been loaned (allowing for its own cost of borrowing over the lifetime of the loans). Only that 32 per cent is therefore recorded as expenditure. Replacing £3 billion of grants with higher levels of loans would therefore save departmental expenditure.

Steve Smith, vice-chancellor of Exeter, and head of Universities UK in 2011, explains:

> the reality is that the government will spend much more on HE in 2014 than it does in 2011. The explanation for this seeming paradox lies in the arcane rules of government accounting. Cash advanced to the Student Loans Company (SLC) to pay to universities on behalf of students does not count as public expenditure: the only part that counts is the estimated amount that will not be repaid ... which is currently estimated at 31 per cent.[4]

Using the government's current figures, revised since Smith wrote, we can see that £10 billion of student loan outlay translates *into only £3.2 billion of expenditure*. Smith continues to set out the basic calculation:

> [W]hile funding to HEFCE reduces by about £3 billion by 2014, public spending on fees and maintenance loans is expected

to increase by about £4.3 billion – and spending on student [maintenance] grants is also likely to increase by about £0.6 billion. This equates to an increase of about £2 billion in public spending on HE by 2014.

Got that? So there is an additional loan outlay of £4.3 billion as compared to 2011/12. If you add that to the extra money for maintenance you get nearly £5 billion to set against the £3 billion cut from Hefce's budget. A net increase of £2 billion. Smith goes on:

> The savings to government ... come from the fact that the reduction in HEFCE funding of about £3 billion is only offset during the year by the increased [maintenance] grant expenditure (of £600 million) and *by the [additional] 'RAB charge' of about £1.33 billion*. Government thus spends about £2 billion more each year, but the national accounts record this as a net reduction of about £1.07 billion. (my additions and emphasis)

'RAB charge' is a piece of technical jargon. It refers to Resource Accounting and Budgeting: the convention used across government since 2001 to set departmental expenditure limits and manage capital expenditure and loans. The 'RAB charge' is shorthand for the *amount of expenditure* recorded to cover the *estimated* non-repayment on the loans issued in 2012/13. In departmental accounts, an 'impairment' is set aside and ring-fenced to cover this estimated cost.

In sum, the loan *outlay* is increased by £4.3 billion, but that only translates into an additional £1.33 billion of *expenditure*. Setting out Smith's calculations in a table may help to clarify what he is driving at.

Table 12.1   Steve Smith's numbers (billions)

Increase in loans for fees and maintenance	+4.3
Cuts to Hefce's budget for undergraduate teaching	–3
Increase to maintenance grants	+0.6
Total Increased Outlay	**+2**
Which results in	
Increase in RAB as a result of higher loans	+4.3
Cuts to Hefce's budget for undergraduate teaching	–3
Increase to maintenance grants	+0.6
Total *Decrease in Expenditure*	**–1.07**

Source: Adapted from Steve Smith's figures, McGettigan 2012.[5]

Smith's calculation is slightly awry: he should take into consideration not just the estimated non-repayment on the *additional loan outlay*, but the *additional non-repayment on the rest of the loan too*. The threshold for repayment has been raised and therefore the estimated non-repayment has moved from 26 per cent to 32 per cent. That said, it gives us a good ball-park figure for the saving from BIS's annual budget – roughly £1 billion. Not exactly a huge saving given the changes at stake.

Coming at this question from a slightly different angle, Paul Bolton's paper for the House of Commons library outlines that the anticipated saving to *expenditure* in Autumn 2010 was £1.3 billion. Expenditure in 2010/11 was £8.8 billion in 2010/11 and that was expected to fall to £7.5 billion in 2014/15.[6]

And that is where most discussion of the impact of loans on public finances has stopped. But there are further implications, not least in relation to what happens to the deficit and the debt over the next few years, but also potential implications for the budgets of other government departments (see Box).

PUBLIC SECTOR FINANCE STATISTICS: THE DEFICIT AND THE DEBT

If we think back to May 2010, the Coalition came together with a clear goal: to reduce the structural budget deficit and slow down the growth rate of public sector net debt. As David Willetts put it, every department was expected to do its bit: 'Higher education cannot be entirely insulated from the savings necessary to reduce the deficit.'[7] It is therefore the saving to the deficit which is the main merit of the new funding scheme.

The Deficit

The 'deficit' is a measure of the government's annual expenditure *minus* the annual income it receives, for example, from taxes. Any shortfall must be funded by borrowing, which adds to the debt.[8] 'Deficit reduction' as a policy is therefore directed at lowering the additional debt needed to meet this shortfall. Reducing the deficit *slows down the rate at which the debt is growing*.

The Debt

Public Sector Net Debt – PSND – is a measure of the UK's balance sheet: its assets set against its liabilities. It is a measure of what the government owns or is owed (assets) versus what *it owes to others* (liabilities, typically borrowing in the form of Treasury

Consumer Price Index and the Impact of Tuition Fees

In October 2012, the new figures for the Consumer Prices Index (CPI), a measure of inflation, registered the impact of the new higher tuition fees. The Office for National Statistics noted that education had contributed 0.32 percentage points of upwards pressure helping to produce a final rate of 2.7 per cent. A similar effect is expected to appear in the next two years as cohorts on the new funding regime replace those on the old one.

Although not expected to be significant in the medium term,[9] there were expected to be knock-on implications, first noted by Simon Ward, chief economist at Henderson Global Investors.[10] In recent years, CPI had been used to calculate the annual increases for tax credits, inflation-indexed benefit payments and state and public sector pensions. There was therefore a potential effect on the *£200 billion* welfare budget overseen by the Department of Work and Pensions, where a small increase attributable to HE reforms could have an effect sufficiently large to outweigh the saving to the small annual BIS budget.

However, in his December 2012 Autumn Statement, the Chancellor George Osborne announced that he was severing the link between those benefits and CPI to fix the annual increase at only 1 per cent for each of the three years commencing in April 2013. This eliminates any potential tuition fee impact from the largest part of the welfare budget. As yet, the link remains for state pensions and public sector pensions, which amount to around £80 billion and £35 billion of annual expenditure respectively. The former benefit from a 'triple guarantee' which sees the annual increase determined by the highest of three measures: wage inflation, price inflation, or a baseline 2.5 per cent. The relevant Secretary of State, Ian Duncan Smith, need not use CPI as the measure of price inflation, nor will the issue arise until December 2013 when decisions need to be made about the increases for 2014. By convention it is *September's* figures which are used for this increase and so the impact seen in October 2012 will not be salient until then.

gilts, government bonds, held by other parties). The preference is to express PSND in relation to Gross Domestic Product rather than nominal terms. UK PSND at the time of writing is around 70 per cent of Gross Domestic Product (or £1 trillion).[11] The Coalition aimed to eliminate the 'structural deficit' by 2015/16 and thereby have PSND begin to fall in relation to GDP, as the latter was to be boosted by economic growth.

The Impact of Loans

Student loans are extremely complicated in accounting terms, and conventions have changed in recent years. The saving to BIS's departmental expenditure described above cannot simply be read across to give a reduction to the deficit in a given year. The headline statistics are based on the national accounts and things work differently there.

In brief, the impairment set aside to cover the loss on the loans does not figure in the national accounts, which instead record the relevant transactions to be covered by the impairment *when they occur*. This splits into two parts over the lifetime of the loans: an interest subsidy and the write-off subsidy. The former is 'unwound' annually, but the latter only occurs in 2046 for the new loans under discussion. In short, this means that the *immediate* reduction to the deficit as a result of the new funding regime *is greater than the saving on departmental expenditure*.

When we consider the normal narrative around deficit reduction, we would expect deficit reduction measures to slow down the increase of the debt. However, loans work differently. The government funds the Student Loans Company. New loan outlay increases the government's borrowing, while repayments received reduce it: the government funds the annual *shortfall*. (Graduate loan repayments do not count as income for the purposes of the deficit calculation.) Therefore much *higher* tuition fee loans mean more upfront borrowing to finance them and that *increases the debt* irrespective of the deficit reduction achieved.

The deficit *is* reduced, but more borrowing is required in the short and medium term until graduate repayments begin to increase.

In its November 2010 *Economic and Fiscal Outlook*, the OBR estimated that the new policy would see the *shortfall* between outlay and repayments *rise* to roughly £10 billion by 2015/16. The increase of debt attributable to higher education therefore *accelerates* in the early years of the new scheme, contributing an additional £25 billion between 2012/13 and 2017/18 inclusive.[12] (Compare this increase to the £1 billion saving from expenditure achieved annually from 2014/15.)

From this perspective, the scheme reaches what might be considered 'operational maturity' at the point when annual repayments begin to come back in significant amounts and *match* outlay on new loans. According to projections offered by BIS and by the OBR, annual repayments will not match annual outlay until sometime around the mid 2030s. In other words, *for the next 20 years, additional borrowing will have to be made to support the loan scheme.*

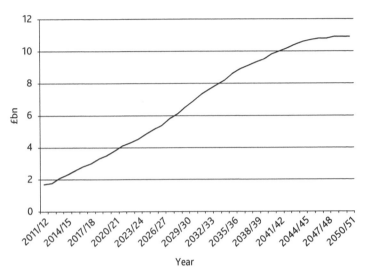

Figure 12.1   Projected repayments (£ billions, 2011 prices)

Source: data provided by BIS, Autumn 2011

Long-range Projections

The Coalition's narrative was rather short-termist, aiming to frame and rectify an economic problem before the 2015 general election. The new student loan scheme is anything but short-term: the loans have 34-year lifecycles, and the scheme only hits operational maturity sometime in the mid 2030s. In order to understand the loans from this latter perspective, we need to distinguish two aspects of the government's balance sheet which are often confused: the liabilities and the assets.

> The Liability: The borrowing the government undertakes to finance the loan scheme is the government's liability due to the loans: it is money the government *owes* to bondholders.
> The Asset: The outstanding balances on individual student loan accounts are *assets*. They are money *owed to the government*. The loan 'book' or portfolio is a *financial asset* that generates income in the form of graduate repayments.

Here are two figures to illustrate the issue. They are for the whole of the UK, not just England. Figure 12.2 is generated from data provided by the Office for Budget Responsibility.

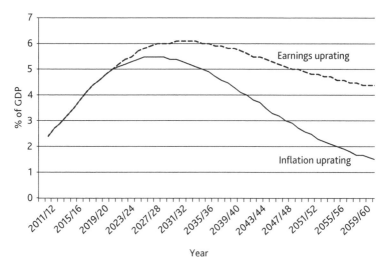

Figure 12.2   The Liability – contribution of gilts to fund student loans to debt as a percentage of GDP

Source: OBR, *Fiscal Sustainability Report*, 2012

The OBR's *Fiscal Sustainability Report* from July 2012 depicts two scenarios. With the solid line, tuition fees increase in line with inflation; with the broken line tuition fees increase in line with average earnings.[13] The OBR assumes the second, more expensive, scenario.[14] What this means is that the liability, government borrowing, peaks at just over 6 per cent of GDP in the early 2030s. The OBR estimates that this is equivalent to £94 *billion* in today's prices. In addition, on the 'earnings' scenario, the debt does not disappear but falls 'to 4.4 percent of GDP (£67 billion) by 2061–62'.

We therefore see something of a debt bubble, but one that has been obscured by the government's focus on short-term deficit reduction. Note the final date! 50 years hence!

Figure 12.3 shows the financial asset: above, the aggregated outstanding balances on individual student loan accounts; along the bottom, total annual repayments which we saw in Figure 12.1 on a different scale. Outstanding student debt, money *owed to the government*, will climb from £35 billion in 2012 to £191 billion by

2046. At this point, the outstanding amounts drop as the 30-year write-offs on individual loans kick in.

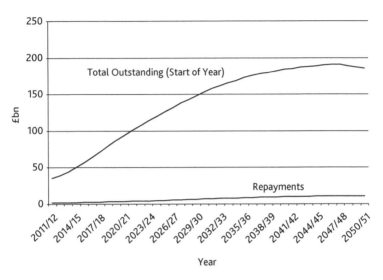

Figure 12.3 The Asset – the loan 'book' (£ billions, 2011 prices)

Source: BIS figures, 2011

People often confuse these two figures, the liability and the asset, but they are not the same. Neither in accounting terms, nor in nominal terms, since the real interest rates on student accounts create an 'interest rate spread'. Outstanding student loan balances increase faster than the government's liabilities. In addition, differing assumptions about the average level of tuition fee loans affects comparisons of the two figures. BIS (the asset, Figure 12.3) estimated the average tuition fee loan for full-time students to be £7,500, while OBR used £7,000 tuition fee loans to calculate the liability (Figure 12.2). It is not clear what underlies this discrepancy; both assumed maintenance loans of around £3,000.

Looking again at Figures 12.2 and 12.3, one could imagine that governments would be tempted to 'sweat' the asset more, so that it produces higher repayments. Those outstanding balances could more than pay down the liability. 'If only the terms on loans could be made less generous!'

From the consideration of our overarching political narrative, this may be more than a temptation. If the electorate is being told that fiscal prudence involves managing the debt (PSND) towards a

---

What is the *Loss* on the Loans?

The loss on the loans is estimated to be 32 per cent. The loss is dependent on repayments made against the original borrowing and related costs. This loss is not to be confused with the nominal aggregated amount written off on accounts which are still outstanding 30 years after repayments first fall due. I will give a simple example to explain the difference between the loss and the amount written off.

Suppose I agree to lend Mack £10 for a year on the condition that he repays me £15. I then borrow the £10 from Fred and agree to give Fred £12 in return a year later. (This is the 'interest rate spread' – the difference between what Fred charges me and what I charge Mack for the loan of £10.)

A year later, I owe £12 *to Fred* – this is my liability. But Mack owes £15 *to me* – this is my asset. Because of the interest rate spread, I should have net gain of £3.

Now suppose I only manage to get £13 from Mack and agree to 'write off' the outstanding remainder. I have written off £2 of what is owed to me, but I am able to pay back Fred and have still made £1. I *made* £1 on the deal, I did not *lose* the £2 I wrote off from Mack's account.

What if Mack only managed to repay me £9? I then need to find an additional £3 to repay Fred his £12. Now I would have *lost* £3. (For the sake of argument, perhaps Mack has died so I have to write off the £6 outstanding.) I have only covered 75 per cent of the cost that I undertook in borrowing from Fred. It is this case that is analogous to the government's situation with regard to loans: it only expects to get 68 per cent back and covers the expected shortfall by setting aside the remaining 32 per cent in expenditure in the year the loans are issued.

What this example is meant to show is that you should not confuse the sum of the outstanding balances that are scrubbed in 2046 with the *loss* to the government on the scheme.

---

target, then we should be aware *how that statistic is constructed.* Its prominence in the narrative frames political decisions.

Although PSND means *net* debt, *only* the liability due to student loans (Figure 12.2) is included in that statistic. The money *owed to* the government on outstanding balances, the asset (Figure 12.3), is excluded from the calculation – it does not 'net against' the liability.

This is because the loan book is classed as an *illiquid* financial asset: it cannot be easily turned into cash!

With only the liability included in PSND, the impact of loans on the headline statistic is *worse* than might be expected. In sum, the new higher education funding regime does not fit the political narrative offered by the Coalition: although the contribution to the deficit is reduced, the contribution to the debt is increased; although BIS departmental expenditure is reduced in the short term, it is not clear how much money the scheme saves overall or in the long run.

ESTIMATING REPAYMENTS

The models above are based on estimates of future repayments, which are then used to *estimate* overall losses. The first actual losses will not be known until 2046, but the *saving recorded today* is based on those estimates. Any variation between actual and estimate is shouldered by future governments, possibly entirely from HE budgets. This is the key risk in the scheme. The question is therefore: how reliable are the estimates of future repayments?

There are many virtues to ICR loans but they are much less predictable than traditional loans (where the amount borrowed is paid back within a fixed period with regular payments calculated accordingly). In the new funding regime, with much higher initial debts and much longer loan lifetimes, these problems are exacerbated.

We do not yet know the amount of loans the SLC will have to issue in 2012. The average tuition fees and the number of students taking out loans are the determining factors here. The government seems to have settled on a particular target: £7,500 as the average loan taken out to cover fees. (The average fee after waivers is estimated to be £8,100, but not every eligible student may take out a loan for fees, currently around 85 per cent do.) On the simplified 'ready reckoner' released by BIS, the assumption is that all graduates study for three years and leave with £35,100 of debt: this equates to £11,700 per year and therefore appears to presuppose an average annual loan for maintenance of £4,200.

We had a brief look at the IFS model in Chapter 3, which examined the distribution of repayments by career earnings. Modelling future graduate earnings and the general shape of the economy for the next 30 years is the key challenge. Typical assumptions include that the economy will revert to trend with earnings experiencing real rises

2 per cent above price inflation and that graduates will continue to prosper as they did previously.[15]

BIS uses data covering 1991 to 2008 from the British Household Survey to piece together 'salary paths' by rank, then uses the Labour Force Survey results from 2001 to 2009 to construct an earnings path in 2009 terms, before using OBR projections of the economy to create a path in nominal terms (relevant in relation to the repayment threshold from 2016 and beyond).[16]

Critics of the government scheme see the official projections as based on over-optimistic assessments of the economy and graduate salaries, particularly in relation to the lower graduate earners who are unlikely to experience the same annual increases as those who enter the highly paid professions (see Figure 12.4).

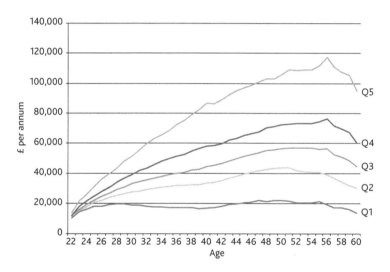

Figure 12.4   Average graduate salary path by quintile

Source: Nicholas Barr and Alison Johnson, 'Interest subsidies on student loans: A better class of drain', Discussion Paper 114, London School of Economics: Centre for the Economics of Education, March 2010 (using IFS data)

The IFS, whose figures the government feels 'vindicate' its scheme, has estimated the non-repayment at 33 per cent, slightly above the government's current estimate. However, IFS have also produced a 'pessimistic' modelling scenario, where average earnings growth is only 1.5 per cent in real terms: there non-repayment increases to 37 per cent. Hepi point out that the IFS 'pessimistic' scenario is closer to the current OBR estimates about future graduate salaries.[17] 37 per cent also tallies with modelling produced by London Economics.[18] Since the annual loan outlay is roughly £10 billion, small percentage shifts of this kind translate into hundreds of millions of pounds. Hepi see an additional £680 million per year of costs resulting from this difference between a non-repayment rate of 30 per cent and one of 37.[19]

Although the IFS believe that the 'graduate age-earnings structures' they use 'appear remarkably stable over time' and that these dynamics will 'continue into the future' for their model, their report twice warns that the focus of the model and the report is the distributional impact across a population, not the *sustainability* of the scheme.[20] In the technical Appendix, the authors write:

It is worth emphasising that *our earnings simulations are not predictions of the future*; they are instead simulations based on a series of assumptions. Predicting the earnings of future graduates poses more severe challenges, in particular because the distribution of earnings of future graduates is likely to change due to underlying changes in the economy, and also may itself be affected by the reforms, for a number of reasons.[21]

This is an important point. The more sophisticated a model is in terms of its population, the more susceptible it may be to changes in that population (career salary paths) in real life.

Real life intervenes in one further respect. In Chapter 3, we saw how Willetts was keen to justify the scheme through the manner in which the burden on those in their twenties and thirties is alleviated by the higher repayment threshold. An effect of that decision is that more repayments are made later in the loan lifecycle. Figure 12.4 illustrates this feature of the new scheme. With repayments further into the future, predicting rates of return becomes harder. It may not be apparent for some time how well the loans are likely to perform. This could mean that several cohorts have been launched on terms where the impairments set aside to cover non-repayment are insufficient.

The government has repeatedly emphasised that forecasting repayments decades hence is a difficult and imprecise job and that the assumptions they use are 'not unreasonable'. But as I emphasised in an exchange with Willetts in the pages of *Times Higher Education*, the responsible approach to relative unpredictability involves differentiating the estimated loss *from the 'impairment' put aside in the accounts to cover it*.[22] One might use a higher figure for the impairment to allow for contingency. Otherwise it is a future departmental budget that will likely have to absorb any adjustments.

Note that whether the impairment adequately covers future liabilities is a matter separate from whether the reforms make savings. For example, if student numbers decline so that fewer loans are issued there would be a substantial saving, but if the impairment is based on 30 per cent non-repayment and it turns out to be 37 per cent, then a future HE budget would likely have to make good the difference.

The Treasury is maintaining one 'hedge' against this potential problem. It charges BIS RPI + 2.2 per cent for access to the lending needed to finance student loans. Its own cost is much lower – currently even below RPI. This current, temporary interest rate spread affords the Treasury some protection against the liability, but at present *it does not benefit the departmental budget.*

Calls for loans to be extended to support postgraduate education need to be reconsidered in light of these factors. But it is not as if governments will wait and see what will happen. There are options for actively managing these associated risks, and these are the focus of the next chapter.

13
Managing the Loan Book

Uncertainty hovers over the new higher education funding regime. However, this government and those to come have the means to manage this uncertainty, even if they are not tempted to completely overhaul the set-up.

Governments are not going allow the build up of potential long-run problems. Some within government expect the new market conditions to exert sufficient competitive pressure so as to drive down fees and lower the cost of the loan scheme. In the interim, the tight control on numbers and fees is likely to continue. Alternatively, cuts could be made to other parts of the higher education budget to compensate for the ballooning borrowing associated with the loan book.

There are several other options here: changing the terms on loans; managing institutions; attempting to sell the loans to third parties.

CHANGING THE TERMS ON LOANS

As discussed in Chapter 3, changing the terms on the loan book for future borrowers is almost to be expected. We have already seen five variants on loans since they were introduced in 1990 (two types of mortgage-style, and three kinds of ICR loan).

The least controversial change would be to freeze the £21,000 repayment threshold in 2017. This would succeed in generating higher levels of repayment without much effort. Indeed, the new regulations have been drafted without any reference to the promised annual up-rating. The current government insists that it is its intention to enact this measure, but that it does not yet need to do so. In which case, it requires whatever government we have in 2016/17 to make the necessary amendment, if they wish to keep to the promise made to the Liberal Democrats in December 2010.

Should such freezing prove insufficient, and the scheme still remains too generous to borrowers, then there will be calls to rectify the situation. We should not underestimate the ideological impact of individual loan accounts with large outstanding balances.

A discourse around 'deadbeats' could see low-earning graduates brought into repayments.

The latest British Social Attitudes survey shows a diminishing sympathy for 'social transfers', and we should not treat the write-off subsidy as immune to these considerations.[1] We have seen far more contentious policies carried out under the guise of necessary austerity since the Coalition came to power. Most importantly, the write-offs are not implemented until several years hence.

Although such changes would alter the distributional effect and the progressive claims for the loan scheme, a suspicious mind might expect a clever two-step. Sell a generous loan scheme to the public, Coalition partners and Parliament, only to make it far less generous when its lack of viability becomes apparent. In this way a scheme that would not have got approval in one go is achieved in two bounds.

MANAGING INSTITUTIONS

More subtle pressure can be placed on universities themselves. The relationship of debt and repayment is between the graduate and the SLC; in so far as one considers universities and colleges, their role in this financial dance might seem to end once they have managed to recruit and see the students through each year in order to collect the fees. Finding ways to bring universities back into the circle is one policy aim.

A generalised loan system has a significant feature: loans generate information. Loans go out into the world and one can measure how they return through repayments. The money moves in different ways – public subsidy is now via individuals not direct to institutions – but that detour is productive in terms of data. Because these patterns are accompanied by a £ sign, we have the first indications of a new powerful performance indicator.

In Chapter 12, we discussed the overall non-repayment rate within the loan scheme. Earlier we looked at repayment rates by sex and by earnings deciles. But repayments can be examined another way. Data on repayments can be examined by institution and even, apparently, by course.

Back in May 2011, Willetts wrote in an article for *Times Higher Education* arguing that the 'RAB charge' would be at the 'core of university financing for many years'.

I expect that, in the future, *as the data accrue, the policy debate will be about the RAB [non-repayment] charge for individual institutions*. One reason why we were not able to accept Browne's ingenious idea of a levy on higher fees is that it was indiscriminate and did not reflect the actual Exchequer risk from lending to students at *specific universities*.[2] (my emphasis)

All along the government has been opposed to a graduate tax, or other tax solution, because it would not create a market with differential fees. Here we have an indication as to why the Browne review was rejected, somewhat disingenuously: it did not have the same ability to individuate institutions such that the repayment rates of their graduates could be monitored.

As opposed to the headline price of fees which confronts the student or applicant, the government confronts different non-repayment rates for different institutions as the Exchequer cost. How is such a measure possible? One method has been outlined by the economist Tim Leunig, who suggests that the data the SLC receives from HMRC could be cross-referenced with the UCAS records for the same individuals.[3] On this basis one could create actuarial style tables matching repayment records to university, course and 'A-level or other academic attainment'. Another economist, Neil Shephard, has been given access to the SLC dataset to see what can be devised from it. Willetts has expressed his 'incredible frustration' that these measures are not yet robust and available.[4]

In this vein, a recent government document announced that:

2.2.12 ... we have worked with the Office for National Statistics to introduce a new question into the Labour Force Survey which will, in time, allow analysis of long-run earnings outcomes from specific institutions.[5]

If Leunig's method does not work, then this might (it might also have overcome the shortcomings Willetts espied in the Browne levy). The main factors determining Exchequer exposure are the level of fees set at an institution and the earnings of its graduates. By assessing both, the government could get a sense of the risk, which could easily be reinterpreted as taxpayer's 'value for money': 'Should we fund this degree course at this university given how little the graduates repay?'

This could work in both positive and negative ways. Universities with low risk might be allowed to set higher fees or have numbers controls relaxed. Universities with poor performances might face sanctions. Under the new powers and duties proposed for Hefce we find: 'A *duty* to ensure not only the proper use of HEFCE's own funding but also that of publicly backed student loans as an essential part of the system to help manage overall government expenditure on higher education' and the power 'to suspend or remove a provider's designation for student support [loans] or HEFCE teaching grant'[6] (my emphasis).

From the Treasury or policy perspective, one can see the attraction: it provides another lever by which to intervene in the decisions universities make. Universities would then be asked to consider lowering their fees or enacting measures designed to boost graduate earning profiles (perhaps by shedding courses which do not perform so well).

The threat of the sanction would prove to be stronger than the execution. Accordingly, loans provide the regulator or government with the means to limit the independence of institutions. On the one hand, loans enable privatisation and, in theory, remove the need for centrally allocated numbers controls, but on the other hand, they empower the centre.

FINANCIALISATION

I use the term 'financialisation' to analyse education in a distinct manner. Generally, the term is used to indicate the domination of finance capital in the modern economy, everyday life, corporate practices, services and production. Here, I use it to show how a public good, education, is placed within a system of accounts via the novel use of data, accounting techniques and political disciplining.

In the UK, public services have been subject to systematic review by management consultants led by McKinsey. Their motto? 'Everything can be measured and what gets measured gets managed.' As De Angelis and Harvie note: 'public managers seek to measure academic labour with criteria that are predicated on values other than the values of teaching, researching and the collective production of ideas and thinking'.[7] Best of all, they would like to measure academic labour in terms of finance.

The fee and loans system brings that possibility closer: students/graduates are the bearer of the unit of accounting. Their passage through the system generates the quantified cost outcomes which enable future forms of public policy intervention.

Roger Burrows summarised the shift to accountability through audit and reporting in academia with the following list of measures bearing upon the individual academic:

> One could, for example: ... publish in journals with an average 'impact factor' of Y; have an undergraduate teaching load below the institutional norm; have a PhD supervision load that is about average; have an annual grant income in the top quartile for the social sciences; work within an academic agglomeration with a 2008 RAE result that places it within the 'top 5' nationally; receive module student evaluation scores in the top quartile of a distribution; work within a school with 'poor' NSS results, placing it in the bottom quartile for the subject nationally; teach a subject where only Z per cent of graduates are in 'graduate' employment 6 months after they graduate, earning an average of just £18,500; work within a higher education institute that is ranked in the 'top 10' nationally in various commercially driven 'league tables', and within the 'top 80' globally, according to others.[8]

Beyond all these, the non-repayment rate associated with a particular course at a particular institution would be the one measure to rule them all. Financing will achieve what direct government control could not, through these more insidious methods, and it will appear that universities are doing it to themselves. The pull of access to the loan scheme may be so strong that institutional autonomy becomes a chimera.

Consider this. I meet many current or soon-to-be students who do not believe they will ever earn enough to begin repaying their loans. 'So why worry about the debt?' Hopefully, I have outlined what could happen: one, that the repayment threshold may move relative to earnings; two, if too many of your peers take the same attitude then certain courses may be deemed to be unviable for loans. This is a particular threat for courses such as philosophy and art and design. The impact may not be felt on the individuals quoted, but on future cohorts who are deprived of certain subjects to study, since they may only be offered at private institutions.

SELLING THE LOAN PORTFOLIO

The third major option for managing the risk or exposure on student loans involves a tale of frustration for this government and the previous one. Both investigated and prepared for selling the new income contingent repayment loans but have been unable to do so. Recounting this somewhat obscure history may give some indications of likely future attempts.

As originally conceived by Milton Friedman, these loans would best be offered by insurance companies or pension funds, but if none were willing to come forward then the government could intervene to create the market and so ensure that there was no 'underinvestment in human capital'. The most important consideration for independent loan schemes is the difficulty and expense of collecting repayments and ensuring that borrowers do not default or disappear: these are loans which are unsecured, they are not backed by any physical collateral that the bank could claim under such eventualities.

One could envisage an independent loan scheme paying the SLC to act as factor on its behalf so as to benefit from the HMRC payroll collection, and this is perhaps the most likely option were any established universities to decide to 'go independent'. This problem is however distinct from underwriting a scheme such as the government's, which is not designed to generate a surplus. Friedman's idea was that such loans would be self-financing and even profitable. In contrast, the progressive and generous loan scheme extolled by the government entails a loss: the risk to the government is that the loss might be bigger than anticipated.

In recent years, governments have looked into the possibility of getting third parties to issue student loans. As one internal government report put it: 'Third party origination of new loans would present a *permanent de-risking*' (my emphasis).[9] Most recently, Santander reported that it had met with Coalition representatives to discuss an independent loan scheme but that talks did not progress. According to Steve Smith, this was because the bank was seeking a guarantee from the government to underwrite non-repayment: precisely the risk that independent loans are supposed to remove! Banks had made similar demands back in the 1980s when loans were first mooted by Kenneth Baker.[10]

An alternative is for the government to issue the loans but find third-party *purchasers* to defray or remove entirely the risk associated with, as the same internal report puts it, 'the growing portfolio of Income-Contingent Repayment student loans on the Government's balance sheet'. Any proposed sale must structure the transaction so that 'sufficient risk and control will be transferred'.[11] Ideally, an 'outright' sale would be the preferred option, but there are impediments to this. We should ask why any purchaser would want to buy what the government is trying to sell. The government has the lowest cost of borrowing and so in the long run would be most likely to generate the best return. By examining the only previous sales of student loans, we may gain some insight into the motivations behind the sale and the structuring of such deals: especially why the government might be prepared to offer a discount or subsidy to the purchaser.

PREVIOUS SALES OF STUDENT LOANS

In the late 1990s, in the early days of the Blair government, two £1 billion tranches of 'mortgage-style' student loans were sold to third parties: Finance for Higher Education Limited, a subsidiary of NatWest, and Honours Trustee Limited, a consortium formed by Nationwide Building Society and Deutsche Bank AG. These loans were for maintenance costs only and had a fixed repayment period of five years once the very generous earnings threshold was crossed.[12] Importantly, this made repayments more predictable than for ICR loans.

Although the full details of the sale are not public, announcements in the House of Commons at the time mean that we know that the government committed to paying an annual subsidy to the purchaser. These subsidies were expected *to exceed* the costs of keeping the loans on the government's balance sheet by roughly *£140 million.*[13]

That is, the government received £2 billion from the purchasers but agreed in return to pay annual subsidies that were estimated to amount to £750 million over the lifetime of the loans. Initially, about £120 million went out in the first annual subsidy but these payments diminished as the loans were repaid. In 2007, a written parliamentary answer estimated the repayments to amount to £635 million in 1998/99 terms. This was lower than originally estimated but at that stage the government had also revised down its discount rate from 6.0 per cent to 3.5 per cent. The cost was therefore revised to £125 million at that stage. (I only paid off my loan, part of these tranches, in March 2012, meaning we have another five years of subsidies to consider.)

The key statement was made by Kim Howells speaking about the first tranche in March 1998:

My right hon. Friend the Chancellor of the Exchequer said in his statement of 10 July 1997 that we would continue the policy of student loan debt sales as part of our pledge to work within the spending plans already announced for this year and next. The sale also underlines our commitment to developing a wide range of public-private partnerships which involve a transfer of risk to the private sector. This sale transfers to the private sector much of the risk of loans defaulting.[14]

There are a few points to pull out of this. First, the spending plans and Brown's two rules, one Golden, were framed around headline public sector finance statistics, as the then Chancellor tried to create an approach to economic policy that was 'open and accountable, based on clearly established rules and discipline'.[15] Tight departmental controls for the first two years of the New Labour administration meant that the income generated from the sales helped Brown meet his 'Golden Rule': that income and expenditure should balance over the economic cycle.

At the time, student loans were treated very differently in the accounts: annual loan outlay was entirely classed as expenditure and graduate repayments as receipts.[16] With the bulk of those receipts somewhere in the future, one could see the attraction of taking £2 billion upfront, and thereby alleviating the short-term restraints, in return for an ongoing annual payment. The resonance with Public Finance Initiatives (PFI) also points to the rationale: the risk of loan default is translated into an annual fee which is more predictable.

Similarly, Brown's 'sustainable investment' rule meant that PSND should not rise above 40 per cent of GDP. Even under different accounting conventions today, one could still see an incentive to take the borrowing used to fund the SLC (the liability) off the balance sheet, particularly as the asset, the loan book, is illiquid and therefore does not feature in the calculation around which an 'open and accountable' policy has been constructed.

The present government has committed to a political narrative of deficit reduction and a slowdown in the growth of PSND relative to GDP. Since loans add so much to borrowing in the short and medium term, finding a way to shift that debt off the balance sheet makes sense politically even if it is arguably economically illiterate. The government may be prepared to take a *fixed* loss in return for reducing the liability on the balance sheet. In terms of risk management, that 32 per cent estimate of non-repayment would be translated into *actual* expenditure, in so far as it appears as an agreed and fixed subsidy or discount on sale, rather than a *provision* in the accounts for future *uncertain* losses.

One potential analogy is the recent sale to Virgin Money of the banking arm of nationalised Northern Rock. Virgin's purchase provided the government with £750 million in 2011 plus potential further payments over the coming years. In terms of overall asset value, the government may have made a loss in the region of £400 million, but as with student loans, the *illiquid* asset has been turned into money. Again, associated liabilities, which do appear in PSND calculation (unlike the asset value), have been removed.

INCOME CONTINGENT REPAYMENT LOANS

Things work differently for income contingent repayment loans, but similar general considerations should apply when considering why the government would be keen on such deals. The key legislation is the 2008 Sale of Student Loans Act brought in by the Labour government.[17] This Act enables the government, technically the relevant Secretary of State, to sell loans to third parties without consultation and without the consent of the borrower. That said, third parties are not able to change the terms and conditions of the loans: no sale can make any borrower worse off nor would purchasers have the powers to change terms. Loans can however be sold subsequently, onwards to fourth and fifth parties, etc., unless the Secretary of State intervenes.

Following the Act, a programme was initiated to achieve sales worth £6 billion in 2008/09 and 2010/11. The idea was to set up a regular and sustainable schedule of sales that would 'continue indefinitely'.[18] The legislation allows loans to be sold in 'tranches' and permits the subsidies to purchasers discussed above in relation to the previous sales. The preferred option at the time was not an 'outright' sale, given the sums involved, but a securitisation-based model (see Chapter 10). The loans would be repackaged through bonds that investors would purchase in return for a share of graduate repayments. One can judge from the dates that all this was being prepared just as the financial crash began to gum up the system. The programme was suspended in 2009 and its planned form abandoned.

In late 2009, the Labour government decided to seek specialist financial advice about 'alternative routes to market'. It was envisaged that a specialist banking consultant would produce a report on options to accompany the Browne review which was also set up at this time. A tender document was published in April 2010 which is reproduced here (see Box).

Procurement Document[19]

The Department for Business Innovation and Skills ('The Department') is evaluating options for a potential sale of its existing £25bn income-contingent student loan portfolio ('The Portfolio').

The Advisor's role would be to advise in the development and assessment of a repeatable sales programme and the potential implementation of the first sale.

The role of the Advisor would cover the feasibility and implementation stages of the transaction and specifically would comprise:

- Conducting detailed financial and credit analysis of The Portfolio
- Developing and structuring a repeatable model for sale
- Evaluating the associated policy, commercial, legal and other risks to, and implications for, the Government
- Assessing market appetite
- Obtaining a credit rating on the proposed structure
- Establishing appropriate governance, legal and servicing arrangements
- Potential implementation of the first sale

The Advisor would be offered the right to compete in a separate and subsequent procurement process in order to appoint institutions to find buyers for any financial instruments that may be issued as part of the sale process.

An Advisor must be able to demonstrate a track record of successfully structuring relevant transactions; provide unbiased, independent advice; provide deep market intelligence; and devote an experienced team to the transaction.

The Coalition appointed Rothschild to the task in May 2010. Its feasibility study has not been released, but had cost the government £700,000 by February 2011. In June that year, the White Paper seemed optimistic that a solution could be devised and that the loan book could be 'monetised': that is, generate significant cash sooner than waiting for the repayments to increase.

The principles of any sale were set out as follows:

We want to find a solution that will manage all current and future ICR loans on an ongoing basis (unlike the one-off sales of the late 1990s). It is fundamental to us that under any solution borrowers would be placed in no worse a position as a result of a transfer of their loans. If the portfolio is sold, further conditions must be met. In particular any sale would need to reduce significantly government's risk exposure to the loan book and represent value for money for the tax payer.[20]

Again, the main aim is to reduce the risk associated with repayments being lower than estimated but that an 'ongoing' or 'repeatable' model would be developed in contrast to the retrospective or 'one-off' sales discussed earlier.

The White Paper and the procurement document indicate the government's interest in an 'originate-to-distribute' model. A 'full range of options' was being considered which included outright sale and 'selling loans to one or more regulated companies set up to manage the loans'.[21] This indicates that each year's new loans could be sold to a 'special purpose vehicle' which could slice or segment the loan book into marketable products for investors.

Like an outright sale this would generate income to offset the borrowing needed to originate the loans (the liability), with investors getting an annual income stream in return for their money. The challenge would have been to match the product to a buyer with a different set of preferences to the government.

RECENT DEVELOPMENTS

However, the challenge seems to have proved too much for Rothschild and BIS. Although the government had been committed to selling off at least part of the loan book,[22] by June 2012 the government's response to the White Paper consultations indicated that it was focusing on the 'pre-Browne' loans. This is a weird shorthand for the loans issued prior to September 2012. As such, we are looking at 'retrospective' sales that they claimed to be aiming to avoid with the new structure.

A Freedom of Information request from the Chaminda Jayanetti at False Economy elicited the following response from BIS: 'A disclosure of the information requested at this stage may also adversely affect BIS's bargaining position during contractual negotiations should a sale proceed which would result in a less effective use of public money.' Later that month it became apparent that the government might only be considering the sale of the final tranche of old 'mortgage style' loans. Willetts told the BIS Select Committee in July 2012 that the ICR loans 'were not a priority'.

As things currently stand, the outstanding balances on ICR loan accounts have already reached £40 billion. The old-style mortgage loans hold a fraction of that, only £750 *million* (under 2 per cent of the ICR value). Given the age of these loans and the terms on which they were issued, any proposed sale will look like the off-loading of bad loans to a debt collector, rather than an *investment* product solution.

Can we surmise from all this that there is a fundamental flaw in the plans to sell off the loans? Admittedly, ICR loans are unusual and investors may be unable to price them with any confidence given the lack of history, or more importantly, datasets, here. The generosity of the scheme with such high losses presents a further challenge.

A sale might be constructed using a large discount or subsidy, but too big and it no longer represents taxpayer value for money. Given that £140 million was required as a subsidy to sell off £2 billion of old loans, what would be needed to monetise a loan book based on issuing over £10 billion every year?

It may be possible to develop a market over time by selling tranches of the most secure, investment grade graduates – doctors or Oxbridge graduates – but this may be politically unacceptable and it would anyway leave government with the rump of non-repayment risk, which is what any sale is meant to dispose of. However if it is really serious, the government would have to act as market maker here, cultivating an appetite and understanding for such products. Or, alternatively, change the current loan terms and thereby reduce the estimated losses, so that attractive investment products can be developed.

An additional problem with securitisation is that it might not sufficiently remove the loans and their associated risk from the balance sheet. Selling investors *the right to a share of income, rather than the loans outright*, is likely to mean that the loan book remains 'on-book' in terms of national accounts classification, especially if the 'special purpose vehicle' that concocts the debt products is arms-length, and owned by government, rather than fully independent.[23]

At root, attempts to sell the loan book generate the same effects of 'financialisation': any investment product would depend on positioning individual graduates as units of account.

CONCLUSION

This survey of broader policy issues is meant to illustrate that loans have significance beyond the question of how they support higher tuition fees or how they serve to open up markets.

With the Labour Party considering its future higher education policy, we need to move the debate beyond whether the maximum tuition fee is £6,000 or £9,000 and force them to recognise that these forms of financing education have much more profound implications than whether a few billion of savings can be cobbled together.

The technocratic dream of self-financing, revenue neutral, student loans passed on to investors in an 'originate-to-distribute' model might seem to fix the financing problem, but also fixes education within a system of accounts that has far more profound implications.

An economic policy driven through headline finance statistics may lead to decision-making around the loan portfolio that may be in nobody's true interests. Financialisation restores powers to the state and its agents on the back of apparent liberalisation.

Conclusion

What does this tour through the backrooms of higher education policy achieve? Hopefully, this account of various piecemeal measures adds up to a bigger picture. To some it may appear more of a shambles than a gamble, but that is to miss the manner in which the game is rigged. The gamble is that the creative destruction of mass higher education as currently provided will be worth it in the longer run.

Education is being re-engineered by stealth through a directed process of market construction, each move designed to protect the elite and expose the majority. At the same time, the gamble involves running the risk of subprime degrees. Existing quality assurance, which has its faults, is supplanted by 'value for money', a 'risk-based' system, and a regulator tasked with promoting competition. Caveat emptor!

The vision has not been put to the public or Parliament. The key reform – the large-scale cuts to the direct public funding of universities and colleges – was achieved by the 2010 Comprehensive Spending Review. A temporary budgetary measure presented as necessary owing to the state of the nation's finances is, in fact, central to a new vision for a marketplace in undergraduate provision. Further progress has been made through instructions to unaccountable quangos, the use of existing powers and secondary legislation or statutory instruments that in themselves grant little opportunity for scrutiny or contestation.

The market extends beyond Willetts's credo, 'I plead guilty to believing in choice and competition',[1] to privatisation: new private providers are encouraged to enter the sector, established charitable institutions must become more commercial and more corporate in their governance, new opportunities are created for private equity. All the while, generalised loan financing weaves its insidious effects through the fabric of higher level teaching and study.

Poor quality may already exist out amongst the courses 'designated' through the shadow scheme for 'student support'. Without a Higher Education Bill, this looks set to expand. *With* a Higher Education Bill, we will see obscure clauses designed to lift the impediments to for-profit expansion: by granting Pearson/

Edexcel, an institution that does no teaching, the power to award degrees; by making it easier for universities to 'adopt a legal form of their choosing'; or completing the process of creating a level playing field for profiteering (VAT exemption and formalising access to student support).

Many of the commercial and market initiatives appear consistent with the Mandelson BIS years. Many of the existing powers being abused by Willetts and co were brought into statute by the Labour administration (most strikingly, the Sale of Student Loans Act). That said, it is the cosy relationship with private equity and preference for profit-driven endeavours which marks out this BIS team.

In the short-term, political activity and organisation needs to be reactive, preventing the unfettered advent of any primary legislation designed to achieve the above. Similarly, any framework that continues to allow the regulatory and legal arbitrage around 'not-for-profit' status is largely worthless: regulation must be devised at the level of group structures.

On the ground, the possibility of 'buyout' looms, especially amongst the companies limited by guarantee, with London Metropolitan now in prime position thanks to the Home Office and UKBA.

But of most concern and least addressed directly in this book is the impact on university staff. This new phase of reforms cannot be resisted from the classroom: good teaching practice will hardly mitigate the new pressures accumulating.

Academics, barely mentioned in the White Paper, seem about to be squeezed by the demands of new student-consumers and the pressures from management to become more efficient, productive and therefore profitable. On some views, they are simply frontline delivery staff, an overhead to be reduced. Staff in other parts of the university know only too well the threats from outsourcing and paring service provision to make efficiency savings.

This is exacerbated by a failure of academics, in particular, to properly defend their profession: pressed by workloads and atomised through research assessment, yes, but too willing to cede difficult chores to bureaucrats. The 'self-critical community of scholars', which is meant to safeguard degree standards, has been eroded to a large extent by an expansionist executive and managerial class, who will now have a new range of performance metrics with which to discipline more and more pliable academics. Collegiality has been displaced by corporatism.

Deprofessionalisation of this kind is a persistent th
privatisation agendas. Casualisation of staff is th
of cheap, for-profit provision, where staff are less
self-directed study groups without supervision are a tea.
'contact time' at some US operations. Of course, there is also a
reserve army of labour, post-docs and PhD students, who are willing
to work for lower wages.

'Affordable' mass higher education may cut corners in a number
of ways; there is enthusiasm about the potential for online learning
to provide 'disruption' to the standard pedagogical practices and
cut staffing requirements further. As Diane Ravitch points out in
a secondary school context, poor students will get computers, the
rich get computers *and* teachers.[2]

That said, at this stage, 'platforms' for revenue generation are
more likely to aim at expanding into a global market, through
distance learning accreditation, than replacing expensive staff
domestically (UK and US).[3] This is why UK degree awarding powers
are such a desirable asset: it is for these that Montagu Private Equity
purchased The College of Law, not because it believes it can run it
more efficiently (see Chapter 10).

Though the general effects may prove hard to predict, the
contours of the emerging market will make decisions about quality
central. There is no requirement on the regulator to concern itself
with disparities and polarisation ('equality of opportunity' – or
meritocracy as talent spotting, 'fairly rationing' limited opportunities
– is not equivalent to social equality).

Any worthwhile alternative also involves a longer range struggle:
one that makes the case and fights for mass higher education not as
'value for money' but as a quality commitment to the population
defined as whoever can benefit. It argues for a breadth of provision
both in terms of subjects offered but also in terms of the content
of those subjects, contesting the demand-led homogenisation of
education and maintaining critical and advanced content.

As a corollary, we must seek more participative provision,
structures and institutions. Neither markets nor remote quangos
provide democratic accountability. Universities and colleges face a
loss of goodwill in so far as commercial imperatives and market
positioning are seen to dovetail with the government's agenda of
polarisation, stratification and the *sorting* of individuals. Few areas
of the public policy reveal the endemic resentments that befoul
education. These threaten to erupt under new pressures.

In contrast, a democracy less beholden to corporate interests ought to be focusing on transforming mass provision through more participative institutions less focused on capturing the market in the 35 to 40 per cent of 18 year olds going away from home. Universities and colleges should be more concerned with local and civic society, providing the opportunity for lifelong, flexible and repeated engagement with education. Regional, civic and local vitality depends on a profound reorientation in this regard and needs to resist 'social mobility' cast as regional exodus.

These are the issues on which we ought to be focusing, not the exact level of the maximum tuition fee cap.

So the book ends where I hope proper public debate, new ideas and resistance will burgeon. My aim has been simply to provide a guide to what is occurring and to persuade you that we should not settle for what will result. This primer might appear bleak, but it is animated by optimism.

Glossary

1994 Group A group of 19 research-intensive universities founded in 1994. The member institutions are smaller than the **Russell Group** in terms of income generation.

AAB+ Applicants who achieve AAB or better at A level (or equivalent). Roughly 79,000 applicants achieved this level in the 2012 entry cycle. See Chapter 5.

Access agreements A publicly funded higher education institution wishing to charge over £6,000 per year in tuition fees must enter into an 'access agreement' with Offa. This outlines how the institution will promote access to university level study and help such students to complete.

Association of Colleges The lobbying body for Further Education colleges.

Articulation arrangements A form of partnership arrangement. A higher education institution agrees to automatically accept students from another course (possibly at another institution) who achieve a set standard in assessment. A student may be able to enter the higher level programme at an advanced stage (e.g., the third year of an undergraduate degree). See Chapter 6.

Band A, B, C and D A categorisation of subjects depending on how costly they are to deliver. See Chapter 2.

Business, Innovation and Skills (BIS) The current government department with responsibility for universities. The Secretary of State in charge is the Liberal Democrat MP, Vince Cable.

Board of governors The body responsible for overseeing the governance of the institution. It can have alternative titles at other institutions, such as Council. To be distinguished from the **executive** who are responsible for the day to day operation of the institution.

Browne review The independent review into higher education financing led by John Browne (Lord Browne of Madingley), the former chief executive of BP. The report, *Securing A Sustainable Future for Higher Education*, appeared in 2010 and presaged the current set of higher education reforms.

BTEC The name for a range of qualifications offered by the for-profit examination board, Edexcel (owned by Pearson). BTEC refers to the former vocational examination board, the Business and Technology Education Council, a precursor to Edexcel.

Bonds A means of raising private investment capital through debt. See Chapter 10.

Chartered corporation A type of corporate form associated with universities formed by Royal Charter. See Chapter 9.

Clearing The process by which unplaced applicants find available undergraduate places after each year's A-level results have been published in August.

Council for National Academic Awards (CNAA) The body formerly responsible for overseeing and awarding degrees at polytechnics. Abolished in 1992. See Chapter 6.

Core The new form of controls on recruitment introduced for 2012. The core determines the number of Home and EU undergraduate students (with grades below **AAB**) an institution is able to recruit annually. See Chapter 5. See also **Margin**.

Company limited by guarantee A *private* corporate form enjoyed by around 20 higher education institutions in England. Examples include London School of Economics and London Metropolitan University.

Consumer Price Index (CPI) A measure of inflation. The rise in tuition fees will have an impact on CPI. See Chapter 12.

Comprehensive Spending Review (CSR) The review of government spending conducted by the Coalition government. Its results were announced in October 2010; it included the large cuts to the institutional block grants used to fund to undergraduate education.

Degree Awarding Powers (DAPs) The 'degree' is a protected qualification title. Only specific institutions have been granted the power to award them, in the majority of cases by Royal Charter or statute. The **Privy Council** currently oversees the process by which institutions can apply for the powers. There are four classes of powers: foundation, undergraduate, taught postgraduate and research.

The Debt The amount of money the government or nation owes: its liabilities. Typically this refers to the Public Sector Net Debt, a measure of liabilities offset against liquid assets. By convention, it is expressed as a percentage of Gross Domestic Product.

The Deficit The amount by which expenditure exceeds income over a determinate period, typically a year. If income exceeds expenditure, a surplus is produced.

'Designated courses' / Designation Private HE providers are able to seek 'designation' from BIS on a course by course basis. Students on designated courses are able to access **student support**. They can access maintenance grants and loans on the same basis as students at established higher education institutions and up to £6,000 per year towards tuition fees. See Chapter 7.

Education Maintenance Allowance (EMA) A means-tested payment made to those aged 16–18 to meet some of the associated costs of staying on in formal education past the school leaving age. It was abolished in 2011.

Exempt charities The majority of universities are not required to register with the Charity Commission. Their public benefit objectives are monitored by **Hefce** and they face fewer restrictions in financial dealings, especially with regard to mortgages and the disposal of assets.

Education Reform Act (1988) The Act which removed polytechnics from Local Education Authority control to create the quasi-public **higher education corporations**.

External degrees Degrees offered by higher education institutions open to anyone who pays to take the examinations (or other modes of assessment). Candidates do not register as students and do not receive tuition from the institution, but make such arrangements privately. See Chapter 6.

Executive Senior management who are responsible for the day to day operation of the university or college, typically led by a **vice-chancellor**.

Fee waivers A reduction in the headline tuition fees offered either as part of **access arrangements** or on the basis of merit.

Financialisation Here, the placing of education into a system of accounting. See Part 4.

For-profit An institution where profits are distributed either to owners or other investors (for shareholders, in the form of dividends).

Franchise arrangements A form of partnership arrangement where a course designed and developed by one institution is delivered by another.

Further and Higher Education Act (1992) The legislation which transformed polytechnics into universities granting those institutions their own degree awarding powers and ending the binary arrangement for funding higher education.

Gross Domestic Product (GDP) A measure of the nation's annual economic output.

GuildHE A 'mission group' aiming for diversity of provision in HE. Its members comprise institutions which have achieved the university title since 2000 or HEIs without university status. Its members and associates also include some private providers, such as Ravensbourne, American Intercontinental University (a **for-profit**), and Anglo-European College of Chiropractic.

HE in FE The term covering the delivery of higher education within further education colleges whether by franchise and validation arrangements or through the Pearson HNCs and HNDs.

Higher Education Funding Council for England (Hefce) The body responsible for distributing grant funding for taught degrees and research money resulting from the **RAE** and **REF** exercises. Under current proposals, Hefce will move from being the main HE funding body to being the main regulator of the new market.

Higher Education Corporation (HEC) A quasi-public form of statutory corporation assumed by many former polytechnics as a result of the 1988 **Education Reform Act**.

Human Capital Theory A theory developed by Milton Freidman and Gary Becker that sees vocational and professional training as analogous to the investment a company might make in physical capital. An individual improves his or her productivity through investing in training.

Highly Trusted Sponsor (HTS) A status accorded to institutions allowing them to sponsor non-EU students for visas under the Tier 4 immigration scheme.

Higher National Certificate (HNC) A qualification offered by Edexcel in England equivalent to the first year of an undergraduate degree.

Higher National Diploma (HND) A qualification offered by Edexcel in England equivalent to the second year of an undergraduate degree.

Income Contingent Repayment (ICR) loans Loans where the size of repayments are determined by the *income* of the borrower. This is in contrast to fixed term repayment loans, where repayments are determined by the amount borrowed and the period by which the loan and associated interest must be repaid. See Chapter 3.

Key Information Sets (KIS) Mandatory information to be provided by institutions about the courses they offer. See Chapters 4 and 6.

London weighting A sum or proportion of grant paid to institutions to reflect the higher costs of operating in London.

Maintenance loans and grants Funding available to individuals to contribute to accommodation and living costs while studying.

Margin A pool of 20,000 places open to tender. Only institutions offering average fees after waivers under £7,500 per year were eligible to bid for these places in 2012. See Chapter 5. See also **Core**.

Mission groups Bodies representing different parts of the higher education sector including **Russell Group, 1994 Group, University Alliance, million+, GuildHE**.

Million+ Now styling itself a 'university think tank', million+ represents the interests of the post-92 universities. Formerly, known as the Campaign for Mainstream Universities and Coalition of Modern Universities.

Monetisation A term referring to the ability to generate revenue from assets or opportunities. See Chapter 13 for the way it is used in relation to the portfolio of outstanding student loan accounts.

National Scholarship Programme (NSP) A government-funded initiative to provide additional resources to widening participation initiatives. It has a budget of approximately £150 million. See Chapter 2 for details.

Not-for-profit An institution which reinvests or retains any surpluses rather than distributing them as profits to investors or owners. Not all not-for-profits are charities.

Office for Fair Access (Offa) The quango responsible for overseeing **access agreements**.

Office of the Independent Adjudicator (OIA) The body officially designated to oversee and arbitrate on student complaints once internal complaints procedures have been exhausted.

Pre-92 / Post-92 A distinction used to differentiate those institutions that were classed as universities before the 1992 **Further and Higher Education Act** from the former polytechnics.

Primary legislation Laws made by Parliament in its legislative capacity (normally requiring the approval of the House of Commons and House of Lords). Primary legislation is needed to create new bodies or to give existing bodies new powers. Cf. **secondary legislation**.

Private provider An institution that offers higher education courses but which does not currently receive any public funding whether for research or teaching.

Private equity Privately owned capital used for corporate investment or buyout. Frequently contrasted with the ownership structures of limited public companies where shares are traded.

Privatisation A complex process by which shifting relations to public and private spheres are transformed. A seven-fold structure for analysing this process, covering e.g., regulation, ownership and financing, in higher education is set out in the Introduction.

Privy Council Nominally, a body advising the Queen. It has executive powers through the use of Orders in Council. It oversees **Royal Charters** and the granting of **Degree Awarding Powers**.

Quality Assurance Agency (QAA) The body tasked with monitoring standards in HE.

Quango Quasi non-governmental organisation. The usual reference for what are officially known as 'non-departmental public bodies'. They are granted devolved powers to use at arm's length from government – in higher education, to avoid direct political interference. Hefce, OIA and Offa are quangos.

Resource Accounting and Budgeting (RAB) The accruals-based accounting and budgetary convention used across government since 2001. The **RAB charge** is the jargon used to refer to amount set aside in departmental accounts to meet the estimated loss on the student loan scheme. See Chapter 12.

Research Assessment Exercise (RAE) / Research Excellence Framework (REF) Complex and unpopular tendering processes by which institutions bid for 'Quality-related research funding' on the basis of the recent 'outputs' of academic staff. The Research Excellence Framework replaces the RAE (which was conducted in 2001 and 2008). The REF will be completed in 2014 and the results will be used to allocate funding from 2015/16.

Repayment threshold The threshold of gross income determining both the point at which borrowers commence repayments and the monthly payment. For those beginning undergraduate study for the first time in 2012, the repayment threshold is set at £21,000 in 2016, when the first repayments fall due. The repayment rate is currently 9 per cent on all earnings above the threshold.

Retail Price Index (RPI) – a measure of inflation. RPI is used to determine the interest rates on student loans. See Chapter 3.

Robbins Report An independent report into Higher Education led by Lionel Robbins and published in 1963. It is widely regarded as setting the blueprint for UK higher education.

Royal Charter See **Charter Corporation** and **Privy Council** above.

Russell Group A group of the 24 most research-intensive and selective universities in the UK. Widely seen as the most influential voice in higher education and the intended beneficiaries of the reforms.

Secondary legislation Legislation enacted by the executive, the government, authorised by and consistent with what is set out by primary legislation. It provides less opportunity for scrutiny by Parliament as compared to **primary legislation**.

Securitisation A means of turning the future income streams of assets into tradeable **bonds** ('securities').

Statutory corporation Any institution formed by statute. Includes the **higher education corporations** and some other universities. They are distinct from **chartered corporations**. See Chapter 9.

Statutory instrument A form of **secondary legislation**.

Student Numbers Controls (SNC) The collective term for measures used to govern annual undergraduate recruitment. Each institution is able to recruit its **core** and **margin** places plus any **AAB+** applicants.

Student support A term covering the loans and grants that students are able to access to support their study.

Supply-side reforms Reforms governing the provision that is offered to the public: the kind of institutions and courses available.

UK Border Agency (UKBA) An agency of the Immigration service responsible for enforcing laws relating to entry into the UK.

University Alliance A mission group which describes itself as the 'voice of the business engaged universities'. It represents 24 universities.

University and Colleges Admissions Service (UCAS) The organisation overseeing the process by which people apply for undergraduate places.

University Grants Committee (UGC) The body that provided funding to universities prior to 1992. Replaced in the unified funding scheme by **Hefce**.

Universities UK (UUK) Although describing itself as the representative body for the UK's universities, it is really an organisation representing the vice-chancellors. It was formerly the Committee of Vice-Chancellors and Principals (CVCP), a more accurate name.

Validation A form of partnership arrangement where an HEI with **Degree Awarding Powers** judges that a course offered by another institution is of sufficient quality to qualify as a degree. Candidates who successfully complete the course are awarded a degree by the HEI. See Chapter 6.

Vice-chancellor (or Principal) The senior executive at an HEI.

White Paper A document setting out the government's plans for reform. In 2011, the Coalition published its Higher Education White Paper, *Students at the Heart of the System*.

Notes

Online sources last accessed November 2012

INTRODUCTION

1. Andrew Lansley, 'The future of health and public service regulation', 9 July 2005, www.andrewlansley.co.uk/newsevent.php?newseventid=21
2. David Willetts, Speech to Universities UK Annual Conference, February 2011, www.bis.gov.uk/news/speeches/david-willetts-uuk-spring-conference-2011
3. In 1993, all former polytechnics took the opportunity to rebrand as universities, with only one retaining the word 'polytechnic' in its title; it is now Anglia Ruskin University.
4. David Willetts, Speech to Bright Blue Conference: 'Tory modernisation 2.0: the future of the Conservative Party', 28 July 2012, http://brightblueonline.com/index.php/medias/speeches
5. BIS, *Higher Ambitions: The Future of Universities in a Knowledge Economy*, November 2009, http://webarchive.nationalarchives.gov.uk/+/http://www.bis.gov.uk/higherambitions
6. Nick Mathiason, 'Hedge funds, financiers and private equity make up 27% of Tory funding', *Bureau of Investigative Journalism*, 30 September 2011, www.thebureauinvestigates.com/2011/09/30/hedge-funds-financiers-and-private-equity-tycoons-make-up-27-of-tory-funding; Sam Jones, Elizabeth Rigby and Cynthia O'Murchu, 'The blue hedge brigade', *Financial Times*, 8 December 2011.
7. Hannah Richardson, 'David Willetts met for-profit university firms', *BBC News*, 2 October 2011, www.bbc.co.uk/news/education-14987073
8. Terry Brotherstone, 'Why Scotland matters: devolution, neoliberalism and the fight for the future of the public university in the UK', 2012, http://andreasbieler.net/wp-content/files/Brotherstone.pdf
9. Anthony Crosland, Speech at Woolwich Polytechnic, 27 April 1965.

CHAPTER 1

1. These figures mask participation through part-time study. Robbins reported in 1963 that participation rates would be around 15 per cent if those pursuing 'part-time and private study' of at least one day per week were included. *The Robbins Report*, Her Majesty's Stationery Office, 1963, §49.
2. Ibid.
3. BIS, *Higher Ambitions: The Future of Universities in a Knowledge Economy*, November 2009, http://webarchive.nationalarchives.gov.uk/+/http://www.bis.gov.uk/higherambitions
4. The Browne review is formally known as the Independent Review of Higher Education Funding and Student Finance. Its report is: *Securing a Sustainable Future for Higher Education*, October 2010.

5. John Morgan, '£6K must be ceiling, survey told Browne', *Times Higher Education*, 3 March 2011, www.timeshighereducation.co.uk/story. asp?storycode=415358

CHAPTER 2

1. The exception is the clauses relating to interest rates on student loans – these were slipped into the back of the 2011 Education Act, which dealt primarily with school reforms. (See Chapter 3 for more details).
2. Campaign for the Public University, 'In defence of public higher education', September 2011, §1.4, text available at http://publicuniversity.org.uk/ 2011/09/27/higher-education-white-paper-is-provoking-a-winter-of-discontent
3. I use the figure used by the Office for Budgetary Responsibility (OBR) since its Autumn 2011 *Economic and Fiscal Outlook*. This appears to be based on data from the Office for Fair Access, which produces a figure of £8,123 for 2012/13. The exact figure will not be known until 2013, though the Higher Education Policy Institute provides an estimate of £8,234. (John Thompson and Bahram Bekhradnia, *The Cost of the Government's Reforms of the Financing of Higher Education*, Hepi, October 2012.)
4. In determining the block grant allowance, use was also made of a 'tolerance band' which provided some flexibility for institutions which over- or under-recruited by offering a 5% margin of error. The grant calculation also assumes a minimum fee of £1,345 is being charged, which is subtracted from the 'standard resource'.
5. BIS, *Guidance to the Director of Fair Access*, February 2011, www.bis.gov.uk/ assets/biscore/higher-education/docs/g/11-728-guidance-to-director-fair-access
6. Hefce, *Student Number Controls and Teaching Funding: Consultation on Arrangements for 2013–14 and Beyond*, February 2012, www.hefce.ac.uk/ pubs/year/2012/201204
7. David Willetts, Speech to Universities UK Annual Conference, 25 February 2011, www.bis.gov.uk/news/speeches/david-willetts-uuk-spring-conference-2011
8. The universities of Oxford and Cambridge told the Browne review that their tutorial model contributed to costs of £16,000 and £15,000 per student per year respectively, far above the maximum cap. Neither published the method used to reach such conclusions, only the figures – not exactly a commendable position for these institutions that are also in receipt of endowments directed specifically at supporting tutorial costs.
9. John Morgan, 'Queries over special funding for Oxbridge', *Times Higher Education*, 2 August 2012, www.timeshighereducation.co.uk/story.asp?secti oncode=26&storycode=420748&c=1
10. Sarah Cunnane, 'Number of academic staff falls 1 per cent in last two years', *Times Higher Education*, 20 January 2012, www.timeshighereducation.co.uk/ story.asp?storycode=418777
11. Offa, 'OFFA announces decisions on 2013–14 access agreements', 26 July 2012, www.offa.org.uk/press-releases/offa-announces-decisions-on-2013-14-access-agreements
12. Ibid.
13. www.direct.gov.uk/en/EducationAndLearning/UniversityAndHigherEducation/ StudentFinance/Typesoffinance/DG_171571
14. Offa, 'OFFA announces decisions on 2013–14 access agreements'.

15. www.offa.org.uk/about
16. BIS, *Guidance to the Director of Fair Access*.
17. From the websites of many universities, one can see additional restrictions on access to NSP bursaries, with limited numbers available even to eligible students and distributed on a 'first come, first served' basis.
18. Harriet Swain, 'New university bursaries tell students what to spend the money on', *Guardian*, 20 March 2012, www.guardian.co.uk/education/2012/mar/16/universities-bursaries-conditions-spend-academic-material
19. www.uel.ac.uk/fees/scholarships-and-bursaries/2012–13-entry/undergraduate/national-scholarship-programme
20. Roger Burrows, 'Living with the h-index? Metric assemblages in the contemporary academy', *Sociological Review* 60:2, 2012, pp. 355–72; John Holmwood, 'TRACked and FECked: how audits undermine the arts, humanities and social sciences', *Research Blogs*, 2 March 2011, http://exquisitelife.researchresearch.com/exquisite_life/2011/03/tracked-and-fecked-how-audits-undermine-the-arts-humanities-and-social-sciences.html
21. Chris Newfield, *Unmaking the Public University: The Forty Year Assault on the Middle Classes*, Harvard University Press, 2008.
22. Steve Smith, 'Afterword', in *Manifesto for the Public University*, Bloomsbury 2011, p. 138.
23. wwwm.coventry.ac.uk/cuc/Pages/CoventryUniversityCollege.aspx
24. Maria Petzler, 'Knock-down university', 20 October 2011, http://pretzler.net/blog/2011/10/20/knock-down-university
25. wwwm.coventry.ac.uk/LondonCampus/Pages/Home.aspx
26. Paul Jump, 'Derby to offer range of tuition fees', *Times Higher Education*, 5 April 2011, www.timeshighereducation.co.uk/story.asp?storycode=415729
27. University of Derby, *Access Agreement 2013/14*, www.offa.org.uk/agreements/University%20of%20Derby%200057%20access%20agreement%202013–14.pdf

CHAPTER 3

1. BIS, *Government Reform of Higher Education: Government Response to the Committee's 12th Report of Session 2010–12*, www.publications.parliament.uk/pa/cm201213/cmselect/cmbis/286/286.pdf
2. A small ICR loan system has become available to US graduates who meet certain conditions on low earnings. Only a tiny minority of graduates have transferred their student loan debts onto this model. The schemes are complex and the ICR terms may only apply for the early years of the loan.
3. Eliot Spitzer, 'Smart loans', in Janet Byrne, ed., *The Occupy Handbook*, Back Bay Books, 2012, pp. 393–96.
4. Claire Callender, Anne Jamieson and Geoff Mason, *The Supply of Part-time Higher Education in the UK*, Universities UK, 2010, www.universitiesuk.ac.uk/Publications/Documents/TheSupplyOfPartTimeHigherEducationInTheUK20100929.pdf
5. Claire Callender, 'Loans for part-time students could end up reducing numbers', *Guardian*, 15 October 2012.
6. John Morgan, 'So long UK, thanks for all the loans: we'll be in touch ...', *Times Higher Education*, 9 August 2012.

7. For loans taken out between 2006 and 2011, outstanding balances are written off after 25 years.

8. www.legislation.gov.uk/uksi/2012/1309/contents/made

9. Haroon Chowdry, Lorraine Dearden, Alissa Goodman and Wenchao Jin, *The Distributional Impact of the 2012–13 Higher Education Funding Reforms in England*, IFS, July 2012.

10. Net Present Value is a method of representing the value of future money in today's terms but allowing for inflation and the interest paid on the government's borrowing. In this diagram, the interest factored in is the cost of borrowing for BIS – RPI + 2.2.

11. David Willetts, Letter to *London Review of Books*, 14 July 2011.

12. From 2012, the repayment threshold for existing borrowers will increase annually in line with inflation (i.e., £15 000 + RPI).

13. David Willetts, Interview in *Oxford Today*, May 2012. Full interview transcript: http://d3gjvvs65ernan.cloudfront.net/David%20Willets%20interview%20 transcript.pdf

14. Nicholas Barr, 'The Higher Education White Paper: the good, the bad, the unspeakable – and the next white paper', *Social Policy and Administration* 46:5, October 2012, pp. 483–508.

15. www.direct.gov.uk/prod_consum_dg/groups/dg_digitalassets/@dg/@en/@educ/ documents/digitalasset/dg_200469.pdf

16. Statutory instruments work in such a way that any scrutiny is limited. Regulations are drafted, laid before Parliament and become law by a set date unless an MP 'moves a prayer' against the instrument. There need be no debate or vote and in fact, for those outside Parliament, it is difficult to work out whether or when such instruments have been 'made'. Moreover, such a prayer can only be 'moved' at the end of the parliamentary day with very little time for discussion. The instrument can be moved repeatedly by the government until it gains a majority and there is no scope for amendment.

17. www.stuff.co.nz/national/education/6853057/Student-loan-repayments-hiked-allowances-restricted

18. David Willetts, Statement to BIS Select Committee, June 2012, www. publications.parliament.uk/pa/cm201213/cmselect/cmbis/uc274-i/uc27401.htm

CHAPTER 4

1. Nicholas Timmins, *The Five Giants: A Biography of the Welfare State* (new edition), Harper Collins, 2001, pp. 418–20.

2. Milton Friedman, 'The role of government in education' (1955), in *Economics and the Public Interest*, Rutgers University Press, 1955. Available at www. schoolchoices.org/roo/fried1.htm

3. Lucy Hodges, 'Has cross-party wrangle hit tuition fees review?', *Independent*, 16 October 2009, www.independent.co.uk/news/education/education-news/ has-crossparty-wrangle-hit-tuition-fees-review-1803985.html

4. David Willetts, Letter, *Guardian*, 7 July 2011.

5. David Willetts, Speech to Universities UK, 25 February 2011.

6. David Willetts, Letter to *London Review of Books*, 14 July 2011.

7. *Securing a Sustainable Future for Higher Education*, p. 23.

8. Roger Brown (ed.), *Higher Education and the Market*, Routledge, 2011.

9. David Willetts, Letter, *Guardian*, 7 July 2011.

10. John Holmwood, 'Code of practice needed to prevent degree-course mis-selling', Research Blogs, 7 February 2011, http://exquisitelife.researchresearch.com/exquisite_life/2011/02/code-of-practice-needed-to-halt-degree-course-mis-selling-.html

11. The government is keen for third parties to provide further work here on provision. The NUS recently announced a team-up with the consumer publication, *Which?* (http://university.which.co.uk).

12. Council of the University of Cambridge, *Response to the Consultation*, 26 September 2011, §26, www.cam.ac.uk/univ/notices/council-white-paper-response.pdf

13. Hefce, *Student Number Controls and Teaching Funding*, §176.

14. Tristram Hunt, 'Universities can't do everything. Reinvent the polytechnic', *Guardian*, 19 August 2012.

15. Gerard Kelly, 'Employers complain, but are they right to?', *Times Education Supplement*, 24 August 2012, www.tes.co.uk/article.aspx?storycode=6278594

16. Campaign for the Public University, 'In defence of public higher education', September 2012, http://publicuniversity.org.uk/2011/09/27/higher-education-white-paper-is-provoking-a-winter-of-discontent

17. New Economics Foundation, 'Degrees of value: how universities benefit society', 15 June 2011, www.neweconomics.org/publications/degrees-of-value

CHAPTER 5

1. This is somewhat simplified as it does not explain the 'tolerance band' which allowed a margin of over- and under-recruitment. Controls have taken various forms since they were introduced in the late 1990s and they were largely used to control the level of *grant*. Where institutions over- or under-recruited, beyond a 'tolerance band' of plus or minus 5 per cent, the *grant* for additional students was clawed back, but the students were still able to access loans. There is no tolerance band in the new system, though Hefce may allow significant over-recruitment in 2011 to be offset against under-recruitment in 2012.

2. The government has determined a list of equivalent grade combinations as well as equivalent grades for other qualifications such as the International Baccalaureate, Scottish Highers or BTECs.

3. www.gold.ac.uk/news/pressrelease/?releaseID=968

4. John Thompson and Bahram Bekhradnia, *Higher Education: Students at the Heart of the System – an Analysis of the Higher Education White Paper*, Hepi, August 2011, §50.

5. Council of the University of Cambridge, *Response to the Consultation*, 26 September 2011, pp. 7–8.

6. BIS, Letter to Hefce, 28 June 2011, §14.

7. www.hefce.ac.uk/news/hefce/2012/margin.htm

8. Hefce, *Student Number Controls for 2013–14: Guidance and Invitation to Bid*, 26 July 2012, www.hefce.ac.uk/media/hefce/content/pubs/2012/201217/2012–17%20Main%20report.pdf

9. Graeme Paton, 'Britain's best universities "failed to fill 11,500 places"', *Telegraph*, 19 November 2012, www.telegraph.co.uk/education/universityeducation/9689004/Britains-best-universities-failed-to-fill-11500-places.html

10. A precursor to this procedure was seen in the 'taskforce' set up to deal with the fallout from the London Metropolitan University debacle.

11. John Morgan, 'Staff put on red alert over Bolton's drastic plans to get into the black', *Times Higher Education*, 29 November 2012.

CHAPTER 6

1. The title 'university college' is also covered in this way, while the government is also considering extending the law to 'polytechnic' too.

2. Government Response to the Consultations *Students at the Heart of the System* and *A New Fit-for-Purpose Regulatory Framework for the Higher Education Sector*, June 2012, p. 4, www.bis.gov.uk/assets/biscore/higher-education/docs/g/12-890-government-response-students-and-regulatory-framework-higher-education

3. David Willetts, Letter to *London Review of Books*, 14 July 2011.

4. Hefce, *A Risk-based Approach to Quality Assurance: Consultation*, May 2012, §121, www.hefce.ac.uk/media/hefce/content/pubs/2012/201211/2012-11.pdf

5. BIS, *Students at the Heart of the System*, 2011, pp. 69–70, http://discuss.bis.gov.uk/hereform/white-paper

6. BIS, *Applications for the Grant of Taught Degree Awarding Powers, Research Degree Awarding Powers and University Title*, www.bis.gov.uk/assets/biscore/higher-education/docs/a/11–781-applications-for-degree-awarding-powers-guidance

7. www.qaa.ac.uk/reviews/dap/QAA_role.asp

8. See Andrew McGettigan, 'Academics and standards: avoiding market failure', in Louis Coiffait, ed., *Blue Skies: New Thinking About the Future of Higher Education* (UK 2012 edition), Pearson Think Tank, 2012, pp. 20–4.

9. www.qaa.ac.uk/Newsroom/PressReleases/Pages/quality-mark.aspx

10. See for example, Nicholas Davy, 'HE in FE: renaissance or reformation?', in Louis Coiffait, ed., *Blues Skies: New Thinking About the Future of Higher Education* (2011 edition), Pearson Think Tank, 2011, pp. 77–80.

11. BIS, *A New Fit-for-Purpose Regulatory Framework for the Higher Education Sector*, 2011, Chapter 4, http://discuss.bis.gov.uk/hereform/technical-consultation

12. David Willetts, 'Putting students at the heart of higher education', in Coiffait, ed., *Blue Skies*, 2011, pp. 17–19.

13. Gareth Parry, Claire Callender, Peter Scott and Paul Temple, *Understanding Higher Education in Further Education Colleges*, BIS Research Paper Number 69, June 2012, p. 12.

14. Vince Cable, Speech to Hefce Annual Conference, 6 April 2011, Aston University, www.bis.gov.uk/news/speeches/vince-cable-hefce-conference-2011

15. Vince Cable, Speech to Association of Colleges Annual Conference, 17 November 2011, Birmingham, www.bis.gov.uk/news/speeches/vince-cable-association-of-colleges-2011

16. BIS, Government Response to the Consultations, June 2012.

17. Bruce Truscot, *Red Brick University*, Penguin, 1951, p. 65.

18. www.legislation.gov.uk/ukpga/1992/13/section/77

19. David Willetts, Speech to HE in FE Conference, Association of Colleges, 31 March 2011, London, www.bis.gov.uk/news/speeches/david-willetts-aoc-conference-2011

20. Roger King, *The Risks of Risk-based Regulation: The Regulatory Challenges of the Higher Education White Paper for England*, Hepi, 2011.
21. Hefce, *A Risk-based Approach to Quality Assurance: Consultation*, p. 16.
22. Ibid., p. 23.
23. BIS, *Applying Student Number Controls to Alternative Providers with Designated Courses*, November 2012, p. 10.
24. Roger Brown, *Everything for Sale?* Routledge, 2013 (forthcoming).
25. Centre for Higher Education Research and Information (for Hefce), *Diversity in the Student Learning Experience and Time Devoted to Study: A Comparative Analysis of the UK and European Evidence*, 2009, www.open.ac.uk/cheri/documents/student-experience-report.pdf
26. BIS, *Students at the Heart of the System*, June 2011, pp. 25–6.
27. www.iconcollege.com
28. For information on MDP, Management Development Partnership, see www.mdpuk.com/pages/new.htm
29. www.pearsoncollege.com
30. www.wales.ac.uk/en/AboutUs/AboutUs.aspx
31. Hefce, *A Risk-based Approach to Quality Assurance: Consultation*, p. 23.

CHAPTER 7

1. David Willetts, *The Pinch*, Atlantic Books, 2010.
2. William Patrick Leonard, 'Private sector capitalises on complacency', *University World News* 197, 13 November 2011, www.universityworldnews.com/article.php?story=20111111214055105
3. David Willetts, Speech to Universities UK, February 2011.
4. The list of designated courses is regularly updated and is available here: www.practitioners.slc.co.uk/policy-information/designated-courses/full-list.aspx
5. Some postgraduate courses have been 'designated' so as to allow eligible students access to the Disabled Students' Allowance.
6. John Morgan, 'Private bodies saddle up for state subsidies', *Times Higher Education*, 12 July 2012, www.timeshighereducation.co.uk/story.asp?storycode=420545
7. BIS, *Applying Student Number Controls to Alternative Providers with Designated Courses*, November 2012.
8. John Browne, Speech to BPP, 26 October 2010.
9. A. Ananthalakshmi, 'Apollo Group to cut jobs, shuts 25 campuses', *Reuters*, 16 October 2012, www.reuters.com/article/2012/10/16/us-apollogroup-results-idUSBRE89F1I520121016
10. David Willetts, Speech to Universities UK, 25 February 2011.
11. David Willetts, Speech to Policy Exchange, 4 January 2012, www.bis.gov.uk/news/speeches/david-willetts-policy-exchange-britain-best-place-science-2012
12. Jonathan White, *Public Service or Portfolio Investment? How Private Equity Funds are Taking Over Post-secondary Education*, UCU, October 2012.
13. Julie Froud and Karel Williams, 'Private equity and the culture of value extraction', *New Political Economy* 12(3), 2007. See also the criticisms made by Sandra Robertson, chief executive of the University of Oxford's investment fund. Sam Jones, 'Oxford investment chief accuses private equity titans of failing clients', *Financial Times*, 9 October 2012.

14. BIS, *Applying Student Number Controls to Alternative Providers with Designated Courses*, November 2012, Table A.2.
15. Matt Robb, 'Here be treasure, but sector unprepared for raiding parties', *Times Higher Education*, 12 May 2011, www.timeshighereducation.co.uk/story.asp?sectioncode=26&storycode=416122
16. White, *Public Service or Portfolio Investment?*
17. 'Tory party donor Peter Hall funded Anthony Grayling's university', *Guardian*, 16 June 2011.
18. Chris Kirkham, 'With Goldman's foray into higher education, a predatory pursuit of students and revenues', *Huffington Post*, 14 October 2011, www.huffingtonpost.com/2011/10/14/goldman-sachs-for-profit-college_n_997409.html
19. www.pbs.org/wgbh/pages/frontline/collegeinc/view
20. Paul Fain, 'The results are in: Harkin released critical report on for-profits', *Inside Higher Ed*, 30 July 2012, www.insidehighered.com/news/2012/07/30/harkin-releases-critical-report-profits
21. David Willetts, Letter, *Guardian*, 7 July 2011.
22. See Nicholas Timmins, *Never Again? The Story of the Health and Social Care Act 2012: A Study in Coalition Government and Policy Making*, The King's Fund/Institute for Government, July 2012.
23. Council of the University of Cambridge, *Response to the Consultation*, 26 September 2011.
24. Suevon Lee, 'The for-profit education industry, by the numbers', *ProPublica*, 9 August 2012, www.propublica.org/article/the-for-profit-higher-education-industry-by-the-numbers
25. www.parliament.uk/edm/2010–12/1999
26. BPP University College, as a not-for-profit, avoids VAT on its tuition fees for higher education courses, which is the 'core issue' determining the group's corporate structure, according to Carl Lygo, BPP UC's Principal and chief executive of the holding company. Retained profits are residing in a bank account (£24 million at September 2012) and cannot be distributed to the parent company while retaining its current legal form and tax status. However, money does leave the subsidiary in the form of service charges and management fees.
27. Grayling founded the original company, GraylingHall, with Peter Hall, the financier mentioned earlier.
28. www.independent.co.uk/opinion/commentators/dominic-lawson/dominic-lawson-a-private-sector-oxbridge-not-exactly-2293915.html
29. Caspar Melville, 'Saving our universities? New Humanist interviews AC Grayling', *New Humanist* 127:5 September/October 2012, http://newhumanist.org.uk/2859/saving-our-universities-new-humanist-interviews-ac-grayling
30. HMRC, *VAT: Consideration of the Case to Extend the Education Exemption to For-profit Providers of Higher Education*, 12 September 2012.

CHAPTER 8

1. Previously unpublished excerpt from Andrew McGettigan, 'Demand would be enormous', *Research Fortnight* 375 (supplement), 21 September 2011.
2. BIS, *Government Response to White Paper Consultations*, June 2012, §2.4.11, www.bis.gov.uk/assets/biscore/higher-education/docs/g/12-890-government-response-students-and-regulatory-framework-higher-education.pdf

3. Suzi Leather, Speech to Almshouse Association Annual Conference, 12 June 2012, www.charity-commission.gov.uk/About_us/About_the_Commission/Speeches/suzi_leather_12062012.aspx

4. James Slack, 'Don't slash visas for foreign students in bid to control immigration, says universities minister', *Daily Mail*, 17 September 2012, www.dailymail.co.uk/news/article-2204310/David-Willetts-Dont-slash-visas-foreign-students-bid-control-immigration.html

5. www.politics.co.uk/comment-analysis/2012/10/09/theresa-may-speech-in-full

6. Simeon Underwood, 'When worlds collide: why the UKBA sends the sector into a panic', *Times Higher Education*, 7 June 2012, www.timeshighereducation.co.uk/story.asp?storycode=420173

7. Andrew McGettigan, 'Middlesex cancels its Delhi campus plans', *Research Fortnight Today*, 9 August 2011, www.researchresearch.com/index.php?option=com_news&template=rr_2col&view=article&articleId=1096520

8. John Elledge, 'Britain, where you can get a flat-pack campus', *Guardian*, 6 August 2012.

9. See http://savemdxphil.com/2010/05/01/faq-on-the-financial-situation-of-philosophy-at-middlesex

10. See Rebecca Attwood, 'Protect cash for access and outreach, Offa argues', *Times Higher Education*, 5 August 2010, www.timeshighereducation.co.uk/story.asp?sectioncode=26&storycode=412889

11. Geoff Maslen, 'The rise of the multinational university', *University World News*, 5 August 2012, www.universityworldnews.com/article.php?story=20120802130423710

12. www.uclan.ac.uk/information/campuses/cyprus/index.php

13. http://rak.gmu.edu

14. David Matthews, 'Empires and allies', *Times Higher Education*, 18 October 2012.

CHAPTER 9

1. Peter Williams, 'Foreword' to David Watson, *Who Owns the University?* QAA, November 2008 (talk given on 4 June 2008).

2. Ibid.

3. The exceptions amongst the pre-92 universities are (i) the University of London; (ii) the University of Durham; (iii) the University of Newcastle formed when it was separated from Durham in 1963; and, (iv) despite its name, Royal Holloway. All four are statutory corporations and bound by ultra vires as per the higher education corporations.

4. The 2004 Higher Education Act moved the Visitor's oversight of student complaints to the Office of the Independent Adjudicator.

5. www.legislation.gov.uk/ukpga/1988/40/contents

6. This process was seen in the summer of 2011, when the higher education corporation, Leeds College of Music, was dissolved into a company limited by guarantee, Leeds College of Music Limited, the wholly owned subsidiary of Leeds City College, an FE college.

7. Universities UK, *Developing Future University Structures: New Funding and Legal Models*, 2009, §5.6. www.universitiesuk.ac.uk/Publications/Documents/PolicyCommentary2.pdf

8. Anthony Barnett, 'Fred Halliday was right: the LSE, Gaddafi money and what is missing from the Woolf Report', *Our Kingdom*, 1 December 2011, www.opendemocracy.net/ourkingdom/anthony-barnett/fred-halliday-was-right-lse-gaddafi-money-and-what-is-missing-from-woolf

9. In November 2012, the University of Central Lancashire, a higher education corporation, announced that it had made a formal request to have itself dissolved and its activities passed to a company limited by guarantee to be known as UCLan Group Limited. The move was in part prompted by its expansion overseas (see Chapter 8).

10. Cabinet Office, 'Appendix A: technical issues', Charities Act Review, 2012.

11. Dennis Farrington and David Palfreyman, *The Law of Higher Education*, Oxford University Press, 2006, §7.13.

12. www.college-of-law.co.uk/About-the-College/Media-Centre/News-2012/17-April-2012--Governors-of-The-College-of-Law-announce-conclusion-of-Strategic-Review

13. Quoted in Jonathan White, *Public Service or Portfolio Investment? How Private Equity Funds are Taking Over Post-Secondary Education*, UCU, October 2012.

14. The College of Law, 'College of Law change of ownership FAQs', www.college-of-law.co.uk/About-the-College/College-of-Law-change-of-ownership---FAQs/?terms=montagu

15. Universities UK, *Developing Future University Structures*.

16. Andrew McGettigan, 'Who let the dogs out? The privatization of higher education', *Radical Philosophy* 174, July/August 2012, p. 26.

17. David Hencke and Frederika Whitehead, 'Tender document details how company will run university', *Exaro News*, 14 August 2012, www.exaronews.com/articles/4551/tender-document-details-how-company-will-run-university

18. 'Private equity firms looking to acquire universities', *Education Investor*, 22 September 2011, www.educationinvestor.co.uk/ShowArticleNews.aspx?ID=2450

CHAPTER 10

1. Simon Baker, 'Bank warns sector of default contagion risk', *Times Higher Education*, 5 January 2012, www.timeshighereducation.co.uk/story.asp?sectioncode=26&storycode=418589&c=1

2. A more detailed account of this history can be found in Andrew McGettigan, 'Demand would be Enormous', *Research Fortnight* 375 (supplement), 21 September 2011.

3. For more detail on the University of California, see Andrew McGettigan, 'Borrowing greatness', *Research Fortnight* 376 (supplement), 4 October 2011.

4. Bob Meister, 'They pledged your tuition to Wall Street: an open letter to UC students' (2010), http://keepcaliforniaspromise.org/404/they-pledged-your-tuition-to-wall-street-summary/comment-page-1

5. California State Auditors Report into University of California, July 2011, www.bsa.ca.gov/reports/summary/2010–105

6. University of California, *Annual Report on Debt Capital and External Finance Approvals*, 2011, www.universityofcalifornia.edu/finreports/index.php?file=debtcapital/debtcapital_2011.pdf

7. Gillian Tett, 'Californian schools could serve up a nasty fiscal shock', *Financial Times*, 10 August 2012.

8. Russell Group, *Funding Higher Education in England: What are the Options?*, May 2010, §4.53, www.russellgroup.ac.uk/uploads/Russell-Group-second-submission-to-Browne-Review-12-May-2010.pdf
9. Ibid., §4.54.

CHAPTER 11

1. John Holmwood, 'With the managers in charge, autonomy isn't what it used to be', *Times Higher Education*, 17 May 2012, www.timeshighereducation.co.uk/story.asp?storycode=419961
2. University of Central Lancashire, internal memo to staff, November 2012.
3. Alberto Toscano, 'The university as political space', in Michael Bailey and Des Freedman, eds., *The Assault on Universities: A Manifesto for Resistance*, Pluto Press, 2011, p. 86.
4. Roger Brown's forthcoming book, *Everything for Sale?* (Routledge, 2013) documents some of the cases of this kind that have reached the public domain.
5. *Report of the Review of Higher Education Governance in Scotland*, 16 January 2012, www.scotland.gov.uk/Resource/0038/00386780.pdf
6. Nicholas Timmins, *The Five Giants: A Biography of the Welfare State* (new edition), HarperCollins, 2001, p. 483.
7. Council of the University of Cambridge, *Response to the Consultation*, September 2011, p. 10.

CHAPTER 12

1. BIS news release, *The Department for Business Innovation and Skills Spending Review Settlement*, 20 October 2010, http://news.bis.gov.uk/content/Detail.aspx?ReleaseID=416110&NewsAreaID=2
2. David Willetts, Speech to Universities UK Annual Conference, 25 February 2011.
3. Simon Hughes's account of the negotiations around the tuition fee vote in December 2010 mentions that 'civil servants' were against the abolition of fees. This is possibly because a 'graduate contribution scheme' would have been even more 'like a tax', such that the government borrowing needed to finance it would not have been treated as 'policy lending'. John Morgan, 'Coalition were close to scrapping fees', *Times Higher Education*, 25 September 2012.
4. Steve Smith, 'Afterword', in John Holmwood, ed., *The Manifesto for the Public University*, Bloomsbury, 2011, p. 136.
5. Andrew McGettigan, *False Accounting? Why the Government's Higher Education Reforms Don't Add Up*, Intergenerational Foundation, May 2012.
6. Paul Bolton, 'Changes to higher education funding and student support in England from 2012/13', House of Commons Library, 6 February 2012, www.parliament.uk/briefing-papers/SN05753
7. David Willetts, 'Universities minister defends higher education reforms', *Guardian*, 19 September 2011, www.guardian.co.uk/education/2011/sep/19/david-willetts-higher-education-reforms
8. In theory, the government could make a surplus, if revenues were greater than expenditure, but this is not the current objective.
9. OBR, *Economic and Fiscal Outlook*, Autumn 2011.

10. www.moneymovesmarkets.com/journal/2011/4/12/tuition-fee-rise-to-boost-cpi-and-cpi-linked-spending-reduci.html

11. This is the normal figure cited. It excludes the liabilities that were taken on when the government intervened to stop the banks from collapsing in 2008.

12. OBR, *Economics and Fiscal Outlook*, December 2012, Table 4.27, http://budgetresponsibility.independent.gov.uk/economic-and-fiscal-outlook-december-2012

13. OBR, *Fiscal Sustainability Report*, July 2012, http://budgetresponsibility.independent.gov.uk/fiscal-sustainability-report-july-2012

14. '2.74 We also assume that student loan fees are uprated with earnings. The medium-term forecast assumes these are uprated with RPIX inflation from 2014–15, but rolling that assumption forward into the long term would imply that university income steadily diminishes relative to the size of the economy.'

15. Phillip Brown, Hugh Lauder and David Ashton, *The Global Auction: The Broken Promises of Education, Jobs and Income* (Oxford University Press, 2011), provides one perspective on why this might not be the case: the changing graduate job market in the global economy.

16. BIS, *Guide to the Simplified Student Loan Repayment Model – Beta Version*, August 2012, www.bis.gov.uk/assets/BISCore/higher-education/docs/G/12-1126-guide-simplified-student-loan-repayment-model.pdf

17. Thompson and Bekhradnia, *The Cost of the Government's Reforms of the Financing of Higher Education*, §28.

18. London Economics, Written Submission to the BIS Higher Education Select Committee Report, *The Future of Higher Education*, 2011, www.publications.parliament.uk/pa/cm201011/cmselect/cmbis/writev/885/m16.htm

19. Thompson and Bekhradnia, *The Cost of the Government's Reforms of the Financing of Higher Education*, §30.

20. Hepi have established that Willetts has been relying on a 2007 report by Price Waterhouse Coopers for his expressed confidence in future graduate salaries. This in turn depended on research conducted on the cohorts who began before 1990 and therefore before the rapid expansion outlined in the Introduction. Thompson & Bekhradnia, *The Cost of the Government's Reforms of the Financing of Higher Education*, Annex A, Footnote 6.

21. Haroon Chowdry, Lorraine Dearden, Alissa Goodman and Wenchao Jin, *The Distributional Impact of the 2012–13 Higher Education Funding Reforms in England*, IFS, July 2012, p. 219.

22. Andrew McGettigan, 'Inflation & Obfuscation', Letter to *Times Higher Education*, 7 June 2012.

CHAPTER 13

1. NatCen, *29th British Social Attitudes Survey*, 2012, www.natcen.ac.uk/study/british-social-attitudes-29th-report

2. David Willetts, 'We cannot be certain about every step. But the journey will be worthwhile', *Times Higher Education*, 26 May 2011, www.timeshighereducation.co.uk/story.asp?storycode=416257

3. Tim Leunig, *Universities Challenged: Making the New University System Work for Students and Taxpayers*, CentreForum, 2011, www.centreforum.org/assets/pubs/universities-challenged-web.pdf

4. John Morgan, 'Wake up to the new world, declares Willetts', *Times Higher Education*, 11 October 2012, www.timeshighereducation.co.uk/story.asp?sec tioncode=26&storycode=421448

5. BIS, *Government Response to Technical Consultations*, June 2012, www.bis. gov.uk/assets/biscore/higher-education/docs/g/12-890-government-response-students-and-regulatory-framework-higher-education

6. BIS, *A New Fit-for-Purpose Regulatory Framework for the Higher Education Sector*, 2011, §1.1.3, http://discuss.bis.gov.uk/hereform/technicalconsultation

7. Massimo De Angelis and David Harvie, 'Cognitive capitalism and the rat race: how capital measures immaterial labour in British Universities', *Historical Materialism* 17, 2009, pp. 3–30.

8. Roger Burrows, 'Living with the h-index? Metric assemblages in the contemporary academy', *Sociological Review* 60:2 , 2012, pp. 355–72, p. 359.

9. HM Government, *Operational Efficiency Programme: Asset Portfolio*, 2009, p. 69, https://consultations.rics.org/gf2.ti/f/196162/3425861.1/PDF/-/oep%20 asset%20portfolio%20dec%2009.pdf

10. Andrew McGettigan, 'Interview with Nicholas Barr', in 'Shifting the Risk', Supplement to *Research Fortnight* 380, 30 November 2011.

11. HM Government, *Operational Efficiency Programme: Asset Portfolio*, 2009, p. 68.

12. Sixty equal payments were then made which covered the total amount taken out. In that way the repayment threshold did not determine the level of monthly repayment, only when (and if) those payments commenced.

13. Sue Hubble and Paul Bolton, 'Sale of Student Loans Bill', House of Commons Research Paper 07/78, November 2007, www.parliament.uk/briefing-papers/ RP07–78

14. Ibid., p. 14.

15. Gordon Brown, 1997 Budget Speech, 2 July 1997, www.prnewswire.co.uk/ news-releases/gordon-browns-july-1997-budget-speech-156180625.html

16. For a discussion of the change to loan accounting, see the Dearing report's (1997) section on 'The Treatment of Student Loans for Public Expenditure Purposes', www.publications.parliament.uk/pa/cm199798/cmselect/cmeduemp/241-i/ ee0305.htm

17. New legislation was required, as when the new income-contingent repayment loans were introduced in 1999 the legislation allowing the earlier sales was repealed, www.legislation.gov.uk/ukpga/2008/10/pdfs/ukpga_20080010_en.pdf

18. HM Government, *Operational Efficiency Programme: Asset Portfolio*, p. 66.

19. Tender document issued by BIS in April 2010.

20. BIS, *Students at the Heart of the System*, June 2011, §1.41.

21. Ibid., §1.42.

22. OBR, *Economic and Fiscal Outlook*, March 2011, §§4.151–4.152.

23. See the *Government Manual on Debt and Deficit* (4th release, March 2012) for further information, especially Part V, Chapter 5 on securitisation and classification, http://epp.eurostat.ec.europa.eu/portal/page/portal/government_ finance_statistics/methodology/ESA_95

CONCLUSION

1. David Willetts, Letter to *London Review of Books*, 14 July 2011.

2. Diane Ravitch, *The Death and Life of the Great American School System: How Testing and Choice Are Undermining Education*, revised and expanded edition, Basic Books, 2010.
3. For a discussion of the investor and start-up excitement about 'edutech', see Kevin Carey, 'The Siege of Academe', *The Washington Monthly*, September/October 2012, www.washingtonmonthly.com/magazine/septemberoctober_2012/features/_its_three_oclock_in039373.php

Index